CompreHending Cults
THe Sociology of New Religious Movements

Second Edition
Lorne L. Dawson

OXFORD
UNIVERSITY PRESS

OXFORD
UNIVERSITY PRESS

8 Sampson Mews, Suite 204, Don Mills, Ontario M3C 0H5
www.oupcanada.com

Oxford University Press is a department of the University of Oxford.
It furthers the University's objective of excellence in research, scholarship,
and education by publishing worldwide in

Oxford   New York

Auckland   Cape Town   Dar es Salaam   Hong Kong   Karachi
Kuala Lumpur   Madrid   Melbourne   Mexico City   Nairobi
New Delhi   Shanghai   Taipei   Toronto

With offices in

Argentina   Austria   Brazil   Chile   Czech Republic   France   Greece
Guatemala   Hungary   Italy   Japan   Poland   Portugal   Singapore
South Korea   Switzerland   Thailand   Turkey   Ukraine   Vietnam

Oxford is a trade mark of Oxford University Press
in the UK and in certain other countries

Published in
Canada by Oxford University Press

National Library of Canada Cataloguing in Publication

Dawson, Lorne L.
Comprehending cults: the sociology of new religious movements / Lorne L. Dawson. — 2nd ed.

Includes bibliographical references and index.
ISBN-13: 978-0-19-542009-8
ISBN-10: 0-19-542009-8

1. Cults. I. Title.

BL60.D38 2005   306.6   C2005-905734-3

Cover Design: Brett Miller
Cover Images: Imtek Imagineering/Masterfile

7 8 9 — 14 13 12

Oxford University Press is committed to our environment.
This book is printed on paper that contains a minimum of 50% post-consumer waste.

Printed in the United States of America

Contents

Acknowledgements   v

CHApter One   **Why Study New Religious Movements?**   1
The Cults in Our Midst   2
The Hostility Towards Cults   5
Box 1 They Come in All Shapes and Sizes   8
Responding to the Suspicions of the Public   10

CHApter Two   **What Are New Religious Movements?**   14
Religion and Its Continuing Significance   14
Churches, Sects, and Cults   26
Creating a Typology of Cults   30
Box 2 How New Religious Movements
     Change with Success   34

CHApter Three   **Why Did New Religious Movements Emerge?**   39
Asking the Right Question First   39
New Religious Movements as a Response to Cultural Change   39
Box 3 Three Models of Cult Formation   60
New Religious Movements as an Expression of
     Cultural Continuity   62
Concluding Remarks   70

CHApter Four   **Who Joins New Religious Movements And Why?**   71
The Stereotypes   71
Getting Involved with New Religious Movements   71
The Social Attributes of Those Who Join   82

Box 4 Why Are American Converts to New Religious
        Movements Disproportionately Jewish?   88
Some Reasons for Joining   90

Chapter Five   Are Converts to New Religious
                Movements 'Brainwashed'?   95
                The Issue and Its Significance   95
                The Case Against the Cults   97
                The Case Against Brainwashing   103
                Box 5 The Active Versus Passive Convert   117
                Reformulating the Issues in the Brainwashing Debate   119

Chapter Six   Why Are New Religious Movements So Often
                Accused of Sexual Deviance?   125
                Sexual Deviance and the Cults   126
                Box 6 Child Abuse and the Social Control of NRMs   132
                Gender Matters   136

Chapter Seven   Why Do Some New Religious Movements
                Become Violent?   142
                Responding to Recent 'Cult' Tragedies   142
                Apocalyptic Beliefs   146
                Charismatic Leadership   152
                Social Encapsulation   162
                Box 7 Surviving the Failure of Apocalyptic Prophecies   168
                Concluding Remarks   175

Chapter Eight   What Is the Cultural Significance of
                New Religious Movements?   179
                Our Skewed Perspective   179
                Modernism and the New Religious Movements   189
                Box 8 Factors Affecting the Success of NRMs   193
                Postmodernism and the New Religious Movements 195
                NRMs: Anti-modern, Modern, or Postmodern?   197
                Concluding Remarks   199

                Notes   200
                Bibliography   216
                Index   258

Acknowledgements

In writing this book and preparing the second edition I have benefited greatly from the scholarship and support of Jim Richardson, David Bromley, and the anonymous reviewers selected by the publishing company. I would also like to thank Phyllis Wilson, Rachael Cayley, and Tom Howell of Oxford University Press for their patience and much appreciated assistance.

Parts of Chapter 2 are drawn from Lorne L. Dawson, 'Constructing "Cult" Typologies: Some Strategic Considerations', Journal of Contemporary Religion 12 (3): 363–81, and reprinted with the permission of the journal. Parts of Chapter 1 and Chapter 4 are drawn from Lorne L. Dawson, 'Who Joins New Religious Movements and Why: Twenty Years of Research and What Have We Learned?' Studies in Religion 25 (2): 193–213, and reprinted with the permission of the journal. Parts of Chapter 8 are drawn from Lorne L. Dawson, 'Anti-Modernism, Modernism, and Postmodernism: Struggling with the Cultural Significance of New Religious Movements', Sociology of Religion 59 (2): 131–56, and reprinted with the permission of the Association for the Sociology of Religion, Inc.

Chapter One

Why Study New Religious Movements?

Two prominent local newspapers lay on my desk. Their headlines read, '48 Found Dead in Doomsday Cult' and '50 from Quebec Cult Found Slain'.[1] According to the stories, the members of a small religious movement called the Order of the Solar Temple (L'Ordre du Temple solaire) had set fire to their own homes and then committed mass suicide by shooting or asphyxiating themselves, an act that occurred simultaneously in three different places: Morin Heights in Quebec and the villages of Cheiry and Granges-sur-Salvan in Switzerland.[2]

I tuned in to ABC's news commentary program 'Nightline' to find host Ted Koppel already interviewing three 'cult experts', two of whom were drawn from the American anti-cult movement; the third was a Canadian journalist. Mr Koppel asked the usual questions: What could make people end their lives in this way? How could they come to join such a group in the first place? What do we know about the mysterious leader of the cult? The show's guests made few direct references to the actual beliefs and practices of the Solar Temple, but informed the audience that the group was like all other 'destructive' and 'apocalyptic' cults. In passing, one of the commentators referred to two other groups, the Unification Church of Reverend Sun Myung Moon and John-Roger's MSIA (pronounced 'Messiah'), failing to mention that neither has ever been associated with either violence or suicide. We were assured that the members of such cults are recruited through deception and mind-control by charismatic leaders who exploit the weaknesses of their followers for wealth and power. The experts had to acknowledge, though, that they really did not know much about this particular cult at all.

The show was an example of how prejudices against cults have been reinforced by the reiteration of the pejorative observations favoured by the media for the last thirty years.[3] Just over a year before the Solar Temple tragedy, the same television host had posed the same questions to similar 'experts' trying to explain the stand-off and eventual massacre of the Branch Davidians under David Koresh in Waco, Texas. He received the same speculative and polemical answers then. Listening to these people, I could not help wondering whether other viewers were as dissatisfied as I was. Might others not also ask why the experts knew so little, or how the groups continue to ply their trade if their sins are so transparent? A large body of information and insights does exist in the academic literature on the beliefs, practices, failings, and significance of cults. Sadly, though, the mainstream of public debate usually chooses to ignore it.

I realized that I had no right to complain if I was not willing to do something about it. This book is the result of that realization. The topic of cults is vast and complex, and plenty more may be said than is contained in my discussions here, but I hope that this text can nevertheless counter some of the suspicion and misinformation. I do not intend to offer an apologia for cults. Instead, I want to contribute to a more fact-based public understanding and an awareness of the limits of our knowledge relating to this issue.

The Cults in Our Midst

Cults, which many scholars now prefer to call 'new religious movements', first emerged into prominence in the 1960s and early 1970s. They later became the focus of public alarm after the mass murder-suicide of 914 followers of the Peoples Temple on 18 November 1978[1] (see Hall, 1987; Chidester, 1988; Maaga, 1998). This tragic and shocking event, sometimes referred to as the 'Jonestown massacre', unleashed years of popular and academic study of new religions. What had initially seemed a relatively harmless spin-off of 1960s counter-culture now appeared to some people to threaten the traditional Judeo-Christian culture of Western society. The cults even signified, some thought, the beginning of the age of false prophets foretold by the Bible as a sign of the end of days. Other people were, and are, willing to perceive the suicide tragedies as aberrations. What we can all agree, however, is that the emergence of cults points to a groundswell of spirituality infiltrating our seemingly ever more secular society (Roof, 1999; Emberley, 2002).[2] Whether good or bad, a sign of degeneration or regeneration, the religious life of North Americans and Western Europeans has clearly been changing over the last several decades, and the birth of new religions provides a unique opportunity for scholars of religion to trace these changes in detail.

Only a small fraction of the North American population has ever been involved with a new religious movement, though the fraction is always growing.[4] The cultural impact of these groups has been far greater than the numbers would suggest, however, particularly in their contribution to the growth of spiritual pluralism. North America was still largely split between Protestantism, Catholicism, and Judaism in the period after the Second World War (Herberg, 1955; Wuthnow, 1988); this picture has since been fractured by the numerous and ever more conspicuous alternatives.[5] After the 1960s, in the evocative words of Robert Wuthnow (1988: 152), 'it was as if the bits of mosaic that had given shape to the religious topography had been thrown into the air, never to land in exactly the same positions as before.'

Within the Christian community alone, North Americans have witnessed such alternatives as Mormonism, 'independent churches' (which do not belong to a particular denomination), groups founded in the ethos of the sixties counterculture (e.g. the Family and other so-called 'Jesus freaks'), and a plethora of other evangelical, fundamentalist, charismatic, and Pentecostalist 'churches'. Even more dramatically, perhaps influenced by immigration and the fact that so many Americans and Canadians have a non-Christian religious heritage, large numbers of Christian people have turned from their tradition altogether, switching either to other major world religions or to a multitude of imported or innovated cults.

In contemporary Western societies, the new religious movements (NRMs) can be divided into five sets:

1. groups associated with various Asian traditions of philosophy, devotion, meditation, and magic, such as Transcendental Meditation, Elan Vital (formerly the Divine Light Mission), International Society for Krishna Consciousness, Osho Foundation (formerly the Rajneesh Foundation), Sōka Gakkai, and Shambhala (formerly Vajradhatu);

2. groups associated with the American 'human potential movement' in popular psychology, such as Erhard Seminar Training (which uses the Latin verb 'est' as its acronym), Scientology, Psychosynthesis, and Silva Mind-Control;

3. groups associated with various forms of occult revival, such as Wicca, Hermetic Orthodoxy, and the Church of Satan;

4. so-called New Age groups, like Ramtha and the Church Universal and Triumphant, blending elements of past western esoteric traditions (e.g. the Rosicrucians, Theosophy) with fringe science, alternative medicine, trance channelling, and other things; and

5. groups that think their salvation depends on contact with UFOs and aliens, such as Heaven's Gate, the Aethurius Society, and the Raëlians.

Our primary concern is with these new kinds of religious life, more than the movements that have developed directly out of mainstream religions. Few groups, however, fit neatly into any of the categories given. Many of the new religions are the product of the ongoing synthesis of different religious traditions and elements of the religious and the secular worlds. Scientology, for example, is an innovated religion inspired by elements of the American human potential movement. But it lays claim to elements of Hinduism and Buddhism too. The Unification Church, which came from Korea, cannot be classified simply as an Asian import or a Christian spin-off; it falls somewhere between the two because its leader, the Reverend Moon, revised the Christian gospel dramatically with his own revelations influenced by the Korean traditions of Confucianism and shamanism. Although I have separated the UFO groups from the New Age ones, they share a common heritage in the esoteric beliefs and practices of Theosophy; one could argue that the UFO groups have transmuted the ascendent masters of Theosophical lore into alien allies from outer space (Partridge, 2003).

These NRMs embody larger processes of cultural integration, transformation, and globalization, which are altering the character of North American and Western European society (and indeed, societies worldwide). Modern mass media, rising levels of education, and changing immigration and economic patterns are ushering in a new era of pluralism and creativity, one that is bringing the East to the West rather as the West was first visited upon the East through economic imperialism and Christian missionaries. Many sociologists (e.g. Tiryakian, 1967, 1972; Hammond, 1987; Robbins and Bromley, 1992) suggest that new religious movements provide sheltering enclaves for social innovations and experiments, with some of these spreading to the larger culture. In any event, the very existence of such opportunities for lifestyle experimentation is bound to alter the self-understanding and values of current and future generations.

Any introduction to the study of new religions is faced with a chicken-and-egg problem in that we can hardly gain a critical understanding of the new religions without prior knowledge of the social-scientific insights into them, and yet the social science will not make much sense without prior knowledge of some specific groups. The only sensible approach is therefore to work simultaneously at both tasks. Readers of this text would also benefit greatly from looking at the case studies listed in the bibliography; these provide very detailed accounts of such prominent groups as Scientology (e.g. Melton, 2000), the International Society for Krishna Consciousness (e.g. Rochford, 1985), the Unification Church (e.g. Barker, 1984), the Jesus Movement (e.g. Chancellor, 2000), the Church Universal and Triumphant (Whitsel, 2003), and the Raëlians (Palmer, 2004); many studies are available on less conspicuous groups like Eckankar, Sōka

Gakkai, Vajradhatu/Shambhala, UFO cults, spiritualism, and various New Age and Neo-Pagan groups (see, for example, Ellwood and Partin, 1988; Melton, 1992a; Miller, 1995). To draw conclusions regarding these groups, we need at least a rudimentary awareness of their concepts of the divine or transcendent, their views on human nature, their beliefs about death and the afterlife, and their definition of 'the good life'—that is, the way in which one ought to live.[6] Seen in the proper context, new religions do not always appear so new, and many of the seemingly irrational aspects of contemporary cult life appear more reasonable, comprehensible, and socially significant.

The Hostility Towards Cults

Before we can begin to talk about cults in a more balanced manner, it is necessary to correct the image of exotic and dangerous 'otherness' that pervades the public perceptions of these new religions. We will begin by looking at a typical media report.

'Nightmare Tales—Why People Join Violent Cults' is the headline of an article in a news magazine.[7] In the first paragraph we are plunged into a gruesome account of a young woman's experience of extreme abuse, as a child and a teenager, at the hands of a Satanic cult. By the end of the second paragraph we are informed of the following 'facts': thousands of people join some 3,000 cults each year, 'dozens' of these cults are violent, and cults can take control of people's minds and brainwash them. Then the article quotes a 'former professor of psychiatry' who says that those of us who stand by and let it happen are no better than the 'regular white middle-class people [who] helped the Nazis murder six million Jews'. In the next two paragraphs we are treated to a recounting of the bloody Manson Family murders and the mass suicide at Jonestown. With our memories of these sufficiently refreshed we are told: 'To lure people into their dark world both violent and non-violent cults often prey on people who are emotionally confused or distraught.' Then another psychiatrist tells us, 'Cult members actually suspend their rational thought processes to do whatever the group leader asks them, even if it involves murder or suicide.' As in much propaganda about drug use, it is suggested that all this tragedy can grow disastrously 'out of a simple flirtation with something different or unknown'. From youthful experimentation with marijuana, heroin addiction follows. From experimentation with alternative religious views, one runs the risk of becoming a zombie enslaved to an unbalanced and immoral cult leader. Once so enslaved, this article explains, you will lose all your material goods and savings to the greed of the cults. Unless, of course, you are as lucky as the young woman from the start of the article, whose parents loved her enough to hire a deprogrammer from California to kidnap her and return her to reason.

Admittedly, the article is about 'violent cults', and much of what it says, in that limited regard, is a matter of record. The problem is that only the most careful and determined of readers could keep from falsely identifying the charges levelled at violent cults with all cults. The article panders to our worst fears and prejudices on the basis of a few aberrant cases. Investigations by social scientists not only fail to substantiate but usually refute most of the suppositions contained in such popular accounts.

Journalists face constraints of time, space, and competition in fashioning their stories about new religions. They are necessarily guided by the demand to attract readers, and often lack expertise in the subject. But as other subjects continue to be newsworthy, the quality of writing about them usually shows a marked improvement. This has not been the case with cult stories. The scholars Barend Van Driel and James T. Richardson (1988: 37) summarize their analysis of American print media by saying that news about cults, 'although not uniformly negative, can best be described as "a stream of controversies" with little attention to the history or human side of the new religions.'

The social scientist Jeffrey Pfeifer conducted a study in 1992 into the effects of the media coverage. He divided 98 undergraduates into three groups and gave each a scenario to read; these texts were identical, a description of a young man who joins an organization and is exposed to its indoctrination process, except that the label given to what the man joined was different for each group of students. One group was told they were reading about a man joining the Moonies (i.e. the Unification Church), another about a man joining the Marines, and the third, a man entering a Catholic seminary to become a priest. Afterwards, each participant filled out questionnaires about the scenarios and his or her knowledge of cults. The study revealed that the participants overwhelmingly preferred the term 'brainwashing' for the experience of a man joining the Moonies, but not for a man joining the Marines or the Catholic priesthood (the results were 71 per cent, 44 per cent, and 29 per cent respectively). Though the scenarios were all the same, more neutral terms like 'resocialization' were preferred for the latter two possibilities. The participants also considered the man joining the Moonies to be less happy with life before joining the group, less intelligent, and less responsible than the one joining the Marines or the Catholic priesthood. The new follower of the Moonies was also more likely to be rated as having been coerced into joining, less able to resist indoctrination, and less free to leave, and it was felt that he was treated less fairly. Similarly, when asked to describe the average cult member, 82 per cent of the participants gave negative descriptions, the rest giving neutral ones (no positive descriptions were recorded). Clearly, the mere mention of a cult produced a significant skewing. Yet the study also revealed that 82 per cent of the participants had never even talked to a cult member, let alone known or been one; 92 per cent said they were basing their opinions on media reports.

How the media has treated cult phenomena certainly seems to have had telling consequences,[8] and such findings have been corroborated by other work such as Eileen Barker's excellent analysis of the Unification Church in Britain (1984: 2–3). In another study, a random national sample of 1,700 Americans found that, despite a long tradition of freedom of religion (enshrined in the First Amendment of the American Constitution), 73 per cent supported the idea of legislation that would prohibit the conversion of teenagers to cults (Bromley and Breschel, 1992). Likewise, in many court cases involving new religions, the jurors have shown a surprising disregard for the constitutional protection of religious freedoms. Media analyst Stewart Hoover (1994: 2–6) believes that the news media contributed to the demise of the Branch Davidians at Waco by reinforcing the conception of David Koresh as a terrorist rather than a religious leader open to theological debate and persuasion. James Richardson (1995a) argues more generally that the FBI was emboldened to override the advice of its own behavioural experts and to proceed with the drastic measures against the Branch Davidians by the highly negative and unrealistic conception of cults that had gained currency in the United States as a result of the media's reliance on press releases from anti-cult organizations.

Indeed, much of the popular prejudice against new religious movements stems from the success of the anti-cult movement (Shupe and Bromley, 1980, 1994; Shupe, Bromley, and Darnell, 2004). This organized response to the newly emergent religious alternatives on the American scene began to take shape in the mid-1970s. It had its origin in numerous grass-roots reactions, particularly those of distraught families of the young adults who joined these unconventional religions. Some groups were also organized by members of the fundamentalist Christian right to defend their vision of the religious culture of America. While the distraught relatives sought the return of their children or siblings to conventional life, the fundamentalists often envisioned themselves to be struggling with the minions of Satan (Cowan, 2003). By the mid-1980s, these anti-cult groups had become a movement in their own right, and an element of professionalism emerged as permanent staff were hired, efforts were coordinated, concerted legal actions were launched, and full-time 'deprogrammers' began to ply their trade. Soon, when the media sought ready information on cult activities, they began to turn to the Citizens Freedom Foundation, Love Our Children Inc., the Council on Mind Abuse, the Cult Awareness Network, the American Family Foundation, and dozens of other anti-cult organizations.

Governments, at least at the federal level, have refrained from formally recognizing or assisting the anti-cult groups, arguing that they are special-interest organizations purveying opinion rather than substantiated claims. But academics who study cults have still found it difficult to have their voice heard. They played no significant role, for example, in advising the author-ities involved in the Branch Davidian stand-off. Later investigations of this tragedy (Ammerman, 1995; Sullivan, 1996) convinced the Department of Justice to set up a scholarly committee to advise them in the future. The FBI and other law enforcement agencies have similarly reached out (Rosenfeld, 2000). But despite this recognition of scholarly expertise, and the denial of the anti-cult movement's legitimacy, the academics still have to fight to be heard in the popular discussion.[9]

BOX 1 THEY COME IN ALL SHAPES AND SIZES

There may be over a thousand NRMs operating in North America, and many thousands more throughout the world. They tend not to be wholly new cre-ations but rather innovative variants of older traditions, the threads of which are ingeniously rewoven to create something different. The remarkable diver-sity of these movements, both doctrinally and organizationally, is evident in the following two examples:

Shambhala International

Shambhala International is an umbrella organization founded in 1992 to unite the different religious and cultural bodies created by the Buddhist teacher Chogyam Trungpa Rinpoche. In Tibetan mythology, Shambhala is the name of a utopian community guided by gentleness and fearlessness, and Shambhala International is dedicated to renewing society through the transformation of the consciousness of individuals.

In the Karmapa subsect of the Kargyupa sect of Tibetan Buddhism, Trungpa was the eleventh *tulku* (supposedly a reincarnation of the abbot of the Surmang monastery). He was forced to flee Tibet in 1959 at the age of twenty after the Communist Chinese invasion. Trungpa studied at Oxford University and went on to establish one of the largest and most successful Tibetan Buddhist communities in the West. This was not enough for him, however. In 1968, after a solitary retreat in Bhutan to seek guidance, he decided to give up his monastic vows and dedicate himself to adapting his traditions to the needs of a Western audience. He soon married a young British woman and moved to the United States, just in time to be carried into spiritual stardom by the tide of youth counter-culture. As a practitioner of 'crazy wisdom', a form of Tibetan instruction designed to shock devotees out of their complacent ways, Trungpa was controversial. He drank, smoked, had affairs, and cajoled and bullied his students, while donning many different public faces. When he died of heart failure in 1987, considerable mystery surrounded the real nature of this much admired and complex figure.

Trungpa freely incorporated into his lectures and work elements of other traditions such as Zen Buddhism as well as humanistic psychology and Western pop culture. This unorthodox approach attracted thousands of followers. By 1974 he had founded several successful monasteries and training centres (e.g. Karme-Choling in Vermont), as well as the Naropa Institute (in Boulder, Colorado), the first accredited Buddhist university in North America. In 1983, fearing the growing influence of materialism in the US, Trungpa controversially moved the international headquarters of his organization to the Canadian city of Halifax, Nova Scotia, and soon built the monastery called Gampo Abbey in a secluded part of Cape Breton Island. With training centers around the world, Shambhala today claims an active membership of approximately 6,000 people. It has successfully survived the death of its charismatic founder and found its niche in contemporary Western society.

Urantia

The Urantia movement is based on the study of *The Urantia Book*, a 2,097-page collection of papers first published in 1935. This book contains the revelations of alien beings about the true nature of the universe, the history of the planet earth (called Urantia), and the life of Jesus. The messages were 'channeled' by a sleeping man, and recorded by Dr William Samuel Sadler (1875–1969), a respected psychiatrist at the University of Chicago and lecturer at McCormick Theological Seminary. The book describes a universe of multiple dimensions containing thousands of inhabited worlds ruled over by gods of varying ranks, with diverse duties. At the highest level of this alternative cosmology is the 'I AM', who resides in Paradise. The last part of the book contains many new claims about the childhood, travels, ministry, death, and resurrection of Jesus. The Son of Man is identified as one of 700,000 'creator sons' incarnated on various worlds, and it is said that he will return

to earth again once humanity is transformed by the new revelations promoted by this movement.

The students of Urantia believe that a 'thought adjuster' dwells in each of
us, seeking to direct our lives to the truth. Upon death our souls enter into a
sleep and are taken to other worlds on a journey of self-discovery, culminat-
ing in admission to Paradise. The sole activity of the membership of the
Urantian movement is to study the book, often in groups. There are no cler-
gy or churches, so it is difficult to gauge the size of the movement or speak of
its structure. This amorphous nature was partly responsible for recent struggles between different groups over the legal ownership of the book, its interpretation, and the reception of new revelations, although these issues have
now largely been resolved.

Reprinted from entries by Lorne L. Dawson in *New Religions: A Guide* (2004), edited by
Christopher Partridge, by permission of Oxford University Press, New York.

Responding to tHe Suspicions of tHe Public

The public controversy over cults poses unique problems for academics,
who often find themselves pitted against active opposition to their findings. Many sociologists, historians, psychologists, and religious studies
scholars have therefore striven to disseminate more neutral explanations
of cult activity; an obvious example of this attempt is their avoidance of
the word 'cult', with all its pejorative connotations, in favour of 'new religions', 'alternative religions', 'emergent religions', 'new religious move-
ments/NRMs', and so on. I still sometimes use 'cult', however, partly for
effect and partly to keep the distinction between cults and other forms of
religious organization, such as sects (see Chapter 2). The generic 'NRMs',
although a useful term, tends to blur the line between these different kinds
of religious groups. (Incidentally, not all NRMs are particularly new, nor are
they all movements.)

Recognizing that the public distrusts the way that cults portray themselves, many NRMs have tried to foster social-scientific interest in their
groups in hopes of countering the misinformation (Barker, 1993: 197–8;
1995a). In turn, the social scientists have sought cordial relations with NRMs
to gain the rapport necessary to conduct their research. This may all easily
be misinterpreted, however, as evidence of pro-cult bias in the research.
Students of NRMs are burdened, then, with a greater than usual requirement

to appear impartial, and their only real protection against such accusations is the depth and quality of their knowledge.[10]

Given these and other difficulties inherent in the study of NRMs, let us conclude this chapter with a vow to keep the following four methodological concerns in mind:

1. We must guard against lumping all new religious movements together. Anti-cult literature is fond of casting aspersions on 'cults' in general, but amongst the many thousands of cults is great diversity. They have different conceptions of our origins, development, and future. They propose different explanations of our existential plight, and they offer different programs to alleviate our woes. They mobilize and organize different resources, in different ways, with different immediate and distant consequences. They may respond to different situations, needs, desires, and constituencies.

We can try to make some useful generalizations about NRMs. When we do, a distinction usually emerges between the more traditionally oriented religions, tending to stress communal life and exclusive commitments, and the religions more oriented to modernity, which tend to be non-communal and open to segmented and plural commitments. This represents a continuum of possibilities rather than two exclusive categories, and we will see later how this generalization becomes problematic. Nevertheless, we might usefully say that the Unification Church, Krishna Consciousness, and most Christian fundamentalist groups lean to the traditional end, while Theosophy, Scientology, Wicca, and most New Age groups lean towards the modern end.[11]

2. We should be wary of treating new religious movements as unique in history or in Western societies. On the contrary, as James Beckford claims: 'They have had counterparts in earlier times and they continue to have them in other regions of the world' (1985: 25). There is something new and yet not so new about the cult activity we are studying, something both home-grown and foreign. The NRMs represent a curious blend of East and West, past and present.

3. We must not indulge in 'reductionistic' analyses of these groups. The social-scientific study of religion confronts a difficulty in that it strives to make objective, empirical, and logical sense of a subject that is highly subjective and claims to be based on non-empirical, 'spiritual' foundations. Religions are often purposefully paradoxical in their basic premises and practices. But it is not the function of social scientists to resolve matters of ontology or theology; that is the concern of philosophers and theologians. Setting aside the question of the truthfulness of the claims of any religion, the function of social scientists is merely to record and explain those aspects of religious life that are susceptible to empirical research.

In practice, however, matters are rarely so straightforward. Attempts to explain elements of religious life may depend on assumptions about human nature and the world that are contrary to the fundamental assertions of the religions. In fact, as Ian Hamnett (1973), Benton Johnson (1977), and others have argued, the sociology of religion seems to be covertly founded on a rather inconsistent assumption: religion is good for society and yet the beliefs of religions are problematic. For most sociologists, belief in the supernatural is implicitly erroneous. Consequently, in seeking to explain religious phenomena, sociologists often seem to be actually explaining them away. In their accounts, where once there were religious processes, there are now merely social, psychological, and even biological processes. However, since social scientists cannot adequately resolve ontological issues, when claims of supernatural agency are involved there is often no sound reason to value the accuracy of their scientifically derived explanations of religious phenomena more highly than the religious explanations.[12]

So, in order to avoid being too reductionist, I will make an effort in this book to treat the doctrines of new religious movements seriously. As Geoffrey Nelson (1984) and others (e.g. Wilson, 1982a; Bateson and Ventis, 1982; Stark and Bainbridge, 1985, 1987) have argued, we must acknowledge that new religious movements grow out a desire to satisfy certain 'spiritual' needs of humanity that have a reality and importance independent of our other social and psychological needs. We should also remember that much of religious life is like the rest of life. Religious choices are usually made on a calculation of apparent benefits and costs (e.g. Brodin, 2003). There is no a priori reason to assume that religious activities are primarily irrational. Rather, we should look for evidence of a reasonable exchange of investments by the convert in return for rewards from the cult.

In our society, the practice of law, education, politics, economics, and daily business is guided by two assumptions: (i) people are predisposed to be rational, and hence once they become aware that they are behaving irrationally, they will adjust their beliefs; (ii) unless we have a reason for thinking otherwise, we should assume the behaviour of others is rational. These assumptions help us explain social life without falling prey to an infinite regress of impractical speculations about the 'real' causes or motivations of other people's actions. In the study of new religious movements, we have no reason to assume in advance that the assumptions no longer hold. We must, however, make sense of the actions of cult members in context. No action can be deemed rational or irrational in ignorance of the circumstances and perspectives of those taking the action (Weber, 1949; Blumer, 1969).

Most of humanity wants a spiritual element in life. A methodological focus on the rational character of people's judgements in no way excludes this possibility. As the philosopher Nicholas Rescher (1988: 9) observes, reason 'recognizes the utility and appropriateness of our higher (aesthetic and affectively social and even spiritual) values. The realm of rationality is as large and comprehensive as the domain of valid human concerns and interests.' Reason and religion are not necessarily antithetical (see Weber, 1963). Thus, 'in addition to the oft repeated insight that people who want to do good work in [the] area [of NRMs] must be able to overcome personal religious commitments, it must be added that it is equally important that people be able to overcome their lack of faith. One need not be a believer, but one must understand how belief is possible' (Stark and Finke, 1993: 123). Accounts of NRMs often give ample attention to the emotional (or 'affective') component of religious actions, and I do not plan to ignore or factor out that component in this text. I am, however, attempting to correct the balance, so to speak, by highlighting some grounds for perceiving the 'relative rationality' of seemingly irrational or even unsavoury behaviour.

4. We should realize that part of the reason for studying new religious movements is that they serve as mirrors for us and our society. In the words of Donald Stone: 'The new religious movements often serve as spiritual inkblots: reports of movements may tell us more about the observers than about the observed' (1978a: 42). Our reactions to religious innovations may reveal much about our individual and collective self-understanding.

Chapter Two

What Are New Religious Movements?

Much of the debate over the future of religion in North America is reproduced in a recent clash of two theoretical paradigms. An understanding of these two perspectives helps clarify many of the issues raised by the study of NRMs. As to the nature of NRMs themselves, we should also look at what sociologists call church-sect theory, which helps us distinguish a cult from other forms of religious organization.

Religion and Its Continuing Significance

The first of the two paradigms is derived from the seminal writings of the American sociologist Peter Berger, in particular his book *The Sacred Canopy* (1967). The second paradigm is from the American sociologists of religion Rodney Stark and William Sims Bainbridge (1985, 1987), developed further in later writings by Stark with Roger Finke and also Laurence Iannaccone.

Berger's theory of religion offers an account of the most essential social grounds of religious belief and practice; his theory is repeatedly called upon in relation to NRMs. Its logic tends to suggest, though, that society is destined to become ever more secular, and that neither old nor new religions will have much importance in advanced industrial societies. In contrast, the theory offered by Stark and his colleagues argues against the demise of religion, breaking with the tendency to equate this with progress towards more rational forms of social management.[1] The result provides alternative criteria for assessing the nature, appeal, success, or failure of various kinds of NRMs. A close reading of the divergent theoretical paradigms of Berger and of Stark reveals some interesting points of convergence, however, which may point the way to an even better understanding of NRMs. We will be discussing this last point further in Chapter 8.

BERGER'S THEORY OF RELIGION

Berger's theory grew out of his earlier and equally important work with Thomas Luckmann on the social construction of reality (Berger and Luckmann, 1966). Building on a masterful synthesis of the insights of foundational thinkers of contemporary social science (Karl Marx, Emile Durkheim, Max Weber, George Herbert Mead, Sigmund Freud, Max Scheler, Karl Mannheim, Alfred Schutz, and others), this theory begins with the simple premise that 'every human society is an enterprise of world-building' (Berger, 1967: 3). The world we live in, the world as perceived by humans, is constantly being created and re-created through a 'dialectical process' that has three aspects: 'externalization, objectivation, and internalization'. Our thoughts become embodied in the things we make and do in the world—they are *externalized*. Once out there, these products of our thought (e.g. machines, art forms, institutions) take on an independent existence as objects of our awareness—*objectivation* occurs—and they act back upon us, shaping and changing our behaviour and our further thoughts. We *internalize* the lessons of living in the world of these objects (physical, social, and cultural), adapting ourselves in thought, word, and deed to the presumed requirements of 'reality'. We are the creators of our world, but we are in turn shaped by our creation and become one of its objects, in part because we are not fully aware of our creativity. This lack of awareness stems from the fact that the creativity is a collective undertaking. World-building is a social process, so complex and dispersed as to defy the ready comprehension or control of any individual or group.

Berger argues that human participation in world construction is an 'anthropological necessity'. Unlike other animals, humans are born 'unfinished'. Since our biological programming is deficient, to survive we must complete our natures by learning how to function in our environment. To this end we have created culture. Culture is the truly 'natural' world of humans, and it stands protectively between individuals and the forces of nature. The problem is that culture is also unstable, fluctuating with the changing conditions of collective life. Thus, Berger proposes, we are eternally trapped between a biologically given imperative to secure a stable and safe environment through culture and the inherent instability of the cultures we create. This is the human predicament.

Religion is the ultimate response to this predicament. The success of a culture in providing a stable environment for human development 'depends upon the establishment of symmetry between the objective world of society and the subjective world of the individual' (Berger, 1967: 15). The upshot of such a symmetry is that the institutions of society and the roles these prescribe for individuals strike us as 'factual', which is to say that we think we must abide by their dictates, by society's traditional ways of doing things, because these are seen as somehow belonging to reality itself. Under such conditions people do not merely perform their assigned roles in social life, they freely identify with these roles. They seek what another sociologist, Ralph Turner, calls 'role-person merger'—they become their roles—and in the process they impart great stability to the received social order. Human activity becomes very regular and predictable, providing practical and psychological reassurance to everyone about their own and other people's behaviour. Hence, under ideal circumstances, which are never actually achieved, most aspects of the social order should come to be 'taken for granted'. The relatively stable human environment that results is what Berger calls a 'nomos', a meaningful world order.

The collective effort to fashion this *nomos* is 'totalizing', in that to become more stable the meaningful order must grow to encompass all aspects of society. The *nomos* does not, however, embrace all the discrete experiences of individuals; on the margins of everyday life are less predictable experiences that can induce 'anomie', an anxiety-inducing sense of normlessness. In dreams, death, defeat, and unexpected events, we are repeatedly threatened with separation from the social world and hence with a loss of meaningful order in our lives. In Berger's words (1967: 23), 'every *nomos* is an edifice erected in the face of the potent and alien forces of chaos'. Religion seeks to provide the 'ultimate shield against the terror of anomie' (1967: 25) by supplying the most effective legitimation of the social order. Religious myths, rites, doctrines, and practices seek to assert the merger of the *nomos* and the cosmos. The social order, in Berger's words, is 'cosmosized' and rendered 'sacred'. It is no longer a human construct, subject to change, but a divinely given order subject to the will of the gods (or other supernatural forces) alone. In such a world, any attempt to deny the order that the religiously sanctioned society imposes is an act of evil as well as madness (Berger, 1967: 39). Of course, it must be remembered that Berger is speaking hypothetically about the earliest stages of human social development, but there has been no real mass awareness of the creative role of humans in the construction of the world until modern times. Rather, as best we can tell, the gods evolved hand in hand with society from the beginning. Historically, 'forgetfulness' is the normal state, and 'awareness' is the modern aberration brought on by philosophy, science, and technology.

In a world where the human microcosm has been merged with the natural macrocosm, where social roles become reiterations of cosmic realities, the experience of anomie is much more tolerable. It is not eliminated, since death, nightmares, and unanticipated twists of fate persist. But these events are given a meaning in light of some larger divine scheme, whether through reference to the will of a supreme God, the struggle of supernatural forces of good and evil, or the consequences of karma. This meaningfulness helps individuals to maintain hope and endure suffering. The promise of ultimate order provides comfort, and more, it ensures that individuals will continue to willingly sacrifice themselves and their own selfish interests for the benefit and survival of the group, the social system, and the culture. The price of this security is 'alienation', or the forgetfulness I just mentioned. For the illusion of world-building to work, humans must 'forget' their own creative role in the dialectic. They must become estranged from their own responsibility for the nature and fate of their society. To consider one's creative role would be to question the objectivity of the social order and hence the ultimate meaning attributed to life. In Berger's theory, every society strikes some balance between the evils of anomie and alienation. The former can only be staved off by a certain amount of the latter.

Berger's theory is full of complexities, such as his description of religions existing in 'plausibility structures'. Just as religion may justify certain habits or institutions of society, a social system can provide a kind of material justification for its religion; a powerful, viable society lends credence to the belief system associated with it. Conversely, the military defeat or social disruption of a society may discredit its religious ideology. (An exception to this pattern would be Judaism, which managed to fashion a new ideology of hope out of disruptions such as the Babylonian exile and later the Diaspora, developing a *nomos* from the notion of redemptive suffering.)

Although Berger meant to provide only broad guidelines, he has decisively influenced the academic study of religion in general and the study of NRMs in particular. Since the 1960s, discussions about the emergence of NRMs have tended to lean heavily on Berger's ideas, partly due to another major aspect of his theory, his analysis of the process of secularization. The differences between this approach and that of Stark and his colleagues has largely framed the debate over the cultural significance of NRMs.

BERGER'S THEORY OF SECULARIZATION

For the first time in history many humans, especially members of the advanced industrial West, live in largely non-religious societies. Our societies have become increasingly secular since at least the middle of the nineteenth century, a process that is the overriding feature of religion in the modern world, and hence the backdrop to all contemporary research in the sociology of religion, in particular the study of NRMs. Berger defines secularization as 'the process by which sectors of society and culture are removed from the domination of religious institutions and symbols' (1967: 107). He suggests that this represents a highly significant break with the dominant pattern of human history.

In a manner that is now conventional, Berger sees all this as beginning with the rise of industrial society. Following the work of Max Weber (1958a, 1958b), Berger links secularization to the processes of 'rationalization' crucial to the capitalist economy. From as early as the seventeenth century, with the economic and then the political spheres of activity in society starting to become liberated from religious tutelage, religious systems have been compelled to adapt to a new social structure. Specifically, Berger argues that religions have met with two new realities. First, religion has become a matter of choice; religious orientations are no longer the legitimating requirements of society so much as the preferences of individuals or nuclear families. Religion has undergone what sociologists call 'privatization' (Berger, 1967: 133–5). In the modern world, as Berger ruefully remarks (1967: 134), 'religion manifests itself as public rhetoric and private virtue. In other words, in so far as religion is common it lacks "reality", and in so far as it is "real" it lacks commonality.' Seen as a private matter, one of individual choice, religious beliefs and practices do not provide a common universe of meaning for the members of society, and thus the traditional task of religion has been ruptured.

Second, while religions must struggle with privatization, they must also cope with 'pluralism' (Berger, 1967: 135–8). Religious choice is possible because the monopolies of the past (such as the nearly universal rule of the Catholic Church in Europe until the sixteenth century) were broken by the Protestant Reformation and the increased exposure of the West to the cultures of India, the Far East, and Africa (see, for example, Fields, 1981; Tweed, 1992; Prebish and Tanaka, 1998; McLellan, 1999).

Privatization and pluralism went hand in hand. By the nineteenth century, religious allegiances had become largely voluntary, especially in North America, and a competitive market for these allegiances emerged. In Berger's words (1967: 138), this means that 'the religious tradition, which previously could be authoritatively imposed, now has to be *marketed*. It must be "sold" to a clientele that is no longer constrained to "buy".' Religious institutions have become marketing agencies and the religious traditions consumer commodities.[2]

This shift has far-reaching consequences, Berger believes, for both the structure and the ideologies of Western religions. In order to compete in the new marketplace, religious organizations have become increasingly bureaucratic, with the result that they have also become more similar in form and functioning. As in other markets, the pressures of competition have led organizations to mute the harshness of competition by forming cartels. This means that, having splintered into many competing smaller groups, the religious landscape then experienced a kind of reverse shift in which small organizations struck agreements with other religions in order to apportion and stabilize their market share. A result of this was the movement of autonomous church communities into larger denominations in the nineteenth and early twentieth centuries, and Berger sees it continuing in the strong ecumenical movement and merger of many American Christian denominations since the Second World War (see e.g. Wuthnow, 1988: 71–99).

The products of religion fall prey to the same irony (i.e. that the growth of pluralism has produced homogenizing pressures). In economic terms, we would talk about 'standardization' and 'marginal differentiation': products are made to suit the same consumer preferences, minimizing of any real differences in substance while maintaining a competitive edge with small differences in style and approach. As with toothpastes and cars, a follower of Berger might say, so with religions. The product must also conform to the dictates of its new location—the private sphere. Religions that place a priority on private matters such as sexuality, marriage, child rearing, and family norms and activities, gain a competitive advantage (or so it is thought). Moreover, so do religions that offer a product 'consonant with the secularized consciousness' of inhabitants of advanced industrial states, for example, by conforming with the findings of science.

The net result, Berger laments, is that in the pluralistic competition of many look-alike religions (at least in the Christian context of the modern West), the plausibility of all is undermined as the content of each becomes seen as a kind of relative version of truth rather than objective fact. The religious beliefs that support a *nomos* 'are "de-objectivated", that is, deprived of their status as taken-for-granted, objective reality' (Berger, 1967: 151). The veracity of religious claims becomes a matter of subjective consciousness and conviction alone. In conclusion, Berger (1967: 153) proposes, two options seem to confront religions in the conditions of the modern world:

> They can either accommodate themselves to the situation, play the pluralistic game of religious free enterprise, and come to terms as best they can with the plausibility problem by modifying their product in accordance with consumer demands. Or they can refuse to accommodate themselves, entrench themselves behind whatever socio-religious structures they can maintain or construct, and continue to profess the old objectivities as much as possible as if nothing had happened.

For most religions, the reality lies somewhere in between these two extremes. And in ways that Berger did not foresee, perhaps could not have foreseen in the mid-1960s, other new options have arisen. Many NRMs (such as Krishna Consciousness) refuse to accommodate themselves to secular modernity, and offer new conceptions of the objective order of the world, in a Western context. Others, like Scientology, fashion new ways of adapting to modernity while reconfiguring the very nature of the religious marketplace (e.g. by openly turning religion into a business). In either case, we get a radicalization of the conditions of religious life compared to the conventions of the denominational Christianity dominant in North America. Some groups tend to become more totalistic in the commitments demanded, while others become more limited in their demands and more consumer-oriented. In other words, we get movement towards the division of types of NRMs mentioned in Chapter 1.

Berger was clearly disturbed by these developments, and *The Sacred Canopy* has been read largely as a prognosis of religious demise, although its author may not have intended that and has since offered a more optimistic view (see Berger, 1969, 1999).

STARK AND BAINBRIDGE'S THEORY OF RELIGION

The fact that some sort of secularization has occurred is a point commonly agreed. Ample debate takes place, however, about its precise nature, causes, and prospects. Berger helped to establish the prevalent view for the last several decades, but his theory presents only one set of possibilities for explaining things like cults. The alternative reading by Stark and his colleagues offers different possibilities and has stimulated renewed debate about secularization and the significance of NRMs.

'At least since the Enlightenment,' Stark and Bainbridge note (1985: 1), 'most Western intellectuals have anticipated the death of religion as eagerly as ancient Israel awaited the messiah. . . . But, as one generation has followed another, religion has persisted.' In response, Stark and Bainbridge have sought to fashion a simple theory that explains this persistence while acknowledging secularization as 'a major trend in modern times' (1985: 1). They suggest that many scholars may be mistaking the secularization of certain traditional forms of religious life for 'the doom of religion in general' (1985: 3).

Stark and Bainbridge's theory of religion grows out of four simple premises. The first is that any meaningful discussion of religious phenomena must acknowledge the pivotal role of the 'supernatural'. Religions, they argue (1985: 5), 'involve some conception of a supernatural being, world, or force, and the notion that the supernatural is active, that events and conditions here on earth are influenced by the supernatural.' Some scholars are inclined to see many things as religious, even though they lack any explicit reference to the supernatural (for example, the fanatical cult of personality surrounding the Communist Chinese leader Mao Tse-tung in the 1960s, or the life-consuming commitment of certain radical environmentalists). But these can only be deemed 'religions' insofar as they resemble activities that actually do refer to the supernatural; the description is the result of drawing an analogy, but an incomplete one.

The second premise is that 'humans seek what they perceive to be rewards and try to avoid what they perceive to be costs' (1985: 5). Stark and Bainbridge claim that this simple utilitarian adage accounts for most human action, including religious acts.

The third premise is that the rewards people seek are often scarce. Throughout human history some of the most desired rewards seem to be things that are not readily available at all, like life after death or an end to suffering.

The fourth and last premise is that, in the absence of real rewards, people often create and exchange what Stark and Bainbridge call 'compensators', promises of reward at some later time or in some other place. These range from the specific to the highly general. When a child is promised a future trip to the amusement park in exchange for chores done now, a specific compensator is being invoked. The promises of a happy life, knowledge of the meaning of life, or immortality, which are common to the religions of the world, are obviously very general; these can be provided only, Stark and Bainbridge assert, with the assistance of some supernatural agency.

Combining these four, Stark and Bainbridge (1985: 8) propose that religions should be viewed as 'human organizations primarily engaged in providing general compensators based on supernatural assumptions'. They see little reason to be pessimistic about the future of religion, arguing that history suggests that

> so long as humans intensely seek certain rewards of great magnitude that remain unavailable through direct actions, they will be able to obtain credible compensators only from sources predicated on the supernatural. In this market, no purely naturalistic ideologies can compete. Systems of thought that reject the supernatural lack all means to credibly promise such rewards as eternal life in any fashion. Similarly naturalistic philosophies can argue that statements such as 'What is the meaning of life?' or 'What is the purpose of the universe?' are meaningless utterances. But they cannot provide answers to these questions in the terms in which they are asked. (1985: 7–8)

Implicitly, like Weber and Berger before them, Stark and Bainbridge are positing that humans need to live in a meaningful world and that neither the wonders of modern science nor the material abundance of advanced industrial societies has displaced this need and the consequent quest for supernatural reassurances. The way in which these reassurances are offered is another matter. Religion, in their opinion, is changing, not dying.[3]

STARK AND BAINBRIDGE'S THEORY OF SECULARIZATION

Secularization, in the sense Berger proposes, is indeed happening. But Stark and Bainbridge introduce an important qualification: continuing the economic imagery introduced by Berger, they propose (1985: 429–30) that secularization is a constant element of all 'religious economies', and not a unique attribute of the contemporary world. The process of secularization is part of the primary dynamic of religious economies, a self-limiting process that engenders religious renewal, and not the sheer demise of religion. Properly understood, secularization refers to the periodic collapse of specific and dominant religious organizations as a consequence of their becoming more worldly, more accommodating to the non-religious aspects of their cultural contexts. Contrary to Berger (and most other sociologists), in this more limited sense secularization should not be confused with the loss of the need for general supernatural compensators. The reverse is true. It is the failure to provide sufficiently vivid and consistently supernatural compensators that accounts for the decline of established religions.

In the modern era, the spread of an increasingly scientific and rationalistic world view has pushed magic (one of the more specific forms of supernatural compensators) out of religion and forced the dominant traditional religions into a full-scale retreat from their essential principles. But the existential questions persist, and hence so does the demand for the kind of totalistic and ultimately unconfirmable responses provided by religions in the past. Commenting on this state of affairs, Stark and Bainbridge (1985: 434) note:

The conception of the supernatural [sustained by the dominant contemporary traditions] . . . has receded to a remote, inactive, almost non-existent divinity. We see bishops and theologians denouncing as mere superstition the notion of a god 'up there'. Does a god who is not 'up there' plausibly preside over heaven and offer triumph over death? Many of the most prestigious denominations offer mixed signals at best in answer to this question. Such religions have reached the point where they can no longer offer the quality of general compensators that has been the historic *raison d'être* of religions. They offer little solace to the bereaved, to the dying, to the poor, or to those who seek to understand the enigmas of existence.

When religions ossify in this way, when their rituals and beliefs become dead and hollow formalities disconnected from any moving personal experiences, there are two possible socio-religious responses: revival and innovation. Stark and Bainbridge associate the revival option with the formation of what sociologists call sects. They associate the innovation option with the formation of cults. Sects tend to be splinter groups from mainstream traditions that are seeking to revive what they think to be the original or pure spirit of the religious tradition they are rebelling against. Cults signify the introduction of a more unconventional mode of religious expression, one that tends to depart altogether from the dominant traditions of the churches that are being secularized. This distinction is discussed more fully below; here we are simply interested in sketching the links that Stark and Bainbridge forge between a more limited conception of secularization and the processes by which new religions are created.

Writing almost twenty years after Berger, Stark and Bainbridge witnessed the unprecedented decline in the 1960s and early 1970s of the size and social influence of the liberal Protestant denominations that dominated North America for centuries, such as Anglicans and Episcopalians, Presbyterians, Methodists, Congregationalists, and Lutherans. They also saw that this decline coincided with the rise, on what might be called the religious right, of more conservative and experiential forms of Christianity (such as Pentecostalism, Charismatic Renewal, and evangelicalism in general; see Wuthnow, 1988; Roof, 1999) and the rise, on the religious left, of NRMs (such as Scientology, Neo-Paganism, and Tibetan Buddhism). Many of the resultant sects and cults were and will continue to be short-lived and inconsequential. But as Stark and Bainbridge are fond of repeating, Christianity, Islam, and Buddhism all began as cults.

To test at least partially whether these developments are linked, Stark and Bainbridge (1985: 444–8) tallied the locations of sect and cult headquarters in the fifty US states (in the absence of accurate state-by-state membership figures) and showed strong negative correlations between the locations of cults and churches on the one hand, and between sects and cults on the other. It seems that where cults abound, conventional churches are weakest; and where either sects or cults abound, the other tends to be absent. The latter observation suggests that cults and sects are not just interchangeable responses to secularization. They would seem to have different constituencies, and hence their presence may mean different things. Sects, it should be noted, are not actually correlated strongly with church decline; in fact, they seem to thrive in the same environments where churches persist. This leads Stark and Bainbridge (1985: 445) to speculate that 'sect formation is, in part, a response to early stages of weakness in the general compensators provided by the conventional churches. Cult formation tends to erupt in later stages of church weakness, when large sectors of the population have drifted away from all organizational ties to the prevailing faiths.' Cult formation reflects, they think, 'the efforts of the unchurched to become churched' (1985: 444). Most interestingly, Bader and Demaris (1996) provided significant empirical corroboration of these findings. Using a sample of 12,415 subjects from the National Survey of Families and Households in the United States, they confirmed that the strength of conventional religious organizations in the subject's area is strongly correlated with the likelihood of cult and sect membership. Where conventional religions are weak, cults, but not necessarily sects, are strong.

Predictably perhaps, the highest rates of cult activity seem to be on the west coast of the United States, particularly in California, and in the sunbelt (New Mexico, Nevada, and Arizona). Those are places to which large numbers of people have migrated in this century, severing their past religious affiliations. On the other hand, the Deep South and parts of the Midwest remain strongholds of sectarianism and conventional church membership (Stark and Bainbridge, 1985: ch. 6 and 9).

Commenting on the value of their theory, Stark and Bainbridge conclude (1985: 455):

> We do not posit a steady-state religious economy in which cults immediately make up deficits in conventional religious affiliation. We argue only that, to the degree a population is unchurched, there will be *efforts* to fill the void. Most such efforts will be abortive. . . . Only once in a while will an effective, rapidly growing cult movement appear. We cannot predict accurately *when* that will happen. But we think we can say where this is apt to happen and *why*.

APPLYING THE THEORIES TO NRMS

One does not have to accept all aspects of Stark and Bainbridge's theories of religion and secularization to see the utility of their views in trying to understand NRMs. The same can be said of Berger's theories. In conjunction, the theories of Berger and of Stark and Bainbridge set the broad context for understanding NRMs in three ways.

In the first place, they guide our understanding of the most fundamental nature of NRMs. Whether or not secularization will ultimately prove to be a permanent condition leading to the near-disappearance of all forms of religion, the evidence discussed in this text supports the view that the rise of NRMs is symptomatic of some sociocultural resistance to recent secularizing trends. Berger's discussion of secularization helps us to see the religious context of the sixties in which NRMs first proliferated. His analysis of the human conditions that require the creation and extension of a sacred canopy clarifies and reinforces Stark and Bainbridge's presumption of a continued need for supernatural compensators.

Second, Berger's theory also alerts us to the reason why many NRMs display the desire to influence, even control, all aspects of the lives of their followers. The attainment of religious monopoly may no longer be possible, but it may remain the expectation of even the most marginal religious group. After all, that expectation is historically rooted in the dominant social function of religion itself. In general, the interpretive frameworks provided by Berger and by Stark and Bainbridge begin to unravel the mystery of why some people turn to NRMs, without presupposing some abnormality or deviant motivation. These theories get us thinking about the context of exchange in which NRMs exist. In every religion, after all, there is an exchange of commitments between individuals and groups, an exchange of sacrifices and benefits, which in most cases can be reasonably delineated and assessed.

Third, it seems that an awareness of these theories sets our options for discerning the social and cultural significance of NRMs and their future. As mentioned above, if Berger is right, NRMs may only be emblematic of the last gasp of religion in the advanced industrial world. Or—and this may amount to the same thing—they may only represent the final triumph of a modern commercial and consumer ethic in the affairs of humanity. From this vantage point, religion has been reduced to just another product to be matched with the private needs and desires of individual consumers. As such, its relative importance has been greatly diminished and the prospects for the survival and growth of most NRMs are not bright (see Wilson, 1976, 1988). Alternatively, if, as Stark and Bainbridge suppose, the rise of NRMs is a sign more of a changing of the guard than of the end of religion, the prospects of at least some NRMs may be brighter than our generation can foresee. And finally, in Chapter 8 we will see that the situation may well be even more complex, for there is a further possibility: many NRMs may be engaged in the process of adapting religion to the conditions of the modern world but in ways that ensure rather than diminish their continuing cultural significance.

Churches, Sects, and Cults

To permit comparisons across time and cultures, sociologists have tried to put particular religious activities into categories according to the dominant form of social organization within which they occur. This process of categorization, which is known as church-sect typology, provides us with the insights we need to understand what kind of religious organization or form of religious life cults belong to.

The first distinction between churches and sects was drawn by Max Weber in 1904 (Weber, 1958a), but it is best known in the form elaborated by his colleague Ernst Troeltsch in 1911 (Troeltsch, 1931). This Troeltschian dichotomy of churches and sects has been broadly accepted and developed in myriad ways, creating a confusing array of types and subtypes of religious organizations. It is out of this process that the concept of 'cults' emerged, and in recent years, with the proliferation of NRMs, many scholars have tried to frame a 'subtypology' of different types of cults (e.g. Campbell, 1978; Bird, 1979; Robbins and Anthony, 1979a, 1987; Wallis, 1984; Lofland and Richardson, 1984; Beckford, 1985; Anthony and Ecker, 1987; Robbins, 1988). We do not need to survey all the permutations and merits of church-sect-cult typologizing here, but some understanding of the procedure and its options is useful in a study of NRMs.[4]

CHURCH-SECT THEORY AND DEFINING 'CULT'

As framed by Troeltsch, with the Christian tradition in mind, the church-sect dichotomy is commonly described as follows. Churches are organizations into which people are born and baptized as infants. Membership is involuntary. Sects are voluntary organizations to which people usually convert, frequently as the result of very emotional experiences. All kinds of people belong to churches; they are inclusive and their membership is heterogeneous. Sects tend to be much more homogeneous in their membership, drawing disproportionately from the underprivileged. This situation often reflects the fact that sects are created by schisms within a church that is aligned with the dominant social structure. The beliefs and practices of sects, then, tend to be more radical and ethically stricter than those of churches, and they constitute an act of protest against the values of the rest of society. Sects tend to be exclusive; that is, individuals must meet and maintain certain clear requirements to belong. Sectarians consider themselves to be an 'elect'—a group of people specially chosen for salvation—and those who contravene the group's precepts are subject to expulsion much more readily than in the case of churches. The leaders of churches are usually hired or appointed on the basis of special educational qualifications. They operate within a hierarchical and impersonal administrative structure. Sectarian leaders tend to be charismatic, and sects tend to have smaller, more democratic, and more personal organizational structures. In theology and liturgy, churches are inclined to be dogmatic and ritualistic. Sects are more inspirational, volatile, and even anti-ritualistic.

In the years since Troeltsch formulated his contrast between churches and sects, two other typologies of religious organizations have won favour amongst sociologists: those of J. Milton Yinger (1970) and Bryan R. Wilson (1970). Yinger divides religious organizations into six types; Wilson has proffered a sevenfold subtypology of sects.

In order of decreasing inclusiveness and also decreasing attention to the social integration of members, Yinger distinguishes the following types: the 'universal church' (e.g. the Roman Catholic Church); the 'ecclesia', or established national church (e.g. the Church of England or the Sunni faith of Saudi Arabia); the 'denomination'[5] (e.g. Baptists or Presbyterians); the 'established sect' (e.g. Jehovah's Witnesses or Christian Science); the 'sect' (e.g. Pentecostalists or the Worldwide Church of God); and the 'cult' (e.g. the Unification Church or Scientology).

The last of these distinctions, of course, adds the sole truly new category to church-sect typology and is the focus of our attention. Cults are placed on a continuum with sects, which makes sense in that, compared to churches, cults indeed share much with sectarian forms of religion. But as Gordon Melton complains (2004: 18), for Yinger and his contemporaries the term remained a rather vague 'catch-all' for groups that did not fit into the other categories. Cults were somehow just more at odds with the religious establishment than sects, and consequently 'their status and role in culture was continually being contested'. They were 'feared, disliked (even hated)' (Melton, 2004: 21). This negative connotation was influenced perhaps by the other context in which the term 'cult' had gained currency since the early twentieth century. Christian writers, particularly evangelical ones (e.g. Martin 1977, Cowan 2003), used the term to identify groups in American society that they thought were deviating dangerously from orthodox Christianity (e.g. Church of Latter Day Saints, Christian Science, Spiritualism, Jehovah's Witnesses). This pejorative meaning was heightened and extended to other new and often non-Christian groups when the 'cult scare' of the 1970s and 1980s gripped North America. By the time sociologists turned to the task of delineating what a cult is, the anti-cult movement had further impaired the scientific utility of the term by identifying cults with accusations of deception, psychological manipulation, and fraud. In fact, the leadership of the anti-cult movement has chosen to integrate these criticisms into the very definition of the word 'cult' (e.g. Hassan, 1988: 55 and Singer, 1995: 7).

Michael Langone (1993: 5), for example, defines a cult as '. . . a group or movement that, to a significant degree, (a) exhibits great or excessive devotion or dedication to some person, idea, or thing, (b) uses a thought-reform program to persuade, control, and socialize members . . . , (c) systematically induces states of psychological dependency in members, (d) exploits members to advance the leadership's goals, and (e) causes psychological harm to members, their families, and community.' Focusing this definition on certain assumptions about the behaviour and effects of a group breaks sharply with the more neutral focus offered by church-sect theory. Langone's definition shows a 'normative' approach, meaning that it tries to establish a norm and then either include or exclude groups from this, implying a common prior understanding of what constitutes the legitimate expression of religion. Such an assumption is problematic, especially when the criteria are not clearly specified; what counts as a 'thought-reform program', for instance, and how is this distinct from more mainstream religions? Such an approach, relying heavily on a set of implicit value judgements, tends to support the inclination to dismiss all new and unusual forms of religion as dangerous.

Even if Langone's definition were not wrongly used to form judgements about the groups, his approach still has a problem. By limiting the use of the word 'cult' to those few groups clearly known to be harmful (in somebody's judgement), he leaves the vast majority of religions that might conventionally be identified as cults undefined. We are therefore returned to the very problem all this classifying was intended to resolve. Yinger and others introduced the term 'cult' to help identify the full range of religious possibilities. The definitions employed by the anti-cult movement are unhelpful, then, for two reasons: (1) they impose a value judgement on cults that is not present in the classification of other kinds of religious organizations; (2) they leave a large number of religious groups unclassified.

There is no consensus amongst sociologists on a satisfactory definition. The sheer variety of new religions poses problems in framing a definition suitable to all or even most of the activities. It would be convenient if cults could just be described as very radical versions of sects but the word is used far too broadly for such a simple solution to be useful.

We need not entirely give up the idea of describing what we might mean by the word 'cult', however. I would venture to say that cults share the following cluster of traits:

1. Cults are almost always centred on a charismatic leader, who is usually the inspirational founder of the religion. The authority of this leader is

relatively unrestricted. Consequently, these groups are subject to gradual disintegration when the leader dies or is discredited (Miller, 1991). Not surprisingly, then, the vast majority of cults are relatively short-lived and small.

2. Cults usually lay claim to some esoteric knowledge that has been lost, repressed, or newly discovered, and they offer their believers some more direct kind of ecstatic or transfiguring experience than traditional modes of religious life.

3. Cults often display no systematic orientation to the broader society, since their primary focus is on the spiritual development of their members. This commonly means they are loosely organized and subject to frequent organizational changes.

4. To borrow from the sociologist Bryan Wilson: In comparison to established faiths, cults tend to 'offer a surer, shorter, swifter, or clearer way to salvation.' They offer a more 'proximate salvation' and, in principle, one more readily attained by more people. 'In new religions,' Wilson explains, 'there is prospect of spiritual abundance' (1982b: 17, 20).

This profile fits most cults, which are relatively unknown. You may have noticed, however, that it does not really describe several of the more famous groups figuring in the public controversy about NRMs. Scientology, Krishna Consciousness, and the Unification Church, for example, are quite long-lived and large. Accordingly, many of their features are sect-like. They are more organized and sophisticated in their relations with the larger world. With the exception of the Unification Church, whose founding leader is still alive, they have also managed to survive the death of their charismatic founder. Originally, though, these groups did display the traits I have suggested, and they do continue to have many of the other attitudes and practices, such as the emphasis on esoteric teachings and the satisfaction of individual needs. Perhaps, then, yet another intermediate category should be added to church-sect typology, that of 'established cult'.

Creating a Typology of Cults

We move now to Bryan Wilson's differentiation between types of sects. Following Max Weber, Wilson thinks we should make sense of religions in light of their manifest function: they offer paths to salvation. Accordingly, he distinguishes sects in terms of the supposedly deviant responses to the world generated by their answers to the question: 'What shall we do to be saved?' (Wilson, 1970: 36–40). Wilson labels as 'conversionist' the sects that view the world and its institutions as evil, with the belief that salvation can be had only as a result of a profound change in oneself (e.g. Salvation Army and Pentecostalists). Sects which 'declare that the world is evil, and that the only prospect of salvation is the overturning of the world by super-natural action', he calls 'revolutionist' (e.g. Jehovah's Witnesses and Christadelphians). Those groups which call the world evil and seek salvation by withdrawing from it, he calls 'introversionist' (e.g. Hutterites and Exclusive Brethren). 'Manipulationist' groups such as Christian Science seek salvation in the world, but by special means not generally known or accepted in the world. 'Thaumaturgical' groups (which could include Spiritualism) are geared to the relief of present individual physical and mental ills 'by special, almost magical dispensation . . . from the normal laws of causality'. Sects which believe that some of the evil in the world might be overcome through reform, in line with the dictates of a divinely inspired conscience, he terms 'reformist' (e.g. Quakers). And finally, he calls 'utopian' the groups that wish to reconstruct society 'by returning to the basic principles by which the creator intended [us] to live,' (e.g. the Oneida and Bruderhof communities). As Wilson demonstrates, in accordance with their ideas about salvation, each of these groups uses different elements of the Christian tradition and adopts a distinctive mode of social organization.

For our purposes, the merits of Wilson's specific typology are not important, nor is an understanding of his distinctions or knowledge of the groups he discusses. Rather, his typology suggests to us that if sects are subject to such subdivision, so might cults be; Wilson's typology could in fact be adapted to this end. Many other writers have devised their own methods of classifying new religions: Bruce Campbell (1978), for example, suggests that cults are marked primarily by their orientation to the 'divine within'. He argues that we can distinguish them according to how they respond to a particular tension between the sacred and the profane, specifically between the sacred ideal of individual potential and the profane world in which one's personality is actually rooted. He divides cults into two main groups plus a rather amorphous third possibility. The two main categories distinguish the 'illumination' cult, 'which emphasizes detachment from the personality and the search for direct inner personal experience of the divine' (for example, Theosophy and Spiritualism), from the 'instrumental' cult, in which 'inner experience is sought for its effects, its ability to transform the everyday personality so that it can better meet the demands made upon it' (for example, Scientology and Sōka Gakkai). The third possibility includes groups resembling either category but with a less individualistic orientation. These he calls 'service-oriented' cults. No illustration of the latter, however, is provided.

Thomas Robbins and Dick Anthony (e.g. 1979a, 1987) choose another approach, dividing cults according to how they deal with metaphysical ideas such as good and evil, and how these ideas affect a group's response to the 'moral indeterminacy' of modern societies. The scholars distinguish 'dualistic' movements, which promote an absolute dichotomy of good and evil forces, and 'monistic' movements, which teach the ultimate unity of all things and a mode of moral relativism. They make another distinction between 'unilevel' and 'multilevel' religions: unilevel groups tend to be literal in their approach to language and texts; multilevel groups display an appreciation of the symbolic and metaphorical aspects of language and regard spiritual teachings as encompassing various levels of meaning. These two sets of divisions are combined with yet another, between 'technical' movements that offer procedures for manipulating consciousness and 'charismatic' movements that stress the emulation of a spiritual leader. The combination of all these sets of categories produces an elaborate array of possible classifications.

Another approach is the much more simple method proposed by Roy Wallis, dividing cults into three types using a modified form of Max Weber's (1963) well-known differentiation between types of religious systems. Wallis distinguishes between cults according to their attitude to the social world in which they emerge: 'A new movement may embrace the world, *affirming* its normatively approved goals and values; it may *reject* that world, denigrating those things held dear within it; or it may remain as far as possible indifferent to the world in terms of its religious practice, *accommodating* to it otherwise, and exhibiting only mild acquiescence to, or disapprobation of, the ways of the world' (Wallis, 1984: 4; emphasis added). Again, each orientation gives rise to a distinctive social structure for the groups.

These examples indicate the riches and confusions born of the typological art. For most purposes, typologies like Robbins and Anthony's are too complex, whereas that of Wallis is too beguilingly simple. Before saying more, however, we should consider two basic features of all church-sect-cult typologies: (1) their 'developmental' and (2) their 'relative' character.

The developmental point is characteristic of almost all church-sect-cult typologies and conditioned by the observations of H. Richard Niebuhr. In *The Social Sources of Denominationalism*, Niebuhr (1929) argues that sects eventually tend to become like churches. As new generations are born and socialized into the sects and their ways become set, the original impetus to reject the norms and activities of the dominant society wanes. Likewise, if a cult is fortunate enough to survive and grow it will tend to take on the features and the increased stability of a sect. As sects become churches, and sometimes as cults become more sect-like as well, a new sect or cult may be spawned out of discontent or loss of interest. We are faced, Stark and Bainbridge (1979: 123) observe, with 'an endless cycle of birth, transformation, schism, and rebirth of religious movements'. Certainly much of the growth of new religions in North America stems from this tendency for established groups to splinter.

Building on Stark and Bainbridge's theoretical perspective, Finke and Stark (1992) argue forcefully in *The Churching of America, 1776–1990* that this pattern accounts for much of the more conventional religious history of the United States as well. In the nineteenth century, long-established religions such as Congregationalists and Presbyterians lost their dominance to younger, more sectarian creeds, such as Methodism. In the twentieth century, Methodism in turn became too church-like and worldly, and it has been surpassed by other new sectarian developments, like the Southern Baptist Convention and the Pentecostal movement.

The second point, about church-sect-cult distinctions being relative, is often forgotten. In most of North America, the Mormons (the Church of Jesus Christ of Latter-day Saints) operate as a sect. At the same time, however, they should probably be considered a church or ecclesia in the state of Utah, where most people are Mormon, and a denomination in southern Alberta, where Mormons account for a third of the population. In other words, the classification of any group depends on the time and place in question. By way of further illustration, let us consider the Roman Catholic Church. In medieval France it was an ecclesia, but in eighteenth-century America, which was dominated by Protestant denominations, it was treated as if it were a sect, or even a cult. By the late twentieth century, in both France and the United States, it is probably best deemed a denomination. In Quebec, the Roman Catholic Church was essentially an ecclesia until the 1960s but is now also better described as a denomination.

So, keeping the developmental and relative character of all church-sect-cult typologizing in mind, what typology should we use to make sense of the diversity of cults in our midst? I favour a typology based on one dimension—in other words, one in which different cults, sects, and churches can be arranged along a continuum based on changes in one variable. As for what this variable should be, I favour Weber's original choice for distinguishing churches and sects: the mode of membership of different groups and the consequent form of their social organization.

Amongst other things, a one-dimensional approach has the theoretical advantage of simplicity. Multidimensional types tend to get confusing because of all the combinations possible, resulting in a kind of infinite regress. This impairs the making of comparisons, and hence the explaining of differences. The one-dimensional approach better accommodates the developmental aspect of typologizing as well, since we can easily envisage groups moving along the spectrum over time. Stark and Bainbridge (1985: 23) stress the need for a common measure theorizing about the movement from sect to church, or cult to sect. I have found Weber's focus on membership and social organization to be the most convenient and reliable for callibrating such a measure, and for making useful comparisons between different groups and types.

In line with this, Stark and Bainbridge differentiate between 'audience cults', 'client cults', and 'cult movements'. Each of these may exist in perpetuity, but as cults gain in size and social stature they will tend to change from the audience type to client and eventually to movements. The same NRM may exist simultaneously in two or more of these forms; it might be a movement in California, but only a client cult in Connecticut or France. But what do these distinctions entail?

'Audience cults' are the least organized, yet perhaps most pervasive expression of cult activity in North America. The label refers to the loosely structured events at which individuals lecture and distribute literature about a variety of esoteric, mystical, eccentric, and occult topics. At various conferences and meetings certain sets of ideas and certain lecturers may attract a consistent following, but no formal and persistent organization results. The audience for the ideas in question remain mere consumers of cultic goods. This level of cult activity is characteristic of much of the interest displayed in UFO-related material and much so-called Neo-Pagan and New Age spirituality. In some respects, however, it also holds true for the early years of even such established sects as the Jehovah's Witnesses (see Penton, 1985: 13–33), an organization that began as a loose network of Bible study groups reading the same new literature about biblical prophecies. Similarly, the Church of Scientology began as a series of spontaneously arising study groups applying the method of psychological therapy developed by L. Ron Hubbard in his best-selling book *Dianetics: The Modern Science of Mental Health* (1975; originally published in 1950).

'Client cults' may emerge from audience cults, or arise independently. Here, 'the relationship between those promulgating cult doctrines and those partaking of it most closely resembles the relationship between therapist and patient or between consultant and client', Stark and Bainbridge suggest (1985: 26). The services of the cult leader or leaders may become highly organized, but little effort is made to 'weld the clients into a social movement. Indeed, client involvement is so partial that clients often retain an active commitment to another religious movement or institution.' In many respects, Theosophy began this way, while Scientology and numerous other popular groups like 'est' (Erhard Seminar Training, mentioned in the previous chapter) seem to have sought to remain at this organizational level. 'In the past, the primary services sold were medical miracles, forecasts of the future, or contact with the dead' (Stark and Bainbridge, 1985: 28). To this list can be added meditation, induced memories of past lives, astral projections to other times and places, UFO contactee accounts, and general experiences and knowledge of an expanded universe or levels of reality.

Finally, with success, a group may become a 'cult movement'. Using the Spiritualist movement of the late nineteenth and early twentieth centuries as an illustration, Stark and Bainbridge (1985: 29) argue as follows:

> When the spiritualist medium is able to get his or her clients to attend regularly on Sunday morning, and thus, in a Christian context, to sever ties with other religious organizations, we observe the birth of a cult movement. Cult movements are full-fledged religious organizations that attempt to satisfy all the religious needs of converts. . . . Attempts to cause social change, by converting others, become central to the group agenda.

Examples of cult movements are Theosophy in its maturity, Krishna Consciousness, the Unification Church, the Raëlians, and the Church Universal and Triumphant.

Box 2 How New Religious Movements Change With Success

To date much of the research on NRMs has focused on the description of the beliefs, practices, and organizational histories of groups that rose to prominence after the 1960s. It is important to realize now that these groups have changed with the passing decades. In fact, NRMs provide scholars with natural laboratories for the observation and analysis of the processes of religious change.

Reflecting on her three decades of research on NRMs, sociologist Eileen Barker (1995b) discusses changes in the characteristics of those NRMs that have survived and grown. First, there has been a shift from familial forms of association to more organized bureaucratic forms, with a corresponding increase in the division of labour and an expansion of the rules governing interaction between different categories of members. Likewise the very range of ways of organizing such movements has expanded, creating a greater diversity of types of NRMs.

Second, there has been a significant shift in the membership of many groups, as the balance of young to old and new to long-term members changes. The number of children now being born into cults has tended to reduce the need for movements to engage in aggressive proselytizing, and also introduced new demands and priorities. In Barker's words, 'It does not take much imagination to recognize that a movement [composed] of enthusiastic and inexperienced young converts with few if any responsibilities will differ fundamentally from one in which middle-aged adults, with 10 to 20 years experience of the movement, have a large number of dependent children' (1995b: 169).

Third, the day-to-day activities and the financial dealings of NRMs have shifted with the need to care for, discipline, and socialize a second generation of members. The children born into the movement also may precipitate changes in the policies and practices of these groups. Again, though, marked diversity is evident in how specific NRMs have actually responded to this challenge.

Fourth, leadership and types of authority have changed, shifting from the charismatic to the more traditional and rational. This often results in a diffusion of power and responsibilities, 'increased accountability for decisions', and 'more room for [the] interpretation and negotiation' of beliefs and practices by different cult members (1995b: 171).

Fifth, the belief systems of these NRMs have become more elaborate, in part because they also tend to become less extreme. Millennial beliefs, for example, are muted in the face of the postponement of the predicted end of the world. As indicated already, a greater diversity of interpretive positions is tolerated within the movements.

Sixth, there has been a weakening of lifestyle requirements and a corresponding softening in the distinction between insiders and outsiders. Groups that were strictly communal and adamant in their rejection of important aspects of the larger society (e.g. higher education) have started to institutionalize many levels of acceptable membership, 'ranging from the totally committed . . . through the rank-and-file faithful to fringe members who accept the beliefs but do not want to commit their whole lives to the movement . . . and, finally, sympathizers who may owe allegiance to another religion' (1995b: 174). Likewise extreme stances on issues like sex or gender relations have drifted 'toward the social norm', and the groups have sought active alliances with other groups in society in the support of various causes.

The moderating effect of these changes is what sociologists and historians would expect. With time, Barker argues, the differences between most NRMs and the wider society will decrease. But along with this, given the highly pluralistic character of contemporary Western societies, the differences among the NRMs may well increase as each group can accommodate itself to a different set of accepted norms (Barker 1995b: 165 and 179). This fact may also partially account for the emergence of 'established cults' as a new order of religious life in the contemporary religious environment.

Drawn from Lorne L. Dawson, 'New Religious Movements.' Forthcoming in Robert Segal, ed., *Blackwell Companion to Religious Studies*. Oxford: Blackwell, 2005. Used with the permission of Blackwell Publishers.

CULT TYPOLOGIES AND THE INTERNAL DYNAMICS OF CULTS

Cult movements are the main subject of this book because their success gives them significance as religions in North America. Their histories reveal different aspects of the path of development suggested by Stark and Bainbridge; each movement grew from humble beginnings, and some, such as Theosophy, have had a reversal of fortunes that has moved them back again into something like the client cult status. As useful as Stark and Bainbridge's distinctions are, however, two anomalous features of cult movements point to the need to modify the typology.

In the first place, as Stark and Bainbridge recognized, there is much variation in degree of commitment and organization, even within the single category of cult movements. These groups entail everything from situations demanding mere assent to the beliefs of a group, regular attendance, and some financial support, to situations of total involvement, where every aspect of an individual's life is given over to the group's maintenance and advancement. Clearly, then, within the category of cult movements itself, there is a range of groups that to some degree replicates the larger contrasts with regard to membership and social organization. Stark and Bainbridge, however, have not followed through on this observation.[6] I believe it would be useful, then, to subdivide 'cult movements' along the same Weberian lines.

That suggestion is supported by the second anomalous feature. As some keen observers of contemporary religion have suggested, NRMs that either have stayed in forms reminiscent of audience or client cults or have returned to these forms may be experiencing neither a failure to develop properly nor a regression to some more primitive form (e.g. Westley, 1983; Bromley and Shupe, 1993; Greil, 1993; Wilson, 1993). On the contrary, religion in the guise of audience or client cults may actually be a sign of things to come, the religious success stories of tomorrow. Whether this is indeed the case hinges, of course, on whether one favours Berger's or Stark and Bainbridge's reading of the overall condition of religion in contemporary society. Is the 'commercialization' of religion evidence of its near-demise or just of its transformation? Whatever conclusion one draws, repeated observations of this kind suggest that cult movements themselves tend to cluster around two poles of a continuum with regard to member-ship and organization, as expressed most clearly in the variant norms of commitment in these groups. Some cult movements tend to resemble audi-ence or client cults in that they are non-communal and more tolerant of multiple commitments. As cults, that is, they display many of the features, with regard to mode of membership and organization, associated with churches. Scientology is a good example. Other cult movements are more communal, and exclusive in their commitment demands. In other words, they are more sect-like; a good example is Krishna Consciousness.

Recognition of this internal subdivision of cult movements can be made to conform even more with Stark and Bainbridge's theory of cults, and implicitly with Weber's theory of churches and sects, by incorporating insights provided by Wallis (1984). He proposes that the tendency of a new religious movement to move towards a more exclusive organizational type depends on the extent to which its message and practices are thought to be (1) important and relevant for a broad range of individual concerns, and (2) unavailable elsewhere. 'That is, a movement is more likely to be exclusive if it is of wide *salvational scope*, or lays claim to a *broad salvational efficacy*, showing the path of truth, salvation or the good life, over a wide range of human preoccupations; and if it lays claim to *unique legitimacy* as the path to these ends' (Wallis, 1984: 125–6). The intent to be comprehensive and the belief in uniqueness lead to a greater exclusivity in commitment demands, a pattern that characterizes the general developmental movement from audience cults through to cult movements, and which is then repli-cated again, like a set of wooden Ukrainian dolls nested one inside the other, as a gradient amongst the cult movements themselves.

In fact, as Wallis (1984: 123–5) persuasively argues, we find this range of membership commitment, from inclusive to exclusive, whenever we look at how individuals are involved in any type of new religious movement, whether audience cult, client cult, or cult movement. The pattern still applies: the more convinced the participants are of the comprehensiveness and uniqueness of the religious message, the greater their involvement with the group. In a kind of feedback loop, this conviction usually grows out of greater involvement.

As a consequence, and replicating the pattern further, most groups con-tain an internal division between a core of devotees engaged in a highly exclusive organizational commitment and a larger group of less exclusively engaged followers or clients. Amongst cult movements, for example,

Scientology certainly appears to be one of the most inclusive in its organizational commitments, allowing its members to freely retain and practice other faiths. But at the heart of Scientology is the 'Sea Org' (Sea Organization), an élite body that originally accompanied the reclusive L. Ron Hubbard aboard a fleet of ships. Members of the paramilitary Sea Org sign billion-year contracts of absolute loyalty and service to the highest leadership of the Church of Scientology; clearly, these members represent the exclusive end of the continuum within the movement. This sort of structural pattern varies in form, intensity, and significance regarding a group's development, according to the influence of other factors. For example, if a group is persecuted, the whole group may implode into the cadre and its more exclusive style; this may have either beneficial or disastrous results for the survival and growth of the new religion. (See, for example, Bainbridge's [1978] account of the Process, Carter's [1990] study of Rajneeshpuram, and Palmer's [1996] and Mayer's [1999] analyses of the Solar Temple.) It is conceivable that the same thing may happen because of the unanticipated and sudden success of a group. Lucas's [1995] account of The Holy Order of MANS comes close to this pattern. With all the complicated dynamics involved, such changes are very difficult to predict.

Having taken such a collection of theoretical tools in hand, let us now use them to consider why so many new NRMs have arisen in the West since the 1960s.

Chapter Three

Why Did New Religious Movements Emerge?

Asking the Right Question First

For most people, the first and most important question asked about NRMs is why someone would join one. This is probably also the pivotal question underlying most studies by social scientists. But the social scientists are more likely to focus on questions that are easier to answer empirically, such as ones about who joins the groups, how they come to join them, and what the organizational structures, procedures, and ideologies are. Enough micro-level analysis has been done to give us good answers to the 'who' and 'how' and 'what' questions; the 'why' remains more enigmatic.

These all relate to a macro-level question: 'Why have so many NRMs recently emerged in North America in the first place?' We can readily answer that it must indicate social and cultural changes in our society; deciding what these are might explain a particular person's choice to join a cult. As Marx (1972: 38) said of religion in general, 'religious distress is at the same time the expression of real distress and the protest against real distress.' Have NRMs arisen in response to some experience of distress? If so, what kind?

The scholarly literature on conversion to NRMs usually deals either with the 'macro-environment' or the 'micro-environment'. This chapter concentrates on the 'macro' under two headings: NRMs as a response to cultural change, and NRMs as an expression of cultural continuity.

New Religious Movements as a Response to Cultural Change

The scholar Thomas Robbins has remarked that academics who think of NRMs as responses to a change usually point to a 'distinctively modern dislocation' which is prompting people to search for 'new structures of meaning and community' (Robbins, 1988: 60). Opinions diverge on the nature of this dislocation but we can distill the common themes into three sets of changes affecting North Americans since at least the 1960s: (1) changes in values, (2) changes in social structure, and (3) changes in the role and character of religious institutions.

One pattern in the academic writing is an eagerness to point out that NRMs offer a complex response to these various types of social change; the groups do not simply provide direct compensation for or an alternative to a person's troubles, as Stark and Bainbridge's theory of religion suggests. Rather, they bring into effect ingenious compromises between the status quo and some alternative state of affairs. If we can discern the nature of the compromises, we may gain insight into (1) why some groups have succeeded better than others, (2) how certain internal weaknesses may account for the failure of so many groups, and (3) why NRMs seem to be subject to the polarization, noted in Chapter 1, into groups that are either more traditional, communal, and exclusive in their commitments, or oriented more to the modern world, geared to the satisfaction of individual needs, and less exclusive in their commitments.[1]

CHANGES IN VALUES

Beginning in the mid-1970s, a number of observers suggested that NRMs were responding to a pervasive crisis in moral certainty amongst North Americans.[2] First broached in Robbins and Anthony's excellent early studies of the American followers of the Indian Sufi mystic called Meher Baba (1972; Anthony and Robbins, 1975), most variants of this explanation have actually taken their lead from a colleague of these two, the eminent sociologist of religion Robert Bellah (1976).

NRMs, Bellah proposed, are best conceived as 'successor movements' to the political protest and cultural experimentation that flourished amongst the youth of the sixties. This was the decade of the counterculture, in which the established order of life and power in society was fundamentally challenged in two ways: by relatively organized movements struggling for political change, and by more amorphous movements of lifestyle experimentation. Both developments, which tended to go hand in hand, deeply eroded the legitimacy of established institutions of business, government, education, religion, and the family. The changes grew out of a unique combination of three interrelated aspects of life in North America in the time following the Second World War: (1) an unprecedented growth and spread of affluence, (2) an unprecedented rise in birth rates, and (3) a resultant expansion and increase in educational attainment.

NRMs *and the Turmoil of the 1960s*

In the United States, the generation of the sixties experienced the civil rights movement, the student power movement, the feminist movement, the war against poverty, the ecological movement, and most important, the often violent protest against the war in Vietnam, and the military draft. They participated, if only vicariously in many cases, in a decade of civil disobedience, riots, and student strikes (see e.g. Gitlin, 1987). All of those events were captured with new thoroughness and urgency by an emerging system of truly mass communication. In 1968, for example, in the face of the brutal attack by the Chicago police outside the Democratic Presidential Convention, young, largely middle-class, protesters chanted, 'The whole world is watching.' And indeed, through their televisions, they were. In late 1969, they were watching again when President Nixon ordered US forces to carry the war across the Vietnamese border into Cambodia, escalating the war rather than bringing 'our boys' home. This led to protests and disturbances (often violent) at over half of all American universities and colleges, 51 of which were closed for the rest of the term (Zaroulis and Sullivan, 1984: 318–21; cited in Kent, 1987: 20). These were stirring times. In the late sixties, much of the largest and most privileged generation of youth the world had known, the so-called baby boomers, vented their discontent and pressed for change, while much of the rest of the United States, Canada, and the world watched in shock and dismay.

This was also the era of extensive experimentation with drugs, liberal sexual mores, alternative living arrangements (such as cohabitation and communes), and new forms of popular music, dress, hairstyles, and psychological therapies. The hippies, with their long hair, beads, beards, peasant clothing, drugs, psychedelic rock, free love, transient lifestyle, organic food, meditation, and incense, were emblematic of the era. American popular life was dominated by the distinct youth culture and the resultant conflict of the 'generation gap'. In its more extreme elements, it was a time to 'turn on, tune out, and drop out' of 'the system'. And as Bellah argues, the two pillars of American ideological self-understanding, of the values people had lived by for decades, came under attack: biblical religion and utilitarian individualism.

In the 1950s, after fifteen years of depression and war, the traditional Christian denominations of North America experienced a rapid and unanticipated growth. More people were attending services than ever before, and there was a boom in church construction as North Americans had babies and moved to the suburbs (see Wuthnow, 1988: Chaps 2–4). Yet by the sixties these same mainstream denominations (e.g. Congregationalists, Presbyterians, Methodists, Episcopalians and Anglicans, Catholics, and Jews) were experiencing a dramatic loss in numbers as many of the baby boomers, now coming of age, ceased to emulate their parents and stopped attending church. Some turned East (Cox, 1977) or elsewhere, to other decidedly unorthodox or un-American forms of religious life. But most simply turned away from organized religion altogether, preferring to guide their lives solely by the principles of utilitarian individualism, the other system of values the young had inherited from their parents (Roof and McKinney, 1988; Wuthnow, 1988; Roof, 1993).

Life from this perspective is primarily a matter of pursuing one's 'interests' by the best means available. The watchwords of the utilitarian ethos are effective organization and freedom from constraint. In this approach to life, rational behaviour is of paramount importance. Yet as commentators on modernity (such as the founding figure of sociology Max Weber, 1958b: 181–3) have observed, the rationality in question seems to be purely formal and devoid of intrinsic ends (see e.g. Wilson, 1982a: 167). In the absence of a clear sense of a larger purpose and meaning to life, the utilitarian preoccupation with means and efficiency has become an end in itself. This, too, was part of the legacy of the newly prosperous postwar society of North America. The parents of the baby boomers had managed to unite the two aspects of American ideology: they pursued their interests, with a passion for efficiency, but within the confines of a traditional Christian conscience, a sensibility still imbued with a more absolute sense of purpose, and of good and evil. But the rapid rise in educational levels attained in North America, the very success, in other words, of the utilitarian ethos, spelled the end of this cultural compromise (see Wuthnow, 1988: Chap. 7; Roof, 1993). Many of the baby boomers, with their unprecedented exposure to university and college education, turned their backs on religion, but only to find eventually that the utilitarian individualism with which they were left was equally unsatisfying. There was ample evidence of the failure of a culture guided by the standards of utilitarian individualism. The United States seemed trapped in an escalating and pointless war in Vietnam. The popular charismatic liberal leaders of the era, President John F. Kennedy, his brother and presidential candidate Senator Robert Kennedy, and Martin Luther King, the great civil rights leader, were all assassinated. On and off throughout the decade race riots raged out of control in the heart of many American cities, notably, Los Angeles, Newark, and Detroit, and in May 1970 several student protesters were gunned down by the National Guard at Kent State University. Then, in 1973, when Americans were beginning to believe in a return to the status quo, the Watergate scandal broke, forcing

President Richard Nixon, the standard-bearer of 'law and order' and 'the silent majority', to resign in disgrace. These public disappointments, combined with the personal struggles many were having with the rising rates of divorce, crime, and drug abuse, and ecological and economic crises, such as the energy crisis and recession set off by the OPEC oil embargo of 1973, fostered among many a new consciousness of the need to reconsider the proper ends of their actions (see Bellah, 1976: 338).

For those engaged in political protest and lifestyle experimentation, these times of trouble gave birth to a new set of 'expressive ideals' with which to guide their lives:

> The counterculture challenged utilitarian culture at the most fundamental level. It asked what in life possessed intrinsic value, and to what ends ought we to act. It rejected money, power, and technical knowledge, mainstays of 'the good life' of middle-class society, as ends good in themselves. Instead, it identified them as means that did not, after all, enable one to experience what is intrinsically valuable—love, self-awareness, intimacy with others and nature. (Tipton, 1982b: 84)

In general, the clamour for change, the experience of disruption, the rising educational levels, and the emergence of new ideals of personal authenticity in the sixties opened the door to a much greater interest in alternative world-views and ways of living. Other readings of 'the good life', like those provided by such NRMs as Scientology, Krishna Consciousness, the Unification Church, Divine Light Mission, Transcendental Meditation, Children of God, Nichiren Shoshu, Vajradhatu, Wicca, and even Satanism, were entertained as serious possibilities. But, as Bellah, Tipton, and other scholars (e.g. Adams and Fox, 1972; Kent, 1987, 1988, 2001a) insist, NRMs are not so much the direct products of the ferment of the sixties. Rather, they are better conceived as 'successors' to the movements of political protest and cultural innovation of this period. People turned from 'slogan chanting to mantra chanting' (Kent, 1988, 2001a), because of both the success and the failure of these movements.

NRMs as a Response to Moral Ambiguity

The revolutionary impulse of the sixties did change the world of Americans and Canadians in many ways. The United States grudgingly withdrew its troops from Vietnam and seemed to acknowledge that it might be guilty of imperialism. Repressive attitudes towards blacks, women, and the poor were displaced by more egalitarian views, while social norms with regard to sex, appearance, language, music, marriage, and religious beliefs were liberalized. However, at the end of the decade and the end of their youth the baby boomers were faced with a more sombre set of challenges. They had to get on with life, and all its adult responsibilities, in a world still fundamentally unchanged. The structural realities of modernity, 'technological production, bureaucratic organization, and empirical science' (Tipton, 1982b: 84) had been left intact by the cultural turmoil of the time, and they continued to necessitate a utilitarian orientation to life. As educations ended and jobs loomed, it was difficult to sustain the 'expressive ideals' of the counterculture, founded on unregulated feeling and pop philosophy. These sentiments were no match for the deeply ingrained demands and aspirations of American utilitarianism. Moreover, the very success of the sixties had, ironically, helped to usher in a more permissive and hedonistic milieu, well suited to the ethic of mass consumption promoted by advanced industrial societies. Accordingly, the sixties gave way to the 'me generation' and the general cynicism of the seventies and early eighties. In American pop culture, disco displaced psychedelic rock, being radical gave way to being a yuppie (young urban professional), and self-help and encounter therapies were substituted for the revolution.

Amidst this 'ideological wreckage', to use Tipton's (1982b: 84) evocative phrase, many of the most committed, who were often the most disillusioned as well, were gripped with anomie—that sense of normlessness, of having lost their way. But some, Tipton and others argue, 'found a way both to cope with the instrumental demands of adulthood in conventional society and to sustain the counterculture's expressive ideals by reinforcing them with moralities of authority, rules, and utility.' Calling on the beliefs and practices of various NRMs, which blossomed in the seventies and early eighties, ways were found to 'mediate and resolve' the clash of moral sensibilities afflicting many young people (Tipton, 1982b: 81). These Americans returned, by new means, to a characteristically American orientation, one rooted in the early Protestant heritage of North America and the experience of conquering the frontier: the path to social revolution must be through the conversion and transformation of the consciousness and conscience of individuals, beginning with oneself. Such was the path of development detailed by Lucas (1995), for example, in his account of how some hippies from the failed Haight-Ashbury enclave of San Francisco flocked to the New Age teachings of a peculiar engineer from Cincinnati and helped him found the Holy Order of MANS, an NRM they eventually transformed into an order of the Russian Orthodox Church.

Proposing a threefold typology, Tipton (1982b: 98) suggests one widely accepted way of explaining the appeal of various kinds of new religions to people who need to resolve their sense of moral ambiguity:

The human potential movement [as reflected in groups like est, Silva Mind Control, and Scientology] recombines the expressive ethic of hip culture with the consequential ethic of utilitarian individualism, with particular plausibility for the middle middle class. Conservative Christian groups recombine the expressive ethic with the authoritative ethic of revealed biblical religion, with particular plausibility for the lower middle class. Neo-Oriental groups recombine the expressive ethic with the regular ethic of rationalized religion and humanism, with particular plausibility for the upper middle class.

In each of these different ways, Tipton (1982b: 98–100) proposes, disoriented elements of the baby boom generation found the rules to live by and an authority they could respect that brought a measure of practical order and peace to their lives, without betraying their countercultural commitment to self-expression and 'love over money'. NRMs like 'est' or Scientology allowed people to return to conventional careers, families, and activities. They conformed to the utilitarian theory of right behaviour, with its emphasis on doing that which yields the most good consequences for oneself (that is, a consequentialist ethic). But these groups invoked elaborate alternative readings of human nature and the real character of the world that radically shifted the definition of good consequences from material acquisition and improved social status to heightened self-awareness, self-expression, and the experience of various supposed spiritual dimensions of existence.

Conservative Christian NRMs, like the Unification Church and the dozens of Jesus Movement groups born of the sixties, resolved the unhappiness of moral ambiguity by replacing the consequentialist ethic characteristic of utilitarian individualism, whereby anything goes if it produces the desired result, with one of biblical authority. Sin is the root of unhappiness, and happiness follows from doing the right thing, from avoiding sin. Our actions should be guided by our principles, and not just by their consequences. Yet the knowledge of the right things to do stems from the development of a deeply emotional and loving relationship to God and the community of fellow believers. An emphasis is placed, over against more conventional expressions of Christianity, on the development and reality of a very personal and often ecstatic relationship with Jesus. Being 'born again in Christ' is the key.

Neo-oriental groups, like Zen Buddhism, Divine Light Mission/Elan Vital, Krishna Consciousness, and Vajradhatu/Shambhala International, replace the utilitarian consequentialist theory of right behaviour with one that stresses the prior need to act in accord with rules that conform to the 'real' nature of reality. Right knowledge of human existence will lead to the abandonment of insatiable desires for some unattainable material happiness. This will result in an abiding sense of peace with oneself and the world. Instrumental to this end is the practice of various activities like rituals and forms of meditation, and a devotional relationship with a guru or some other spiritual master.

NRMs *and Social Reintegration*

Whatever the merits of Tipton's particular formulation of these relationships, most scholars agree that his basic approach is workable. Clearly many of the NRMs that suddenly surged into public awareness in the sixties and seventies were responding to a moral malaise felt by the young adults and adolescents of North America. In varying degrees these new religions were also involved, like other puritanical or fanatical religious groups throughout the ages, in reintegrating these estranged young people back into society, or at least redirecting their protest from the realm of overt political confrontation to the less threatening realm of socio-religious experimentation. Robbins, Anthony, and Curtis (1975) specify four ways in which this social reintegration of religious converts is facilitated: (1) adjustive socialization, (2) combination, (3) compensation, and (4) redirection. Any particular religion may influence its followers towards integrating back into society by means of any combination of these processes, and using this more generic set of possibilities can be helpful if we want to avoid the typecasting of groups that may result from Tipton's tripartite classification of NRMs.

These four categories need some explanation, of course. 'Adjustive socialization' refers to the way in which some religious groups resocialize individuals to the dominant values and norms of society (Niebuhr, 1929; Holt, 1940; Johnson, 1961). They do so through their emphasis on the strict moral standards required to win salvation. The traditional prohibitions against drinking, gambling, fighting, and laziness have been complemented in many of the new Jesus groups and Eastern religions with admonitions against, and programs to correct, drug abuse, sexual promiscuity, and selfishness. Devotees are encouraged to do everything for the glory of Krishna, God, or their true inner nature in ways that place a high value on hard work and service to others. 'Combination' is the term used by Robbins, Anthony, and Curtis, independently of Tipton, for the fusion of expressive and utilitarian orientations discussed above. In the Divine Light Mission of Guru Maharaj-ji, for example, the return to 'straight' morality and work habits in the everyday world and a rather uncritical acceptance of modern technology were blended with a self-styled 'revolutionary' ethic of universal love and the daily inducement of ecstasy through meditation

(Downton, 1979; Galanter and Buckley, 1983). 'Compensation' and 'redirection' are described by Robbins, Anthony, and Curtis as processes that

> do not require the presence of explicit norms either proscribing deviant involvements (e.g. drugs) or legitimating non-deviant commitments (e.g. to conventional 'careers'). Compensation refers to the renewal of commitment to conventional vocational routines, that derives from having the expressive needs that these routines cannot gratify, gratified elsewhere (i.e. in religious groups). Redirection is more exclusively negative and refers to the substitution of socially legitimate religious activities and satisfactions for stigmatized activities and satisfactions (e.g. spiritual 'highs' for drug induced 'highs'), from which the convert is thusly 'redirected' (1975: 52).

The scholars suggest that all of these processes, operating in various combinations in diverse groups, may serve the function of managing tension in advanced industrial societies. Modern affluent and increasingly automated societies, it is argued, need an even smaller portion of their populations in the labour force. By inducing a segment of their population to resist the quest for material success and prestige, NRMs are helping to stabilize the social systems; they may alleviate the unrest that arises when too many qualified people wish to participate meaningfully in the workforce and in political and economic decision-making. The monastic orders of the Catholic Church, for somewhat different reasons, are said to have served a similar function during the Middle Ages.

One merit of this theory is that it draws our attention away from the kinds of micro-analyses that tend to predominate in the study of these small and idiosyncratic groups. We clearly need 'macro-speculations' like this to help explain the situation in the early 1970s, by which time, as Wuthnow (1988: 152) observes, 'the various new religions may have resulted in the organization of more than 3,000 local groups of one kind or another, with perhaps as many as a tenth of the entire population [of the United States] having participated in at least one.' But such speculations are best approached with great caution. We must remember that in the late 1980s the activity of NRMs tapered off, and membership in the relatively well-established groups like Scientology, Krishna Consciousness, and the Unification Church has stabilized at levels well below those achieved in the early to mid-seventies. Fewer new religions are being formed now, and they are attracting fewer followers. And yet we have little reason to believe that there have been any significant changes to the basic conditions of advanced industrial society, conditions that are thought to have precipitated either a state of moral ambiguity or a systemic need for tension management. From another angle, though, the drop in support for NRMs could be interpreted as evidence for the 'moral crisis' thesis. As times have changed and the baby-boom generation has grown older, leaving the counterculture behind it, the need for NRMs has seemingly become more peripheral.

The Continued Appeal of NRMs

All the same, some young people continue to seek out such organizations, and we can probably relate this to moral ambiguity in our rapidly changing society. Moreover, while direct experience of the turmoil characteristic of the sixties is no longer pertinent, North Americans continue to struggle with the cultural legacy of those years. In his extensive interviews of members of the baby-boom generation, Wade Clark Roof (1993, 1999) found that people who actually took part in some of the protests, drugs, and rock festivals of the sixties are far more inclined, even now, to practise or at least accept alternative religions. Within the confines of their otherwise relatively conventional lives, these people have continued to carry the more liberal and expressive values of the sixties, and they have tried to pass them on to their children. But only about half of the baby boomers ever actually 'experienced' the sixties. Many others, Roof reminds us, lived through the sixties in harmony with mainstream society, largely unaffected by the changes that wrought the generation gap. In fact, for a sizable portion of this 'straight' group, the little exposure they had to the counterculture helped to turn them to the more conservative forms of Christianity that culminated in the cultural and political activism of the New Christian Right that emerged in the late 1970s and continues to the present. Of course, an even larger share of the baby boomers simply abandoned any participation in organized religion altogether.

In the end, it is probably safe to say, in agreement with Tipton (1982b: 105), 'that many converts to alternative religions, in the past and the present, 'are people who experience ethical contradictions of unusual intensity and as a result look for unusually coherent solutions to them.' Historically, it is a matter of chance that the crisis of meaning experienced by so many baby boomers struck at a time when North America was opening up to an unprecedented measure of cultural and religious pluralism. The gurus happened to be in place, in search of new ideological markets, when the need for their spiritual goods arose. The unexpected explosion of non-traditional religions ensued.[3]

It is worth reiterating at this point the warning against falling into overly reductive lines of analysis. To argue that part of the appeal of NRMs is in their ability to integrate alienated people back into society in some way, we cannot assume that this function is essential to the existence of these groups. People may join these groups for any number of other reasons, and the groups conceive themselves to be serving decidedly other purposes. Even though integration may be a valued by-product of involvement, we must guard against treating the spiritual and other accounts that believers give for their involvement as less significant than the apparent social or psychological benefits of participation.[4]

CHANGES IN SOCIAL STRUCTURE

A different explanation of cult activity in North America focuses on changes in social structure, and appears in three varieties.[5] In its most immediate and simple form it links the rise of NRMs to a search by young adults for 'surrogate' families in the face of the demise of what sociologists call 'mediating structures' in society. The scholars who advance this explanation point to the widening gap between our childhood experience of family life and the ever more compelling demands of the educational institutions, places of employment, and so on. In a more abstract form, this type of explanation also links the rise of NRMs to the diffuse mental and emotional disorientation stemming from the 'de-institutionalization' of many aspects of 'private life' in advanced industrial societies (Berger et al., 1974). This type of explanation can further relate the rise of NRMs to even larger social psychological consequences of structural changes in society associated with late modernity.

As you can see, what varies here is the scope of the social structural problem described. In the more recent form of the argument, the issues are confined less to the experience of adolescents and young adults, and consequently seem more difficult to deal with. A larger structural dilemma is at issue, which shapes the social environment in which all religions, new or old, must operate for the foreseeable future.

The Search for Surrogate Families

We are being raised, sociologists and historians argue, in more humane and 'personalistic' families than in the past. Present-day families cater more to the individual needs of their children, trying to promote their independent identities. This greater personal attention is the result of the decreasing likelihood of death during childhood, smaller families, increasing affluence, higher levels of education, and more leisure time. It is also the result, however, of the increasing isolation of the nuclear family in an urbanized, suburbanized, and geographically and socially mobile North America. The family is becoming the sole, or at least the primary, provider of the kind of everyday psychological and social support that once came from homogeneous and stable neighbourhoods, extended families, churches, voluntary associations, social clubs, and more personal workplaces. These traditional extra-familial sources of support are what sociologists call 'mediating structures', which stand between the world of the nuclear family and the world of large corporate and government bureaucracies. On the one hand, these mediators help to buffer the family from the mega-structures of modern life. On the other hand, they ease the socialization of the young away from the personal world of the family and into the more impersonal adult world. They perpetuate many of the kinds of face-to-face contact and personal bonds typical of childhood and family life, while simultaneously introducing the young to the more detached and utilitarian procedures of larger organizations. The trouble is, in the face of the continuous expansion of the responsibilities of large corporations and government bureaucracies, the mediating structures have diminished. Moreover, the expanding functions of such larger social institutions as schools, social welfare agencies, social-control agencies, and the medical profession, have undermined the legitimacy and integrity of the family by performing many of its traditional functions.

In the last several decades many sociologists have argued that the resultant polarization of social life between the extremes of public and private life has set the stage for a new, intense, and pervasive identity crisis amongst adolescents and young adults (e.g. Erikson, 1968; Wilson, 1982a: 177). The crisis in question is rooted in the jarring transition now experienced by young people between the 'expressive' values, roles, and relationships of the familial milieu and the 'instrumental' values, roles, and relationships of the adult milieu. These terms derive from the work of Talcott Parsons, who analysed the institutional changes that mark the emergence of 'modern' societies (e.g. Parsons, 1951, 1971). By 'expressive' relationships, Parsons is referring to relations that tend to be (1) ends in themselves, (2) diffuse, (3) idiosyncratic, (4) particularistic (i.e. they involve exclusive devotion), and (5) emotional in nature. Instrumental relationships are (1) means to ends, (2) functionally specific, (3) performance- or achievement-oriented, (4) universalistic, and (5) emotionally neutral. For many young people, long immersed in the expressive atmosphere of the isolated suburban family, the struggle to adapt suddenly to the instrumental demands of university or the work world is disconcerting. For those who are particularly sensitive to this, joining an NRM may offer a way to cope. As with the closely related experience of moral ambiguity, NRMs may appear to offer some individuals a compromise between the expressive affectivity of childhood and the instrumental orientation of adulthood.

Most NRMs, especially those of a more communal type, stress the affectionate, loving, family-like character of their internal bonds—for example, the Children of God/The Family, Hare Krishna, the Unification Church, the Holy Order of MANS, and even the Catholic Charismatic Renewal and the Neo-Pagans. They are 'spiritual families', held together by ties of brotherly and sisterly love. Charismatic religious leaders present themselves as parental figures, or they are treated as such by their followers. Many members of the Catholic Charismatic Renewal speak of 'daddy God' and 'brother Jesus', Moonies literally see Reverend Moon and his wife as their new parents, while the use of family symbolism is self-evident in the Children of God, now called the Family, founded and led by Father David (David Berg, known also as Moses David—after another great father-figure). In these groups, diffusely affective and expressive relationships, like those of a true extended family, are reiterated in dozens of ways but in a wider context geared to the service of some greater cause. Through dedication to the cause, the real family of the convert is transcended and left behind. Yet symbolically and experientially, a highly personal and integrated way of life is sustained. In some cases, independence, with its fearful burden of responsibility and detachment, is held off or sacrificed in favour of continued child-like obedience to a presumably benevolent authority. Arthur Parsons (1986) points out that such child-like respect for superiors is central to the Confucian-like patterns of order and emotional intimacy expected in the Unification Church. Jacobs (1989: 5) goes so far as to suggest that the 'rise of charismatic religious movements . . . can be understood as the desire to experience both the ideal family and the fathering of a protective and loving male authority figure. . . [Conversion] reflects the failure of the middle class family to meet the needs of contemporary society . . . and the attending disillusionment with the nature of fathering in American culture.'[6]

In broader and less contentious terms, the British sociologist of religion Bryan Wilson (1982a: 134) captures the appeal of NRMs by speaking of a return to a greater sense of 'community':

In the modern world, natural community has largely disappeared: [people] no longer live, learn, work, play, marry, and die in the same community. Yet there is no doubt that [they] hanker after the benefits of community, seek contexts in which they are personally known, and in which they share responsibilities with others. New religious movements can supply precisely this context in a way that no other social agency can do. Other activities—politics, economics, even recreation—are dominated by specific interests and exchange relationships—only the family shares with religion the idea of community as an end in itself, and the modern family, now nucleated, is too small to fulfil the functions of a community. Because religious activity is predicated on transcendental concepts, because sharing and caring are the core of its operation, because the celebration of the transcendent truth is also a celebration of the community in which the truth is cherished—for all of these reasons, religious groups provide the intrinsic, as well as the symbolic, benefits of community.

Robbins and Anthony (1972: 132) also say that the transcendental values and objectives of the NRMs make a post-adolescent return to expressive roles feel legitimate by 'universalizing' their nature and significance. On the one hand, this universalization means seeing the dominant instrumental demands of the secular culture as much less important than some divine purpose or greater cosmic plan, opening the door to more expressivity in daily life. On the other hand, the universalization of expressive roles actually borrows its aura of legitimacy from the 'universal' significance associated with the instrumental roles pursued in the modern secular adult world. In this way, NRMs combine and transform two negatives, childish expressivity and impersonal universalism, into a single positive. Functionally, the NRMs through which this transformation is accomplished are acting as substitutes, for a time, for the traditional mediating structures that have been driven from advanced industrial societies. They maintain some of the personalism of the family in structures dedicated to larger, more impersonal goals. They provide a way to reintegrate the expressive and the instrumental in a single cohesive social unit and, hence, provide a stable identity for their young members.

Coping with Deinstitutionalization

James Davison Hunter (1981) and Benton Johnson (1981) add important nuances to this tale of modern youthful fear and alienation. The tension felt by the young, in transition into adulthood, is in fact structurally endemic to life in advanced industrial societies. Building on Berger's basic understanding of the human condition and the social construction of reality (Berger, 1967; Berger et al., 1974; see Chapter 2), Hunter concentrates on a crisis of meaning and personal security stemming from the 'deinstitutionalization' of the modern world. As Berger stipulates, humans are born biologically incomplete. As a species we have sought to fashion a stable cultural order to compensate for our lack of instinctual programming. Ideally this culturally fabricated order will come to be taken for granted and will hold the ever-present threat of anomie at bay. The aspects of human life that become so routinized and so habitual as to be beyond ready questioning are said to be institutionalized. Most of life in traditional societies is institutionalized in this sense. 'Modernity', Hunter (1981: 4) proposes, 'is characterized by an unprecedented degree of de-institutionalization.' This problem is exacerbated by the uneven distribution of the deinstitutionalization process in modern society.

On the one hand, modern individuals live in an environment where more and more aspects of their so-called 'private' lives are being converted from the realm of taken-for-granted experience to that of choice. Courtship, marriage, child rearing, sexuality, gender relations, consumption, vocation, and spirituality are being de-institutionalized. In the private realm, there are no set and secure behaviours. In these spheres of activity traditional institutions have, as Hunter says (1981: 5), 'lost their grip on the individual', and struggles with anomie are common.

On the other hand, in the 'public' sphere of activity, dominated by massive bureaucracies that organize and operate our governments, the law, business and commerce, labour, health care, communications, the military, and even religion, the processes of institutionalization are continuing unabated. The institutionalization in question, however, is distinctive. In the modern world, as Weber stressed (e.g. 1958b: Chaps 4, 5, and 8; 1964: 35–55), institutions are guided increasingly by a strictly 'formal rationality', which is geared to the satisfaction of the functional requirements of social systems, with little or no regard for the desires, needs, or even character of the individual members of the institutions. The effective performance of 'roles' in the service of the institution matters more than any personal features of the incumbents of the roles or the quality of relationships experienced in the institutional environment. One's integrity or simple contentment is secondary to one's accomplishments for the organization (see Wilson, 1982a: 159–68). Consequently, as Hunter comments (1981: 4), there is a profound disjuncture between people's private and public experiences and neither is very satisfying.

In the private sphere everything is seemingly a matter of choice; yet many people yearn for more guidance. In the public sphere, on the other hand, one is compelled to conform. Guidance is manifest, but in ways that belie the meaningfulness of participation for the individual. In this situation, personal identity, promoted as all-important at the private level and as the natural end-product of making the right choices, is frustrated by a structurally diverse public realm that demands an elaborate differentiation of social roles and restricts real choices. It is hard to know who we are when the social system requires us to be many different people in many different functional circumstances, but none with any depth. We are expected to be one person at home, another at school, another at work, and yet another in the store or on the street. In the modern world, so the argument runs, identity is fragmented or at least pluralized. Either way, for many, having a meaningful identity at all has become problematic. In the face of this, so the argument runs, the proliferating new religions provide a holistic sense of self that transcends the constellation of limited instrumental roles recognized by modern mass society (see also Campbell, 1978; Westley, 1978, 1983; Beckford, 1984).

> The dilemma of modernity, in which all individuals are variously caught, is an oppressively formidable public sphere, which is structurally incapable of providing individuals with concrete and meaningful social confirmation of their sense of reality (including their understanding of social processes, subjective meaning and personal identity), and an enfeebled private sphere, which is distressingly under-institutionalized, and which is structurally unable to provide reliable social parameters for the more mundane activity of everyday life and a plausible, well-integrated system of meaning which gives location and purpose to the individual's total life experience. (Hunter, 1981: 5)

I think Benton Johnson (1981) does an even better job of capturing the structural dilemma of modernity. The contours of his argument are pretty much the same. But he speaks more concretely of the worlds of 'work' and of 'love'. Johnson (1981: 54) traces the rise of NRMs and related new forms of psychotherapy as a response to 'a widespread distress that is produced by an inability to achieve and sustain heightened demands for satisfactions in the areas of work and intimate relations.' The acuity of his analysis is such that it warrants being quoted at length. His descriptions, written twenty-five years ago, still ring true. Here is the enervating quandary in which modern North Americans are caught every day, and which some people intuitively seek to flee by turning to NRMs.

With regard to the world of work, the node of most people's involvement is the public sector, Johnson says (1981: 54–5):

> The development of modern economies has opened up a great many new opportunities and has encouraged people to expect increasing levels of material and psychological rewards for occupational achievement. Success in the workplace for many people has become the single most important test of personal worth. But the proliferation of new opportunities for occupational achievement is largely the result of the growth of large-scale organizations. Self-employment has declined steadily for over a century, with the result being that most of us today are dependent on the wages and salaries paid to us by employers. The character of our jobs, including our prospects for success, is

increasingly governed by considerations that are systemic in character and therefore beyond our personal control. Work takes place in formal organizations that are hierarchical in structure and are primarily responsive, through their top-level control centers, to the requirements of the market and government. Work relations are therefore highly inegalitarian. Workers tend to be evaluated individually and competitively on the basis of their contribution to the goals of the enterprise. In the world of work there are winners and losers, and those who are winning today may be losing tomorrow. The sense of achievement, and hence the feeling of self-worth, is placed in constant jeopardy because of the uncertainty of the outcome of our efforts. The search for a secure sense of self-worth based on work is made difficult by the structure of work itself—a structure that Americans by and large do not understand and that they do not control.

Faced with what Marxists would call the alienating nature of work in the modern world, Johnson proposes that people tend to increase their demands for satisfaction in their private lives. In their personal relations they demand more emotional support, love, and sexual gratification. But this compensatory move is to no avail, for the private sector is drawn into the same vortex.

The insistence on higher levels of gratification has brought with it a higher potential for dissatisfaction with one's personal relationships. Whereas our ability to control the conditions of work has progressively shrunk, our ability to control the conditions of love has expanded. It is now possible to abandon intimate relationships that are not satisfactory. But this freedom has its costs. It is exhilarating to find fulfilment in a new love, but it is not exhilarating to be abandoned by an old love. To the risks of work are now added the risks of love. Moreover, the risks of the latter are exacerbated by the increasing economic independence of women. For years men have intuitively understood that it is safer to act-out the frustrations of work at home than it is to act-out the frustrations of home life at work. Women's participation in work has not changed the structures of work. It is still risky to act-out home-life frustrations at work, and it now becomes unsafe for either sex to do much acting-out at home. Finally the perils of love are also made more difficult by the competitive character of the workplace and by the tendency to make invidious comparisons in an effort to assess personal worth. Just as the success of competitors can make people envious, the success of loved ones can make people question their own worth. The anarchy of work is reflected in intimate relationships.

For theorists like Hunter and Johnson, the new religious consciousness that emerged in the sixties is quite simply a sociocultural protest against these anomic and alienating conditions. In Hunter's view (1981: 7–9), NRMs represent a 'demodernizing impulse': an attempt to reconstruct the world socially by 'reimposing institutionally reliable meanings upon existence.'

Adapting Life in Late Modernity

In previous work, I have tried to gain some insight into the changing religious sensibilities associated with the rise of contemporary NRMs (Dawson 1998a) by turning to Anthony Giddens' analysis of the consequences of the social changes marking the shift into 'late modern' society (Giddens 1990, 1991).[7] I break Giddens' argument into three parts: the social-structural conditions of modernity; the social-psychological consequences of these conditions; and the different possible responses (social, cultural, and political) to these consequences.

In Giddens' view modernity is marked by three primary structural changes that have permanently altered the social environment in which religions must operate: (1) the 'disembedding' of social life in conjunction with a reliance on 'abstract expert systems'; (2) the 'institutionalization of reflexivity'; and (3) the process of globalization.

The development of rapid and mass transportation and communication, monetary systems, standardized time, and expert systems of all kinds—ranging from meteorology to surgery to computer science—has lifted people out of the more immediate frames of reference that have traditionally shaped their lives and identities. Life has become increasingly detached from the cycles of nature, the dictates of geography, and the customs and features of local social contexts. This disembedding of social life has been helped along by the progressive rationalization of all social practices. Everything we do is subject to an ongoing critique based on our commitment to reason, oriented towards justifying our beliefs and actions in the light of incoming knowledge rather than past custom. Such radicalized reason has even called the certainties of science into question (e.g. in postmodernist thought). But in the mundane world, science and the expert systems associated with it have penetrated all aspects of our existence, rendering daily life an exercise in perpetual self-reflection based on the latest findings of sociologists, psychologists, medical experts, and others. Giddens refers to this as the 'universalization of reflexivity'. All of this is happening, of course, within a globalizing context in which events and developments in distance places have complex effects on our lives and attitudes. Economic upheavals in one part of the globe are reshaping the prospects of others thousands of miles away overnight, just as watching the news every evening embroils thousands of people, intellectually and emotionally, in tragedies and triumphs happening half a world away.

Giddens envisions the social-psychological consequences of living under these conditions in terms of a dialectic of 'trust and risk' (building on Beck, 1992). At the heart of the modern global social order is trust in the abstract systems of expertise that make our world work. It is these systems that guarantee a social and technological order to the relations between the local and the global, individuals and social systems, nature and humanity. This trust is essential, yet it is imperiled by the very institutionalized reflexivity that warrants its existence in the first place. We are encouraged to question everything, even the expert systems. What is more, the modern societal need for trust happens in a new collective environment of risk unlike anything experienced by past societies.

The risk profile of modernity has a number of unique features. First, we are subject to risks that have been globalized, both in terms of the intensity of the risks (e.g. nuclear holocaust or planetary ecological disasters) and the expanding number of contingent events that can affect almost everyone on the planet. Second, we are subject to risks stemming from our interventions into nature, plus the 'institutionalised risk environments' we have developed, like investment markets. Third, our perception of the risks has been altered in at least three ways: there is an ever wider awareness of the risks to which humanity is subject, there is less confidence that the risks can be averted by supernatural or magical means, and people are increasingly aware of the limitations of expert systems to cope with the risks, even those they created (Dawson 2004: 84–85).

In the face of these stark realities, Giddens argues that people have sought compensation in the intense cultivation of personal relationships and a heightened sense of subjective identity. Friendships, romantic relationships, and parent-child relationships have taken on a magnified importance as forums for the continued cultivation of the security first imparted to all of us (normally) in the earliest years of family life. In a globalizing, risk-riddled world, people have turned inward to a 'reflexive project of identity construction' to create the necessary sense of meaning in their lives. Self-actualization has become the new norm of maturation and success. But identity construction requires the co-operation of others; it is the product of social interaction. As we become disembedded from the traditional collective contexts of identity formation, attention has turned to the cultivation of a new ideal, what Giddens calls 'the pure relationship.' Life is becoming a series of such relationships, characterized by an unprecedented ethic of 'mutual self-disclosure.' These idealized relationships have become the natural forums for the creation of the self-narratives that are used to impart a sense of purpose to our lives.

But in the end, Giddens worries, we may be asking too much of our intimate relationships, and some people have trouble finding such relationships at all. The reiterated promise of the exaggerated mythology of romantic love that suffuses our society is subject to episodic failures that can bring on 'fateful moments' when the harsh realities rush in upon us, shattering the trust that is central to our continued and willing participation in the given social order.

In the face of the ceaseless anxiety that constitutes so much of late modern life, Giddens recognizes that many people will still seek refuge in the order provided by a religious worldview. On the whole religion is still closely associated, Giddens asserts, with the provision of trust. Religions tend to 'remoralize' life, providing the reassurance required to make important commitments when only partial information and understanding is available. New religions in particular try to creatively reassert the greater transcendent, even supernatural, significance of our most personal acts, providing a safer forum for both identity experimentation and the quest for pure relationships. In some more reactionary cases they also provide a new kind of collective and traditionalist context to guide the social processes of identity formation and protection. Of course, in the contemporary globalizing context, the many different religions on offer tend to relativize the claims of all. But the fit between the socially structured needs of many people in late modern societies and certain religious choices would seem to be sufficient to assure the survival of numerous religious sub-cultures.

Much like the two previous scenarios, however, such conjectures are strictly theoretical. The link between the search for surrogate families, or the deinstitutionalization of private life, or our struggles with the dialectic of trust and risk in late modernity, and the motivations of individuals who have joined NRMs is empirically unknown. We are in the realm of creative speculation. But at present no other means of understanding is at hand.

Whatever the nature of modern society's structural malaise may be, the response of the NRMs tends to be concentrated on treating the symptoms. The causes are addressed only indirectly, by one of three means: (1) by removing people from the existing social system (that is, from the conventional pursuit of careers and romantic relationships) into alternative communal arrangements and livelihoods, (2) by giving people alternative life goals that take priority over work and love (for example, achieving various spiritual skills and states of being), (3) by encouraging people to abandon their traditional quest for security and instead to seek growth and self-actualization in the flexible acceptance of change and the cultivation of spontaneity. In different groups these strategies appear in various combinations and in a myriad of specific forms.

CHANGES IN THE ROLE AND CHARACTER OF
RELIGIOUS INSTITUTIONS

The third related theme of cultural change commonly reiterated in the literature that tries to explain why NRMs emerged returns us to the issue of secularization. Where once almost all aspects of social life fell under the influence, if not direct rule, of religion, over the last several centuries ever larger segments of daily life have been segregated from religious authority and relegated to other institutions. Such a transfer of authority accompanied the development of independent economic, political, medical, educational, recreational, and even family institutions. This process not only stripped religious institutions of their manifest power in social affairs, but also subverted the latent social functions that religions have long performed as well. Although offering assurance of ultimate salvation has always been the primary function of religion, before the Industrial Revolution religion was also the primary agency of social cohesion and social control in society, the chief source of knowledge about the world, the foundation of personal and group identity, and a major force for the cultivation, expression, and regulation of emotions. These functions are now the prerogative of national governments, legal systems, science, public education and health systems, professional sports, and the mass media and entertainment industry (see Wilson, 1982a: 32–46). Following in the footsteps of Ferdinand Toennies, Emile Durkheim, Weber, and many other sociologists of note, Bryan Wilson characterizes the overall change as a shift from community to societal system (1982a: 125 ff., 153 ff.). As life became less religious, it also became markedly less local and personal and more national (even international) and impersonal. In the long term, it is this comprehensive shift in the basic configuration of social life that lies behind the more specific changes in values and social structures associated with the rise of NRMs from the 1960s onwards. It is this shift that is thought to account ultimately for the experiences of moral ambiguity and anomie that made North Americans receptive to the NRMs. The difficulties of the baby boom generation were only a recent phase of a much larger and longer process.

Much like Stark and Bainbridge, then, and Berger in some measure, Wilson suggests that the decline in the social prominence of conventional religions was a necessary precondition for the rise of nationally significant and relatively exotic NRMs. This is true in at least two senses. First, the religious tolerance that came with religious pluralism and the increasing privatization and institutional segregation of religion is a *sine qua non* of cult growth (Wilson, 1982b: 26). Second, the incongruity sensed between systems of religious beliefs and practices born of an earlier, different, and simpler age and the new horizons opening to the educated members of advanced industrial societies undermined the credibility of traditional religious ideas. Unlike Stark and Bainbridge, and more like Berger, however, Wilson thinks that the macro-social changes associated with secularization have limited the capacity of NRMs to reverse the privatization of religion in Western culture. Why? Because he believes that most of these movements are largely the products of the modern social system, rather than its opponents.

> New religious movements, whether in the Christian, Buddhist, or any other tradition, are not in the strict sense revivals of a tradition: they are more accurately regarded as adaptations of religion to new social circumstances. None of them is capable, given the radical nature of social change, of recreating the dying religions of the past. In their style and in their specific appeal they represent an accommodation to new conditions, and they incorporate many of the assumptions and facilities encouraged in the increasingly rationalised secular sphere. Thus it is that many new movements are themselves testimonies to secularization: they often utilise highly secular methods of evangelism, financing, publicity and mobilisation of adherents. Very commonly, the traditional symbolism, liturgy and aesthetic concern of traditional religion are abandoned for much more pragmatic attitudes and for systems of control, accountancy, propaganda and even doctrinal content which are closer to the styles of secular enterprise than to traditional religious concerns. The new religions do evidently indicate a continuing interest in, perhaps need for, spiritual solace and reassurance on the part of many individuals, but, in the West at least, they are also very much the creations of a secularized society. (Wilson, 1988: 965)

Who is right, Berger and Wilson or Stark and Bainbridge? Do NRMs represent the remnant of religion as it once was, adapted to a reduced existence in a secular context, or are NRMs simply new religions, with the potential in some cases to be the precursors of a true revival of religion? We will explore this question further in the final chapter.

BOX 3 THREE MODELS OF CULT FORMATION

Early in the study of contemporary NRMs, William Sims Bainbridge and Rodney Stark (1979) presented three fascinating, if cynical, models of how cults form. These were simplified constructs meant to highlight some of the existing theories; in reality, new religions may originate from a combination of the different elements identified with each model. In line with their larger theory of religion, Bainbridge and Stark treat cults as systems for the production and exchange of rewards and compensators.

The first model, the 'Psychopathology Model of Cult Innovation', suggests that NRMs are in essence the inventions of individuals 'suffering from certain forms of mental illness' (p. 285). The religions represent new packages of compensators born of visions experienced by the creator during psychotic episodes, which serve to ameliorate that individual's symptoms or focus their anxious energies on a constructive task. The power of the hallucinations assures the budding prophet of the veracity of his or her new understanding of the world, launching them on the road to convince others. The acceptance of others will further legitimate the vision, helping the new religious leader to achieve a greater measure of relief from his or her underlying psychological problems. The individual will succeed in creating a cult 'if the society contains many other persons suffering from problems similar to those originally faced by the cult founder, to whose solution, therefore, they are likely to respond'. Once in place all the members begin to receive the therapeutic benefits of their shared alternative reality, as well as the more direct and real benefits that come from success. This model implies that cults are most likely to arise when societies are enduring crises, causing many people to experience 'similar unresolved problems'.

The second model is the 'Entrepreneur Model of Cult Innovation.' Here the motivation for the creation of a new package of general compensators is quite simply the desire to profit materially from satisfying an apparent market need. The founders of cults are skilled sales people with an eye for new opportunities, and they have usually acquired the particular skills and experiences they need to succeed through 'a prior career as the employee of an earlier successful cult' (p. 288). Consequently, the new religion created is often only a reconfiguration of other existing religions, with developments designed to better suit the product to emerging market conditions. This helps to explain why so many 'cults tend to cluster in lineages', why their beliefs and practices bear such close 'family resemblances' (p. 288).

According to the third model, the 'Subculture-Evolution Model of Cult Innovation', cults are often the by-product of the novel social systems that arise in small groups of people dedicated to obtaining scarce or unusual rewards (e.g. some therapeutic objective or environmental cause). The intense interactions and exchanges of affection born of their efforts may become the focal point of an alternative culture, especially in the face of the failure of their efforts to achieve their original goals. The intrusion of ideas from the occult milieu or some other religious orientation may then offer another justification for their continued interaction, providing a new reason for being and sense of purpose. As the intra-group exchange of rewards and compensators becomes ever more satisfying in itself, the group may become 'relatively encapsulated' (p. 291). With time and the emergence of leadership, a novel religious culture will develop that turns its attention to the mobilization of new material resources and new members.

As the cults in question achieve some success, they may come to operate in autonomy from their original impetus, developing into legitimate religions. Emile Durkheim (1982), one of the founding figures of sociology, long ago advised that we must guard against confusing origins with functions. Things change with time.

Drawn from William Sims Bainbridge and Rodney Stark, 'Cult Formation: Three Compatible Models.' *Sociological Analysis* 40, 1979: 283–95.

New Religious Movements As An Expression of Cultural Continuity

Having looked at the changes that contributed to the rise of NRMs, we now turn to a set of views united by the claim that NRMs are not as new or different as most scholars and the public think. In fact, much that contemporary secular and conventional religious culture finds objectionable in NRMs has its roots in the history of American religious dissent and the mainstream religious traditions.

NEW RELIGIOUS MOVEMENTS AND AMERICAN RELIGIOUS HISTORY

The history of religion in North America is marked by periods of sweeping change and fervour that have come to be known as the Great Awakenings. Historians widely agree that many aspects of fundamental cultural identity of Americans were forged during two times of intense religious revivalism, the First Great Awakening, which spread throughout the American colonies from 1730 to 1760, and the Second Great Awakening, which gripped the new nation from 1800 to 1830. To these, some other historians, most notably William McLoughlin (1978), have added a Third Great Awakening, from 1890 to 1920, coinciding with the birth and popularity of modern urban revivalism, and, even more speculatively, a Fourth Great Awakening, coinciding with the rise of NRMs and of the New Christian Right, from the 1960s to the present (see also Lucas, 1992). In other words, McLoughlin and others (e.g. Pritchard, 1976; Moore, 1985) are suggesting that the recent rise of NRMs may be only the latest manifestation of the cyclical pattern of cultural development that has characterized American religion from the beginning. The United States has always been a land of 'new lights', as opposed to the 'old lights' of the established churches, and hence in broad perspective the new religions of today are not so new.

However one chooses to date, number, categorize, or explain these periods of religious tumult in American history, it is clear that social change and religious change have gone hand in hand in the New World and that the pattern of change has tended to be episodic.

> The . . . great awakenings [mark] periods of fundamental ideological transformation necessary to the dynamic growth of the nation in adapting to basic social, ecological, psychological, and economic changes. The conversion of great numbers of people from an old to a new world view . . . is a natural and necessary aspect of social change. It constitutes the awakening of a people caught in an outmoded, dysfunctional world view to the necessity of converting their mindset, their behavior, and their institutions to more relevant or more fundamentally useful ways of understanding and coping with the changes in the world they live in. (McLoughlin, 1978: 8)

In the first three awakenings, the focus and vehicle of change was evangelical Protestantism. The first awakening broke the hold of the 'old light' Puritan ethos and institutional order of New England, ushering in a 'new light' religious pluralism of other forms of Protestantism marked by the positive valuation of individual piety and personal conversions over denominational loyalty and doctrinal formalism. Socially, the experience of revival helped to weld the people of the American colonies together in a spirit of independence from the old order that resulted in the American Revolution. The second awakening furthered these same processes and gave birth to the Methodists, Baptists, and many other evangelical sects (such as the Disciples of Christ). Over the course of the rest of the nineteenth century and the early twentieth century, these new evangelical forms of Christianity set in motion the true 'churching' of America, rendering it the most religious of nations in the modern West (Finke and Stark, 1992). The Third Great Awakening was designed to save this largely Protestant America from the cultural contamination thought to stem from the massive influx of Catholic and Jewish immigrants into the cities of the United States and

Canada in the late nineteenth and early twentieth centuries. From this third awakening emerged the modern style of mass evangelism now so familiar to most North Americans through the contemporary crusades of Billy Graham, Oral Roberts, Jimmy Swaggart, Pat Robertson, Benny Hinn, and many other televangelists (see e.g. Frankl, 1987; Schultze, 1991). But there also arose the recognition of America as a land of Judeo-Christian pluralism. As the sociologist Will Herberg (1955) documented, by the early 1950s being Protestant, Catholic, or Jewish was simply seen as different ways of being American. For most Americans, to be 'American' required at least a belief in God and the Bible, and some fairly regular participation in the services of a church or synagogue.

From the beginning, each of the first three awakenings helped to define the collective sense of America as a nation destined to serve some special and probably divine purpose. By doing so, these revivals worked to bring the nation together and fashion what McLoughlin calls 'a constant cultural core' (1978: 10). Yet the intensity of religious feeling and conviction stimulated by the spirit of revival also gave rise to a plethora of new Christian sects and even cults. With each awakening, old denominations were subject to repeated schisms, and some altogether new revelations came into being (for example, Mormonism, Spiritualism, Christian Science, and Pentecostalism). Through recurrent religious change, adjustments were made to the collective self-conception of Americans, resolving the distortions that periodically emerged between the values and social conditions of daily life in North America. The overriding effect has been to generate a new unity out of diversity. One is reminded of the old adage: '*Plus ça change, plus c'est la même chose*' (Karr, 1849).

But what of the Fourth Great Awakening? Are the NRMs that have emerged since the 1960s characteristic of this pattern? Or are they antithetical and evidence of the end of this kind of American religious history? The marked increase in Americans drawn to evangelical Christianity, Pentecostalism, and Catholic Charismatic Renewal conforms to this pattern. But what of the turn East, to use Cox's adroit phrase? How does the spread of Krishna Consciousness or Tibetan Buddhism reflect an ideological adjustment to the collective self-conception of Americans? What are we to make of the creation and popularity of Scientology or diverse forms of neo-paganism? Noting the obvious parallel in the pattern of social and ideological change, McLoughlin says they do point to a shift in the self-conception of Americans, and many others are sympathetic to his reasoning. Writing in 1978, however, he lacked sufficient historical perspective, and in truth he does more to declare and describe the elements of this Fourth Great Awakening than to demonstrate convincingly the commonalities linking the present to the past.

Expressing a view of the ferment of the sixties much like that already discussed, McLoughlin argues that the post-sixties period was marked by a self-doubt and pessimism about the American way that was different from the previous awakenings only in the depth of its assault on the core culture: 'When men become self-conscious and analytical about their most cherished cultural myths, they have ceased to believe in them.' The sharp turn of the counterculture away from continued faith in 'the self-reliant, morally free, and responsible individual (acting in a special covenant with God), . . . signalled that . . . [a]nother era of cultural distortion had begun' (McLoughlin, 1978: 185). The 'new lights' of this awakening were more truly new, though, starting with the Beat poets and writers of the fifties (Allen Ginsberg, Lawrence Ferlinghetti, Alan Watts, Gary Snyder, and Jack Kerouac), moving through the hippies of the sixties, and on into the oriental philosophies and practices of the seventies. McLoughlin sees a common spirit of social reform linking the aspirations of the hippies and Jesus freaks to those of Ralph Waldo Emerson in the Second Great Awakening or the exponents of a Christian socialism in the Third Great Awakening. He argues that each awakening simply seeks new ways 'to express the transcendent spirit of the cultural core, to find the universal fraternalism of the primitive Christian church before it became bogged down with doctrines, dogmas, rituals, and institutional restrictions upon the Spirit that moves the world' (McLoughlin, 1978: 211). The legacy of counterculture is a turn to the vision of a more humane Godhead, greater human possibilities, and more social harmony. But McLoughlin thought it would take a generation or more for this Fourth Awakening to work itself out, since it must grow with the young (1978: 214–16).

McLoughlin (1978: 216) describes the anticipated change as follows:

> The beginning of a new belief-value system springing from [a] new respect for life and its mysterious source and continuity is found not only in the current distaste for defoliation weapons, carbon monoxide, insecticides, preservatives, fluorocarbons, detergents, nuclear fission, and toxic dyes but in the concern to preserve whales, dolphins, and other endangered species. It is found in the greater respect for the helpless aged and the battered wife, the oppressed races and the incarcerated prisoner, in respect for the materials of craftsmanship and the patient skill with which the craftsman works. Today's countercultural behavior strives for relationships that are tolerant, soft-spoken, respectful of the feelings and opinions of others; it frowns on the aggressive, defensive, hostile, and possessive attitudes of the cultural past; it likes what men and women have in common as individuals and as groups and finds no 'specially chosen people.' It does

not measure success in terms of money, status, or power but in terms of friendship, generosity, and the ability to empathize and give. It is concerned pre-eminently with the quality of life, not its quantity. In that direction the awakening is moving and changing American life.

We can recognize elements of this vision in our world today, but we have plenty of ambiguity to deal with. In the first place, it is not clear that these features are so new to the culture of North America. Nor is it clear that these changes have happened, or to what extent and effect. All we can safely say is that a new air of legitimation arose for religious innovation and lifestyle experimentation, and in that respect the rise in new religious activity is in continuity with other times in the American past.[8]

J. Gordon Melton (1987) and others (such as Raschke, 1980; Werblowsky, 1982; Ellwood and Partin, 1988), have simply argued that 'the blossoming of the alternative religions in the 1970s is not so much a new event in Western culture as the continuation of the flowering of occult mysticism and Eastern thought that began in the nineteenth century' (Melton, 1987: 47–8). With specific reference to the United States, these scholars and others[9] document the founding and spread of Eastern religious groups, for example, the Vedanta Society of Swami Vivekananda amongst native Westerners, since at least the 1890s. By 1900, the Theosophical Society was well established and was educating many Americans about Eastern philosophies and religious principles. The many groups that have splintered off from Theosophy in the twentieth century constitute a vast network of occult bodies heavily influenced by Eastern religions. To these Eastern elements of the not-so-new 'new religious consciousness' can be added a welter of Spiritualist, New Thought, Swedenborgian, occult, and other psychical research groups that were thriving in North America by the turn of the nineteenth century (Stillson, 1967; Campbell, 1980). And as Melton (1987: 49) comments in passing, 'lest we come away with the notion that this alternative religious community grew among people alienated from the mainstream of American culture, let us take note of the center of the alternative religious community in the 1880s: Boston and its environs.'

The virulent attack against the NRMs of today, viewed in historical perspective, indirectly provides further evidence against the 'newness' of NRMs. In their innovative and playful study, 'The Tnevnoc Cult', Bromley and Shupe (1979a: 365) conclude:

As even a cursory review of American history reveals, virtually every major denomination and religious body was met initially with some degree of skepticism, ostracism or persecution. Indeed, the parallels with contemporary religious groups are striking. Much as the Unification Church, Hare Krishna, Children of God, and People's Temple are currently labelled 'cults,' the Tnevnocs once were pejoratively lumped together with groups such as the Mormons and Masons despite their enormous doctrinal and organizational diversity. The stereotypes and litany of charges levelled against contemporary 'new religions' also are remarkably reminiscent of allegations against the earlier 'new religions': political subversion, unconditional loyalty of members to authoritarian leaders, brutalizing of members, sexual indiscretions, and possession of mysterious, extraordinary powers. . . . And the atrocity stories told by apostates from earlier groups . . . read much like the lurid tales told by former members of contemporary 'new religions'.

What is the Tnevnoc cult? As you may have guessed, Tnevnoc is 'convent' spelt backwards, and Bromley and Shupe demonstrate that the beliefs and practices of Catholic monasticism were the object of suspicion and persecution by the Protestant majority of nineteenth-century America. Other studies of even greater historical detail have developed similar comparisons with regard, for example, to the treatment of Quakers, Mormons, and other new religions of the past (Swatsky, 1978; Robbins and Anthony, 1979b; Kent, 1987; Lewis, 1988; Jenkins, 2000).[10]

More recently, however, Melton (1987, 1995), and Stark and Finke (1993), have radically called into question the entire presumption that there has even been an upsurge of new religious activity rooted in the social discontents of the sixties. Stark and Finke (1993: 114) declare that 'whether or not there have been cultural crises in recent times, they did not prompt significant religious reactions because the alleged eruptions of cult and sect activity never took place.' Citing some rather limited statistics that Melton has compiled on the number of cult movements founded for each decade between 1950 and 1990, these writers point to what Melton calls the 'steady pace of the founding of new religions' (Melton, 1995: 270). In other words, they argue for a pattern of 'continuity' and 'stability' (Stark and Finke, 1993) and not sudden change. There is no significant increase in the number of new religions founded in the sixties or seventies over the fifties. Reinforcing this interpretation, Stark and Finke call attention to the evidence available (limited again) that indicates the consistently small size of the new religions in question, whether founded in the fifties, sixties, or seventies.

But if such is the case, how did the misconception of a sudden increase in cult activity arise? Stark and Finke (1993) simply claim that such mistakes are far from uncommon in the history of American religion and then go on to note that the prominence of today's cults on university campuses in combination with the disproportionate cultural impact of the baby-boomer generation may well account for the exaggerated significance attributed to recent groups by scholars. Furthermore, with Melton they stress that the sudden yet quiet repeal of restrictive US immigration policies against Asians in 1965 removed a barrier to the natural development of the various long-established Eastern religious traditions in the West. The influx of gurus in the 1960s and 1970s, that is, did not so much set off a dramatic 'turn East' as simply encourage the 'normalization' of Hinduism and Buddhism. Due to a lack reliable data we cannot tell if this is the case, and the arguments of Melton, Stark, and Finke remain controversial.

NEW RELIGIOUS MOVEMENTS AND THE HISTORY OF RELIGIONS

In their well-known book, *Religious and Spiritual Groups in Modern America*, Ellwood and Partin (1988) try to place contemporary NRMs in the context of the same esoteric religious traditions discussed by Melton, Werblowsky, and others. They expand the context, however, beyond America to the full history of Western civilization, pointing to a long lineage of alternative religious and philosophic groups in the West—such as Pythagoreanism, Neoplatonism, Hermeticism, Gnosticism, Kabbalah, witchcraft, and alchemy—of significant size, diversity, and sometimes considerable social influence, that have persisted in whole or in various partial forms since pre-Christian times. These groups have drawn their beliefs from a variety of ancient and invented Greek, Egyptian, and other Middle Eastern religions and European traditions like the Celts. These 'perennial philosophies' (Huxley, 1970) tend to emphasize the continuity between humanity and the divine or supernatural, as opposed to the strict Christian dualism of God and humanity. In each of us, they believe, there is a 'spark of divinity'. Thus, true knowledge of the world comes as much from intuitive or mystical insight into our inner self as from conformity to the doctrines of science. The pursuit of this inner awareness reveals little-known and unexpected human capacities. Contrary to the dominant traditions of Christianity and science, with their stress on the rule of reason over feeling and the methodical discovery of the impersonal and law-like character of the physical universe, these more esoteric traditions envisage a world that is as much a mental as a physical place. It is a world that humanity shares with many other, largely spiritual, forms of intelligent life. In this alternative world-view, the boundary between the realms of spirit and matter are much more porous or blurred. Over the centuries the 'truths' and relevance of these other worlds and beings to the well-being of humans has been 'revealed' by a long lineage of esoteric masters, seers, and prophets whose writings provide the key to self-fulfilment and life beyond death: in modern times, Emmanuel Swedenborg, Comte de Saint Germain, Helena Blavatsky, Annie Besant, Georges Ivanovitch Gurdjieff, L. Ron Hubbard, and Elizabeth Clare Prophet come to mind. Many of the ideas attributed to the most ancient of these mystical figures can still be readily found, in whole or in part, in the plethora of 'metaphysical' or 'New Age' NRMs in our midst, such as Rosicrucianism, Eckankar, Scientology, and the Church Universal and Triumphant.[11]

In fact, many of the supposedly Christian new religions (such as the Solar Temple, the Church Universal and Triumphant, and the Holy Order of MANS) participate in this alternative tradition by incorporating similar esoteric teachings about Jesus into their doctrines. In this sense the truly 'cult-like' nature of the origins of the Christian church is preserved. But it is also useful to remember that the Christian community was indeed original-ly a cult, in relation to the dominant Greco-Roman world of the time. To most of his contemporaries, Jesus must have seemed but an uncouth and lowly peasant from a backward and distant part of the Roman Empire (that is, the civilized world), who was bizarrely presumed to be the son of God and future king of the world. His early followers were few in number and socially inconsequential. Some of his teachings, such as the Sermon on the Mount, must have seemed simplistic, and others, such as the doctrines of the incarnation and of the resurrection, dangerously fantastic. It was said that he had risen from the grave and could and would eventually raise oth-ers, and his devotees regularly met to eat his 'blood' and 'flesh' in mysteri-ous rituals. For these and other presumed practices, and out of sheer fear of the unknown and different, the early Christians were severely persecuted. But with a moment's true reflection the parallels with the plight of many contemporary cults should be clear (see Atwood and Flowers, 1983).

Finally, it must be duly recognized that the history of Christianity itself is littered with the corpses of thousands of 'new religions'—supposedly heretical variants of the Christian message and community of the most diverse type, longevity, and significance (see, for example, Cohn, 1961). As the American theologian and historian H. Richard Niebuhr (1951) so mas-terfully shows in *Christ and Culture*, there is no definitive way to discern the truth of any one of the many possible alternative readings of the cultural consequences of Christian belief. Each has been supported by different emi-nent leaders of the church through the centuries, such as Tertullian, Abelard, St Aquinas, St Augustine, and Martin Luther. Christianity can exist, normatively and factually, in all manner and degrees of tension with the rest of society. The differences in people's experiences and interpretations have fuelled endless disputes, schisms, and wars in the past, and continue to do so today. The emergence of new religions, as sects or cults, would appear to be the norm of the human condition and not an oddity.

Concluding Remarks

The social and historical forces influencing what seemed to be a sudden flowering of new religious activity in North America in the closing decades of the last millennium (i.e. pre-2000) are exceedingly complex. The reasons for the emergence of contemporary new religious movements are many— no one factor appears to be crucial. As is now also apparent, the claims of change and of continuity are not essentially incompatible. The new religions of today both continue and change ancient, and not so ancient, traditions of esoteric beliefs in response to the novel circumstances of modern society as well as the perennial questions about the meaning of life.

In closing, I think it is important to reiterate that we must guard against reductionism. Sociological and historical explanations of the conditions that spawn religious innovation can only carry us so far. We must give due consideration to the inherent appeal of the religious systems under study in accounting for the emergence of NRMs. To explain the continued vitality of these religious movements long after many of the initial conditions of crisis have passed, we need, as Jamie Hubbard (1998) asserts, to give more serious attention to the doctrines of these new religions. Part of their success surely lies in their ability to provide satisfying explanations of the crises buffeting people, both social and individual, and how to move beyond them (1998: 83).

Chapter Four

Who Joins New Religious Movements And Why?

The Stereotypes

The popular conception of who joins NRMs and why is riddled with stereotypes. Sometimes those who join are thought to be young, idealistic, and gullible people duped by cunning cult recruiters. Sometimes they are maladjusted and marginal losers who have found a safe haven in the controlled life of a cult. Other times it is suggested that everyone is susceptible to being recruited. The popular press and the anti-cult literature tends to blend together all these stereotypes using anecdotal evidence. In thirty years of systematic studies, however, academics have offered a very different picture. This chapter looks at what the systematic approach can tell us about how people become interested in new religious movements, and about the social attributes of those who choose to join.[1]

Getting Involved with New Religious Movements

Much that we know about who joins NRMs (and how and why) stems from the application and criticism of two theories: relative-deprivation theory (Glock, 1964) and the Lofland-Stark model of conversion (Lofland and Stark, 1965). The results of studies prompted by these theories can offer a fairly reliable set of generalizations.

RELATIVE-DEPRIVATION THEORY

In line with a broader range of popular conservatism and prejudice regarding the bringers of social change, early studies of such things as riots, demonstrations, panics, and so on, often assumed or implied that participants were irrational. Those who joined social movements, particularly radical religious movements, were deemed to be deviant. They were presumed to have been recruited from marginal segments of society or at least from groups experiencing bad times or a decline in their fortunes. People's involvement in acts of collective protest or in unconventional lifestyles was even described as the result of a pathological personality (e.g. Freud, 1921; Adorno et al., 1950; Blumer, 1951; Toch, 1965).

With the sweeping social disruptions of the 1960s, particularly the student-led anti-war movement, these attitudes and interpretations began to change. The university students who marched in the streets, fought with the police, and shut down campuses across the United States did not seem to fit the image that the social scientists had fashioned. Unlike the Communists, Jehovah's Witnesses, or other groups associated with social protests just before and after the Second World War, these proponents of change could not be readily dismissed as mentally disturbed or deficient, nor could it be readily said that they had been deprived of the benefits of American life (Skolnik, 1969). Rather they were the 'children of privilege' (Levitt, 1984). In the end, moreover, the wisdom of many of the changes for which these students and others fought, such as an end to the war in Vietnam, greater civil rights, female equality, sexual liberation, and ecological awareness, was accepted by the majority of Americans. In the face of these developments many sociologists turned away from 'irrationalist' theories of the origins of social movements and collective behaviour to theories of 'relative deprivation' (e.g. Aberle, 1962; Glock, 1964; Gurr, 1970). This largely set the agenda of the sociology of NRMs from the 1960s well into the 1980s. Since the 1980s, relative-deprivation theory itself has been harshly criticized (see Gurney and Tierney, 1982) and largely displaced by ideas labelled as resource-mobilization theory (e.g. McCarthy and Zald, 1977), new-social-movements theory (e.g. Hannigan, 1991; Mauss, 1993), and rational-choice theory (e.g. Stark and Iannaccone, 1993). But its influence shaped much of the literature on NRMs, and it continues to have an effect on most popular conceptions of why people join cults (see, for example, Pfeifer, 1992) and on some academic conceptions (e.g. Levine, 1984; Kent, 1987; Deikman, 1990; Stark and Bainbridge, 1987). So let us briefly look at the relative-deprivation approach as developed by Charles Glock (1964), probably the most prominent exponent of the theory in the sociology of religion.

In studies of why people joined new religions of a predominantly Christian sectarian type in the nineteenth century and the first half of the twentieth century (for example, Seventh Day Adventists, Jehovah's Witnesses, Pentecostalism), sociologists and historians argued that the primary 'push' was simply economic deprivation. The 'pull' was thought to be the promise of reward in the next life for proper Christian humility (that is, acceptance of one's lowly lot in life), in combination with both the compensatory spiritual legitimation that results from faith in this promise (the belief that 'while we may be poor, we are virtuous') and the more immediate psychic compensation of ecstatic and highly emotional religious experiences. People were seeking an escape from the hardships and humiliations of life. Sociologists and historians reached this conclusion in large measure because the members of these organizations came disproportionately from the lower socio-economic strata of society. Just as attitudes to social protest have changed since the 60s, so have views about sectarians, due to growing evidence that their socio-economic status is rising (e.g. Wilson, 1961; Calley, 1965) together with the emergence of the new cults whose participants seem to be drawn from university and college campuses, not from the poor and abused sectors. As we will see, the successful cults of today seem to 'skim more of the cream of society than the dregs' (Stark and Bainbridge, 1985: 395).

Glock (and others) tried to account for this by distinguishing between 'absolute' (or real) deprivation and 'relative' deprivation. Whether people really are deprived or not, it is argued, may not be very important in determining who joins either social or religious movements. If people think there is a discrepancy between the social rewards they feel entitled to and the rewards they think they are getting or they believe others are getting, and if they do not accept some rational explanation for their deprivation, then there will be an incentive to launch or join a movement that promises change or compensation. The deprivation in question is subjective (though it may also be real), and Glock greatly expands the scope of analysis by proposing that there may be several different forms of this subjective sense of being deprived (1964: 27–8): (1) it may be 'economic deprivation', related to the unequal distribution of income; (2) it may be 'social deprivation', related to the unequal distribution of social status, prestige, and the markers of power; (3) it may be 'organismic deprivation', related to the unequal distribution of mental and physical health; (4) it may be 'psychic deprivation', relating to unequal distribution of various kinds of psychic rewards, like love and affection; (5) it may even be 'ethical deprivation', related to an individual's feeling that the dominant values of society no longer provide a sufficiently meaningful way to live.[2]

Glock argues that relative deprivation in some form is a 'necessary' condition for the rise of NRMs. It explains why even relatively privileged individuals would be willing to make sacrifices to join a movement and change their lives. It is not, however, a 'sufficient' condition—it is not enough, by itself, to explain the emergence of an NRM. To bring an NRM into being it is also necessary 'that the deprivation be shared, that no alternative institutional arrangements for [the] resolution [of the relative deprivation] are perceived, and that a leadership emerge with an innovating idea for building a movement out of the existing deprivation' (Glock, 1964: 29). Nevertheless, a study of the beliefs, practices, and organization of particular groups, Glock implies, should tell us quite a bit about what kinds of deprivations probably motivated people to join the groups in question (Glock, 1964: 33).

There is a common-sense appeal to the relative-deprivation thesis: 'The view that movements of all types arise out of deprivation, however it is defined, is almost universal' (Hine, 1974: 651). Clearly, elements of this view can be detected in Berger's theory of religion and even more explicitly in Stark and Bainbridge's theory. But regrettably, decades of research using this approach have generated a host of theoretical and empirical criticisms, and scholars have been unable to establish the causal links claimed with sufficient consistency or exactitude. In an excellent review of the literature, Gurney and Tierney (1982: 40) conclude that most applications of the theory 'take as given the very link which must be empirically established to render [relative-deprivation] theory plausible. Their failure to link convincingly psychological states with antecedent societal conditions on the one hand and with subsequent movement participation on the other hand is the Achilles heel of [relative-deprivation] research.'

Even if the necessary causal links were isolated, however, a more fundamental theoretical objection remains: we can never be certain whether there are not just as many non-participants as participants in social and religious movements that are experiencing some kind of relative deprivation (see Gurney and Tierney, 1982: 38; Stark and Bainbridge, 1985: 308). In fact, there is the possibility of 'greater variation in [relative-deprivation] levels among participants than between participants and nonparticipants.' So the evidence that many converts to NRMs may have experienced some type of relative deprivation does not give us any very specific information about why these particular movements arose. It does not allow us to discriminate effectively between joiners and non-joiners, and hence the concept of relative deprivation loses much of its explanatory value. Contrary to Glock's assertion, in other words, it cannot even be said with confidence that the experience of relative deprivation is a 'necessary' condition for joining an NRM.

Wilson (1990: 195) drives the point home with a few adroit questions: 'Why . . . do some people not feel deprived when by all objective criteria, they are deprived, and why, even of those who feel deprived, do only a proportion become absorbed by religious groups? Do none of the undeprived become religious?' Picking up on the last point, Hine (1974: 654) observes scathingly, 'In refining the concept of deprivation, [researchers] seem at times to be going out of their way to avoid the possibility of positive motivation!' Theoretically, that is, the search for some explanatory form of relative deprivation to account for every unconventional religious choice smacks of reductionism, and the approach comes dangerously close to being self-fulfilling and irrefutable (that is, non-scientific).[3]

Even our peripheral examination of the many different typologies of cults revealed the variety of NRMs in existence. There are pronounced differences in their beliefs, practices, organizations, and patterns of commitment. It is folly to try to account for the many motivations that may exist for joining different groups on the basis of one highly generalized theory like relative deprivation. Matters are more complex, and the diverse claims of the religious people themselves warrant more consideration.

In pursuing the question of who joins NRMs and why, we must turn to another model, one having some similarities to relative-deprivation theory but which takes account of a greater diversity of factors.

THE LOFLAND-STARK MODEL OF CONVERSION

This model grew out of field research into what was then a small and obscure deviant religion, newly imported to the United States from Korea. Dubbed the 'Divine Precepts' by Lofland and Stark, the group in question was in fact the early Unification Church (that is, the Moonies) in the United States. Gathering the accounts of converts to this cult and observing the many other attempts made to recruit others, Lofland and Stark charted the seven factors they thought must come into play in order to transform a potential recruit into a 'verbal convert' first and then eventually a 'total convert'. Verbal converts are 'followers who [profess] belief and [are] accepted by core members [of the group] as sincere, but [who take] no active role in the [movement].' Total converts are those 'who [exhibit] their commitment through deeds as well as words.' It is only with the onset of the last stage of the seven-step conversion process, Lofland and Stark assert, that a verbal convert becomes a total or true convert (1965: 864).

The model stipulates that for persons to convert to a cult they must (1) experience enduring, acutely felt tensions in their lives, (2) within a religious problem-solving perspective (as opposed to a psychiatric or political problem-solving perspective), (3) which leads them to think of themselves as a religious seeker. With these three 'predisposing conditions' in place, the individuals must then (4) encounter the cult to which they convert at a turning point in their lives, (5) form an affective bond with one or more members of the cult, (6) reduce or eliminate extra-cult attachments, and (7) be exposed to intensive interaction with other converts. With the completion of the latter four 'situational contingencies', the new convert can become a 'deployable agent' of the cult. It is the cumulative effect of all of these experiences, Lofland and Stark believed, that produces a true conversion. Each step is necessary, but only the whole process is sufficient.

Over the years this model has been tested repeatedly, in different contexts, with mixed results. In the study of quite a large NRM imported to America from Japan, Nichiren Shoshu (also known by the name of its lay organization, Sōka Gakkai), Snow and Phillips (1980) found reason to be suspicious of all but two of the seven steps of the Lofland-Stark model of conversion. Greil and Rudy (1984) arrived at a similar conclusion after scrutinizing the data on conversion available from ten case studies of widely divergent NRMs. On the other hand, Merrill Singer (1988) and to some extent Knox et al. (1991) found almost all aspects of the model to be relevant to the study of the Black Hebrew Nation and of Dutch adolescents who had converted to either the Unification Church or the Pentecostal Church. The debate over the merits of the theory has become complex. The Snow and Phillips study rejects the claims that potential converts must experience enduring and acutely felt tensions and some turning point in their lives (such as failing at school, experiencing a divorce, taking a long trip). Looking at the Nichiren Shoshu NRM in Britain, however, Wilson and Dobbelaere (1994) found that many members at least say that they experienced chronic or acute crises in their lives and a turning point. This disparity in findings can be explained in many ways, but the divergent results suggest, as Knox et al. (1991) propose, that the steps outlined by Lofland and Stark should be viewed less as a model and more as a fairly adequate statement of some crucial 'conditions' of conversion (which may be of varying significance for different religions).

Although many scholars have clearly overgeneralized the relevance of the Lofland and Stark model, the research it inspired has consistently confirmed some of these 'conditions' and led to the formulation of some systematic reasons for why they may vary. Those insights constitute the body of what we can say confidently about why people become involved with NRMs.

Seven Empirical Insights

In order, roughly, of the degree of empirical support (that is, research consensus) that exists, the availability of particular people to cults is conditioned by the following seven generalizations.

Social Networks

In the first place, studies of conversion and case studies of specific groups have found that recruitment to NRMs happens primarily through pre-existing social networks and interpersonal bonds. Friends recruit friends, family members recruit each other, and neighbours recruit neighbours. Contrary to public belief and the 'brainwashing' theory of cult conversion, the figures available support neither the proposition that everyone is equally susceptible to recruitment nor that most converts are recruited through individual and single contacts in public places. Groups like the Unification Church, Krishna Consciousness, and Children of God/The Family (to name but a few) have been condemned for their aggressive and persistent forays into public places to proselytize and disseminate literature. Yet the evidence strongly indicates that these recruitment drives are not very successful, that in fact in some regards they are dismal failures in relation to the effort invested in them (with regard to the Moonies, see the figures in Barker, 1984: 141–8, and Galanter, 1989: 140–1). Rather, the majority of recruits to the majority of NRMs come into contact with the groups they join because they know one or more members of the movement.[4]

The results of a recent and quite comprehensive study of Nichiren Shoshu (Sōka Gakkai) in Great Britain are characteristic:

> Only 6 per cent of those in our sample had encountered [the Nichiren Shoshu] through the impersonal agencies of the media—through exhibitions, concerts, the movement's own publicity, or the various media accounts of the organization which had appeared in Britain. Ninety-four per cent met the movement through social interaction. Friends represented the largest category of people who introduced members, amounting to some 42 per cent; 23 per cent were brought into contact with it through their partners or family members. The remainder were first presented with information by acquaintances, work or student colleagues most particularly, but 14 per cent owed the encounter to casual acquaintances. (Wilson and Dobbelaere, 1994: 50)

Even the anti-cultist Margaret Singer supports the proposition that most converts are recruited through social networks (Singer, 1995: 105). She cites a figure of 66 per cent, but does not seem to detect any inconsistency between this claim and another made on the same page, namely, that 'all of us are vulnerable to cult recruitment.'

In the study of NRMs, however, as stressed in Chapter 1, there are exceptions to every rule. Barker (1984: 95–100) denies that existing personal networks accounted for the majority of converts to the Moonies in Britain in the 1970s and 1980s. But she does note that networks account for over a quarter of the British membership and for a third of the membership in the rest of Europe, and does not clearly explain how the majority of members are recruited.

Affective Ties

Second, as some of the harshest critics of the Lofland-Stark model admit, Lofland and Stark were correct in specifying the importance of affective ties with members of an NRM in the recruitment of new members (e.g. Snow and Phillips, 1980; Greil and Rudy, 1984; Stark and Bainbridge, 1985; Knox et al., 1991). Again, Wilson and Dobbelaere's findings with regard to the Nichiren Shoshu in Britain are typical: over a third of the respondents in their study stressed 'the quality of the membership' as the primary reason for their initial attraction to the group. Wilson and Dobbelaere provide numerous quotations from their questionnaires and interviews full of praise for the vibrancy, warmth, openness, joy, and positive outlook of the members first encountered by the respondent. Studies also show that, beyond the moment of recruitment, affective bonds with specific members are crucial in leading recruits into deeper involvement.[5]

Intensive Interaction

The same studies make it equally clear that the intensive interaction of recruits with the other members of the group is pivotal to the successful conversion and maintenance of new members. A good example is found in 'Waiting for the Ships', Robert Balch's (1995a) last academic paper on the Bo and Peep UFO cult before it was catapulted from obscurity into the international spotlight under its new name, Heaven's Gate. In this paper Balch describes how the leaders systematically reversed the rapid disintegration of their fledgling group, by introducing daily routines that promoted intensive interaction between all members of the group. Conversely, the apparent loss of such intensive interaction is often decisive in the deconversion or 'apostasy' of members of NRMs (Jacobs, 1989).

On these first three points, then, there is little disagreement in the academic literature.

Weak Social Ties

The fourth insight is that cult involvement seems to be strongly correlated with having fewer and weaker extra-cult social ties (e.g. Lofland, 1977; Downton, 1979; Stark and Bainbridge, 1985, 1987; Balch, 1995a; Bader and Demaris, 1996). Part of the reason for the disproportionate representation of adolescents and young adults in NRMs is simply that this segment of the population is relatively free of other social and economic commitments. They have the time and the opportunity to indulge their spiritual appetites and to experiment with alternative ways of living. The more freedom one has in that regard, the more likely one is to accept the 'invitation' of a cult recruiter to dinner, a lecture, or a meditation session (see Snow et al., 1980). This also helps to explain the popular image of cults preying on the lonely. Students who are away from home to attend university, or who are 'on the road', are more susceptible to cult recruitment. But the condition of being temporarily unattached is not the cause of being recruited. Although the experience of intense loneliness is pervasive amongst self-conscious young adults, most individuals who join an NRM do not do so simply out of loneliness (a most direct form of relative deprivation). Their being alone— that is, their lack of social attachments—is due largely to the transitional and unencumbered status that our society tends to accord to its youth, and as such it is merely an aspect of the increased availability of this segment of the population. Stark and Bainbridge (1987) develop this point, arguing in general that people with relatively 'low stakes in conformity' (that is, with few attachments, investments, involvements, and beliefs) are more likely to join NRMs that are in high tension or philosophical conflict with society. This is quite simply because these people are likely 'to incur minimal costs by deviating, and may, in turn, have much to gain from it' (1987: 190–1). Bader and Demaris (1996) have independently confirmed this claim, demonstrating statistically that low stakes in conformity increase the likelihood of membership in cults and sects.

Evidence from Barker's analysis of a large sample of participants in Unification Church recruitment workshops suggests that 'non-joiners' are actually more likely than 'joiners' to be in a transitional state in life (for example, unemployed or travelling) (1984: 199), a point that appears to conflict with Stark and Bainbridge but does not necessarily do so. With regard to the growth and success of NRMs, everything is a matter of degree and balance. As Stark and Bainbridge (1987: 225–8) further specify, empirical studies suggest that too low an investment in conformity can lead to a condition of 'chronic seekership' that prevents certain people from forming lasting bonds with any religious group. Structurally, those most likely to convert to an NRM will have relatively few extra-cult social ties but they will not be complete loners. Otherwise, it would be difficult to explain why studies have shown social networks to be so important in recruiting. As we will see in Chapter 7, if for various reasons an NRM becomes almost totally isolated from outside social networks, as did the Peoples Temple at Jonestown, Guyana, it is likely to become too extreme in form and be in danger of becoming violent or of failing.

Weak Ideological Alignments

Fifth, cult involvement seems to be strongly correlated with having fewer and weaker ideological alignments. Most researchers now discount Lofland and Stark's suggestion that converts to NRMs were probably pre-socialized to adopt a religious problem-solving perspective. In fact, the data actually suggest that the 'unchurched', as Stark and Bainbridge (1985) call them, are more likely to join. In many cases, lack of prior religious education and family life seems to leave young people more open to alternative spiritual explanations of the world and its hardships (Snow and Phillips, 1980; Stark and Bainbridge, 1985). There are clear exceptions to this generalization. As Richardson and Stewart (1977) suggest, for instance, in the case of many neo-Christian movements (such as the Unification Church) and Jesus movements we may be dealing with the phenomenon of 'returning fundamentalists'. Recruits to these groups often do seem to have been raised in strict religious households from which they lapsed or rebelled as adolescents (see also Tipton, 1982a). Similarly, it would seem that recruits to the Catholic Charismatic Renewal and its offshoots are overwhelmingly from Catholic backgrounds (Neitz, 1987).

Seekership

Sixth, while 'seekership'—the active search for religious answers to one's problems—does not seem to be as necessary as Lofland and Stark thought, it does precede many conversions. People interested in even the possibility of joining an NRM have been reading related religious and philosophical literature and giving some serious thought to the 'big questions' in life (What is the meaning of life? Is there a God? Is there life after death?). Indicatively, several studies have discovered that a little fewer than half of the converts to NRMs were either actively practising a religion other than that in which they were raised, or had previously been members of another NRM (e.g. Rochford, 1985: 54; Wilson and Dobbelaere, 1994: 88; Balch. 1995a: 147–8). Here again, though, Barker found aspects of seekership to be far more prevalent amongst the 'non-joiners' in her sample of people participating in Unification Church workshops than amongst 'joiners' (Barker, 1984: 199), and in a detailed survey of the members of ten Eastern meditational groups in North America, Gussner and Berkowitz (1988) found little evidence of any notable period of seekership.

Direct Rewards

Seventh and lastly, as Stark and Bainbridge (1985, 1987) stress in their theory of religion, we should be careful when trying to account for the conditions of conversion not to neglect the obvious. Whether one wishes to postulate a degree or kind of relative deprivation to explain why any individual joins an NRM, it should be recognized that such groups provide many direct rewards or 'specific compensators' to their members. They commonly offer such positive inducements as affection and heightened self-esteem, knowledge that provides a sense of power and control over one's life, as well as simple material and social aid, security, new career opportunities, and prestige. Sometimes, in fact, the rewards of participating in the new reality constructed by the group may become more important than satisfying 'the ends such participation was originally intended to procure' (Wallis, 1984: 122).

Other Complicating Factors

The degree to which these factors are involved in recruitment to any particular NRM can vary. The requirement that potential converts have weak extra-cult ties or ideological alignments depends on how deviant and particularistic (i.e. exclusive) the group is and the extent of the commitment demanded (Snow and Phillips, 1980; Snow et al., 1980; Stark and Bainbridge, 1987). If joining an NRM does not entail a dramatic transformation of one's values and lifestyle, as in the case of Scientology, there is less need to sever extra-cult bonds to effect a conversion. On the other hand, if there is a pronounced difference between the orientation and activities of the new religion and the family and friends of the recruit, as is usually the case with Krishna Consciousness, then the weakening of prior ties is more crucial to the conversion process. Groups stigmatized by the dominant society because of the peculiar or revolutionary character of their world view may choose a strategy of isolation to neutralize the stigma. The use of this strategy may also depend on the extent to which a group insists that it has the exclusive path to truth and salvation. The more particularistic a religion is, the more it will demand a sharp separation from the world and from the convert's past social and ideological attachments. Finally, the more complete the commitment demanded by a group, the more likely it is that new members will be recruited through contact in public places rather than through interpersonal bonds and social networks. This latter linkage may explain Barker's findings for recruitment to the Unification Church in Britain, findings that seem to be at odds with the strong role of social networks in recruitment detected in most other studies of NRMs.

A similar correlation has been found between seekership and the degree to which an NRM is stigmatized by society (Greil and Rudy, 1984). Seekership is far more likely to be relevant in conversion to seemingly 'deviant' religious groups than to others. For groups like the Moonies and Krishna Consciousness, personal ties with the 'outside world' are minimized, hence it is less likely that individuals will find and join these groups 'unless they have defined themselves as being "in the market" for conversion' (1984: 317).

Judging from the small number of people in NRMs, these factors are not sufficient in themselves to predict who will join. They must be set against a backdrop of yet more contingent and situational factors. For example, recruitment can be influenced by the degree and type of hostility to NRMs in the dominant culture, the presence or absence of missionaries, and the presence of competitor groups (Stark and Bainbridge, 1985, 1987). It makes a world of difference whether an NRM arises in the relaxed and experimental atmosphere of modern California or the highly conformist social and religious environment of Ireland or Iran. Contrasting Japan and the United States, Wilson (1982b: 24) points out that we must be careful not to assume even that new religions fulfil the same functions in different cultural and historical circumstances (see also Werblowsky, 1982). To the convert it often seems miraculous that a representative of a particular new religion happens to be at hand at the crucial moment of doubt or decision in their lives. If other similar kinds of groups, competitor religions, or functional equivalents to religion (such as a cathartic encounter therapy group, a revolutionary political movement, or an idealistic social service organization) were present instead, the conversion in question might never happen (see Levine, 1984).

A further possibility is that 'in some measure, movements may awaken needs in particular individuals, giving them increased specificity in the terms of the movement's own ideology, and so defining the situation for prospective adherents, supplying both the sense of needs and the means of its fulfilment' (Wilson, 1982b: 25). New religions, like many new commercial enterprises, are in the business of 'consciousness raising' about needs and how they can be satisfied. But in any event, this still means we 'need to know why people should accept the proposed definition of their situation and the proffered solutions' (Wilson, 1982b: 25). In other words, this valuable insight merely reconfigures the problem of explaining conversions.[6]

THE Social Attributes of THose WHo Join

Before we can attempt to draw conclusions about the individual psychology of people who join an NRM, we must assess what information the academic community can offer in terms of more general social profiles. Two things are clear from the numerous studies: (1) because of the different recruitment methods of different cults, each new religion tends to attract a rather homogeneous group of followers; (2) the overall membership of

NRMs is much more heterogeneous than commonly expected, since each group tends to attract somewhat different kinds of followers (e.g. Latkin, 1987; Poling and Kenny, 1986; Palmer, 1994). Given this diversity, what kind of generalizations might we usefully make?

Disproportionately Young

The members of most NRMs are disproportionately young. In the 1980s Barker (1984: 206) found that 50 per cent of the members of the Unification Church in Britain were between twenty-one and twenty-six years of age. The average age at which people joined the movement was twenty-three (pp. 199, 206). Rochford (1985: 47) reported that 56 per cent of the members of Krishna Consciousness were between twenty and twenty-five and that more than half had joined before their twenty-first birthday (see also Judah, 1974). Wilson and Dobbelaere (1994) found that the members of Nichiren Shoshu (now Sōka Gakkai) in Britain were also young, although the statistics were not as dramatic: 68.2 per cent of the members were under the age of thirty-four and 88.4 per cent were under forty-four. For the most part, the new religions have until recently been a game for young people, with middle-aged and old people markedly under-represented.

As some of the NRMs of the 1960s have aged, these figures have changed (e.g. Palmer, 1994: 39; Barker, 1995b: 168–9; Bainbridge, 2002: 25–26). The first generation of converts to Krishna Consciousness, the Unification Church, and the Family are now in their late forties and early fifties. But many people drop out of these organizations when they reach middle age or before, especially in the case of NRMs that are more communal and more exclusive in their commitments, for the demands and desires that accompany family life and the raising of children often conflict with the obligations of membership.

New religions that are less exclusive and extreme in their commitment expectations, like Scientology, Eckankar, Sōka Gakkai, Neo-Paganism, and so on, may maintain a better spread in the age distribution of their members as the groups grow older. For example, on the basis of an admittedly small sample, Wallis (1977) found that the average age of recruitment to Scientology in Britain was about thirty-two. Similarly, Wilson and Dobbelaere (1994) report a mean age for starting the practice of Nichiren Shoshu Buddhism (in the Sōka Gakkai movement) of thirty-one. In their survey of the American followers of Sōka Gakkai, Hammond and Machacek (1999: 45) found the median age of members was forty-five, reflecting the disproportionate presence of aging baby boomers. Similarly, Latkin et al. (1987), Carter (1990), Palmer (1994), and Goldman (1999) place the average age of followers of Bhagwan Shree Rajneesh in the mid-thirties. This is also true of the Raëlian UFO cult (Palmer, 2004: 117), and American Neo-Pagan/Wiccan groups (Berger et al., 2003: 27). In another instance, the Church Universal and Triumphant seems to be aging along with its leaders: in the 1990s approximately 53 per cent of the members were between forty and sixty (Jones, 1994: 42).

In the popular press there was some surprise expressed at the more mature age of the membership of the Solar Temple and Heaven's Gate groups. Palmer (1996: 305) says that the Solar Temple 'seemed to attract a clientele of predominantly middle-aged, prosperous and highly cultured professionals'. In line with popular expectations, the first news reports of the Heaven's Gate tragedy stated that thirty-nine identically dressed young men had taken their lives. Yet soon it became clear that twenty of the thirty-nine were actually women, and the ages of the dead ranged from 24 to 72. The majority were certainly middle-aged, and many had been with this new religion for over a decade. Similar observations have been made with regard to the Church of Satan (Alfred, 1976), 'est' (Babbie and Stone, 1977), and many Eastern meditational groups (Gussner and Berkowitz, 1988: 154). It still seems likely that most people convert to new religions when they are young, relatively free of other social obligations, and interested in experimenting with lifestyle options and alternative identities. To my knowledge, however, no systematic studies have been done in the last ten years or so to document whether the age profile of converts to NRMs is changing.

Better Educated

Most studies have found that recruits to NRMs are on average markedly better educated than the general public. Wallis (1977: 163) reports that in his admittedly rather small sample, 56.7 per cent of the Scientologists had either professional training or college or university degrees (29.7 per cent were university graduates). Likewise, Wilson and Dobbelaere (1994: 121–4) found that 24 per cent of their large sample of the membership of Sōka Gakkai in Britain had attended university, whereas in 1990 only 8 per cent of the population had a university education. In the United States, Hammond and Machacek (1999: 52) discovered that Sōka Gakkai 'members are considerably more likely than the American public (66 per cent versus 33 per cent) to have completed at least some college, more likely to hold a baccalaureate degree (40 per cent vs 26 per cent), and they are twice as likely to have an advanced degree (17 per cent vs 9 per cent).' Jones (1994: 43–4) actually found that a quarter of her respondents from the Church Universal and Triumphant had an advanced technical or professional degree. In surveying the membership of ten American religious meditational groups,

Gussner and Berkowitz (1988: 154) found that a striking 79 per cent had completed four or more years of college, 28.6 per cent had master's degrees, 10.3 per cent professional degrees, and 8.0 per cent PhDs. In fact, in their study of over 12,000 subjects, Bader and Demaris (1996) discovered that each year of educational attainment increased the likelihood of cult membership and decreased the likelihood of sect and church membership.

Why do NRMs tend to attract the well educated? Wilson and Dobbelaere suggest the answer is fairly obvious: 'To be properly understood, the teachings [of most NRMs] demand literate intelligence, a willingness to study, and lack of fear in the face of unfamiliar concepts and language' (1994: 123).

Disproportionately Middle to Upper Class

Unsurprisingly, given the educational levels, recruits to NRMs are also disproportionately from middle- to upper-middle-class households. The findings are similar for Scientology (Wallis, 1977), the Unification Church (Barker, 1984: 198, 206–8), the International Society for Krishna Consciousness (Judah, 1974; Rochford, 1985; Poling and Kenny, 1986; Palmer, 1994), Rajneesh (Latkin et al., 1987; Carter, 1990; Palmer, 1994; Goldman, 1999), other Asian-based meditational groups (Gussner and Berkowitz, 1988), the Church Universal and Triumphant (Jones, 1994) and Neo-Pagans (Berger et al., 2003: 31–32). The fathers of converts come primarily from the professional, business-executive, or administrative segments of the occupational world; skilled or unskilled manual labourers are clearly under-represented. In a rare exception, Palmer (2004: 117–118) reports that most of the early membership of the Raëlians came from working-class households. But most of the actual members were upwardly mobile individuals, and since she began studying the group in 1987, it has become solidly middle class.

Gender Balance

On questions of sex there seems to be some dispute. Machalek and Snow (1993) suggest there is an over-representation of women in NRMs. At some points, Stark and Bainbridge (1985: 413–17) do as well. But the evidence, as Stark and Bainbridge themselves admit, is highly variable. In the past, women were disproportionately present in fringe religions: for example, Christian Science in the 1920s was 75 per cent female (Stark and Bainbridge, 1985: 413), and Wilson and Dobbelaere (1994: 42–3) found about 59 per cent of the Sōka Gakkai movement in Britain to be female, Hammond and Machacek (1999: 4a) report a 2:1 ratio for Sōka Gakkai in the USA. Latkin et al. (1987), Palmer (1994) and Goldman (1999) also report a disproportionate number of women in the Rajneesh movement, which is also true for American Neo-Pagans (Berger et al., 2003: 27–28). Barker (1984: 206), however, reports a two-to-one ratio in favour of men for the Moonies in Britain, and Wallis's (1977: 165) sample of Scientologists is 59 per cent male. Likewise, Palmer (2004: 119) reports a strong gender imbalance in favour of men in the Raëlians. Others imply that there is little substantial discrepancy between the sexes in the groups they studied. On the whole, it would seem that while some cults may attract more of one sex than the other, there is no strong evidence that women are any more susceptible to joining NRMs than men.

It does appear that many groups undergo a kind of developmental shift in their sex ratios as they mature. Krishna Consciousness began life in America as a largely male phenomenon, but this imbalance in sexual representation has been corrected as the movement has aged and become an order of 'householders' and not strictly priestly ascetics (Palmer, 1994: 32). In Korea and Japan, before its emergence in America, the Unification Church actually appealed more to women, as did the Rajneesh movement in its beginnings in India (Palmer, 1994: 62, 90). These imbalances also adjusted with time. Reliable membership figures, though, especially ones that differentiate between the sexes, are hard to come by.

Religious Background

Did recruits to NRMs grow up religious? Here there is ambiguity as well. On the one hand, with the limited evidence available, Stark and Bainbridge (1985: 400) conclude: 'Church membership and membership in a conservative denomination are preventives against cultism. The unchurched and those affiliated with the more secularized denominations are more open to cult involvement.' The level of participation in NRMs of American Protestants, Catholics, and Jews varies from group to group. On the whole, though, Stark and Bainbridge think that Protestants are under-represented, reflecting the strength of right-wing evangelicalism in the United States, whereas the participation of Catholics is roughly proportionate to their numbers in the population. Jews are another matter. They are extraordinarily over-represented in many NRMs. Latkin et al. (1987), for example, found the following distribution in religious backgrounds for members of Rajneeshpuram: 30 per cent Protestant, 27 per cent Catholic, 20 per cent Jewish, 14 per cent 'none', 4 per cent Hindu or Buddhist, and 4 per cent 'other'. Jewish people, however, make up just 2.5 per cent of the American population. Why the over-representation? Stark and Bainbridge (1985: 402–3) suggest this might be explained by the secularization of the American Jewish community compared to other religious groups (see Box 4). Support for this stress on the relatively 'unchurched' character of converts to NRMs comes from the British followers of Nichiren Shoshu Buddhism (i.e. Sōka Gakkai): 'Fully 76 per cent of the respondents said that they had not belonged to any religious organization before they joined' (Wilson and Dobbelaere, 1994: 79). In fact, 47 per cent declared that, let alone belonging to an organization, they had not previously been religious at all, leading Wilson and Dobbelaere to call into question the contention that religious 'seekership' is a necessary precondition for conversion to NRMs (p. 88). Latkin et al. (1987) report that only 40 per cent of the members of Rajneeshpuram saw themselves as religious before joining, and a survey of the Church Universal and Triumphant revealed a slight over-representation of religious 'nones' (13.67 per cent). But in the latter instance, seekership would seem to be a significant factor since 49 per cent of the sample reported one or more previous associations with other non-traditional religions after childhood, such as Rosicrucians, Theosophy, and various Hindu and Buddhist groups (Jones, 1994: 49–50). Goldman's intensive interviews with eleven committed female members of the Rajneesh group highlights the important role played by seekership as well, as do Chancellor's (2000) interviews with over six hundred members of the Children of God/The Family.

American followers of Krishna seem to have come from fairly religious households; in Rochford's study, more than 50 per cent of his sample said religion was stressed in their childhood homes, 77 per cent had received formal religious education as children, about 50 per cent had attended religious services regularly, and another 30 per cent had attended irregularly (1985: 51–7). Likewise, Barker detected a strong correlation between high levels of church attendance and a general emphasis upon religious beliefs and values in childhood and joining the Unification Church (Barker, 1984: 212–13). Like the British members of Nichiren Shoshu (i.e. Sōka Gakkai), at the time of conversion most of Rochford's and Barker's respondents had lapsed in the practice of their childhood faith (Barker, 1984: 217) and only 25 per cent of Rochford's sample were practising some other religion. But the contrast with Stark and Bainbridge's conclusion remains pronounced.

It may well be that different NRMs draw people with different kinds of religious backgrounds—some being more attractive in their style of religious expression to individuals with more pronounced religious educations in their youth. We lack the kind of systematic data and comparisons to be more precise at this point. On the whole, though, Stark and Bainbridge's assumptions seem warranted. In reading the accounts of converts offered in detailed studies like Goldman's (1999) analysis of the women who joined the Rajneesh movement, Chancellor's (2000) interviews with converts to the Children of God/The Family, and Palmer's (2004) investigation of the

Raëlians, one gets the impression that the situation is often more complex than whether one's family was religious or secular. Many converts appear to have had reasonably strong and pleasing involvements in conventional religious practices in their childhood. But as they entered adolescence and became more critical they found the increasingly nominal religious practices of their families unsatisfactory. Turning away from organized religion for a time, they found themselves excited by new and more enthusiastic forms of religion they encounter, almost by accident, as young adults. Coping with the personal crises so characteristic of the quest for self-identity in our individualistic societies, some converts are clearly more open to the siren call of new spiritual possibilities because of their fond memories of the comforting effects of their childhood religiosity.

BOX 4 WHY ARE AMERICAN CONVERTS TO NEW RELIGIONS DISPROPORTIONATELY JEWISH?

Althought they constitute only 2.5 per cent of the American population, it was estimated in the 1980s that Jews comprised about 15 per cent of the membership of Krishna Consciousness, about 11 per cent of the Neo-Pagan community, 9 per cent of the Church of Scientology, and 6 per cent of the Unification Church (Melton and Moore, 1982: 30–31; Stark and Bainbridge, 1985: 398–404; Rochford, 1985; Shinn, 1985). Latkin et al. (1987) discovered that about one-fifth of the members of Rajneeshpuram, the utopian community established by Bhagwan Shree Rajneesh, were Jewish as well. What accounts for this curious over-representation? Are Jews more susceptible somehow to special techniques of recruitment used by NRMs? The issue has sparked a keen interest in the anti-cult movement on the part of the Jewish community (Kelly, 1990; Bretton-Granatoor, 1997); one of the most prominent deprogrammers in the United States, Rick Ross, has estimated that about 30 per cent of his clients are Jewish (DeRosa, 1989).

Stark and Bainbridge (1985: 402–3) hypothesize that the answer lies not with what the cults are doing, but rather the heightened secularism of the American Jewish community. It is the lack of a sufficiently religious family life that inclines young Jews, proportionately more than Protestants and Catholics, to turn to new and more intense forms of religion. In his unique study of American Jewish converts to NRMs Charles Selengut (1988) has found strong evidence to support this view. But his data also suggest that Jews may be over-represented simply because they tend to epitomize the social attributes typical of most converts to NRMs regarding higher education and class.

Selengut gathered information on one hundred young Jewish converts to the Unification Church (forty-two of them) and the International Society for Krishna Consciousness (fifty-eight of them). He found that the Jewish converts came overwhelmingly from educated middle- to upper-middle-class families. Fifty-seven of the converts had university degrees; eighty-eight had attended an institution of higher learning for at least two years; and three had doctoral degrees (p. 97). The typical convert grew up in a broadly Jewish home. The family identified itself as Jewish, celebrated the High Holy Days and occasionally attended other religious services. The children had participated in some Jewish rites at home and received some religious training. But 'nearly all respondents claimed that their parents were not observant . . . They described the Jewishness of their families as ethnic or cultural but not religious' (pp. 97–98).

Most of the converts had been religious seekers. They claimed prior involvement in a variety of new religious or quasi-religious movements before joining the Unification Church or the Hare Krishna group. Their conversion represented only the last step in a long and difficult search (p. 100). The converts to both NRMs 'frequently referred to their feelings of unease and psychological discomfort before their conversion. They had no sense of community either with their Jewish milieu or the wider society. Most of them said that they felt something was wrong with their life even if they had achieved some measure of conventional success in their college or in their place of work and even if they had pleasant relations with members of their families; they felt that they should be doing something different but did not know what . . . ' (p. 102).

Affiliation with either group 'was claimed to have resolved outstanding moral dilemmas and to have provided an experience of the ultimate, of God, of absolute truth. It enabled the new converts to become full members of a community in which they were at ease both philosophically and emotionally' (p. 102).

The converts, then, are not rejecting the Jewish religion so much as making a break with their family and Jewish secularism. The NRMs 'speak openly and unabashedly about God or Divine Presence and about God's relationship with the faithful. They stress God's directives to humankind, God's demands for ethical and ritual observance, and the need for personal discipline and obedience to religious authority. Above all, the new religions provide powerful Messianic visions that are to be realized only if the faithful, and others who can be converted, come together in devotion to these ideals. For the first time in their lives, these Jewish converts have experienced a sacralization of mundane reality. All action, all experience, all relationships now take on a sacred dimension' (p.104).

Selengut concludes: 'There is no doubt that various cults practise extensive proselytizing and resocialization techniques, but such activities would not succeed if they did not find fertile ground' (p.105). Contrary to the assumptions of the anti-cult movement, for the Jewish converts to NRMs at least, apostasy precedes the encounter with the NRMs; it is not caused by them. When these young people reject their familial religion, it is from a need for a richer spiritual life, and it is this need that draws them into the 'interactive' process by which they become converts to the new religions.

Drawn from Charles Selengut, 'American Jewish Converts to New Religious Movements.' *The Jewish Journal of Sociology* 30 (2), 1988: 95–109.

Some Reasons for Joining

The Theories of Barker and Levine

We cannot claim to know definitely why people join NRMs. What scholars offer instead are various profiles that describe a certain number of converts, or which work well for particular cults. For instance, in *The Making of a Moonie*, Eileen Barker suggests a profile of the typical convert to the Unification Church in Britain (Barker, 1984: 210–16, 221). She states that Moonies she came to know often seemed idealistic people from fairly happy, conventional, and highly 'respectable' families that placed a higher value on public service and duty than on simply making money. They had grown up in sheltered environments, in which they were encouraged and rewarded for being over-achievers at school and in other activities, but seem to have had their emotional development retarded so that they failed to experience the usual crises of adolescence until later in life than most of their peers. Consequently, it seems that many of them experienced 'disappointments, hurt and disillusionment' when they 'first ventured out into the world'. They may have found the transition to life at university or on the job and away from home more difficult than expected. The implication is that they may have joined the Unification Church to re-establish themselves at least temporarily in more satisfying circumstances (that is, in a more structured and idealistic environment).[7] Her comments call to mind the speculations discussed in Chapter 3 about the search for surrogate families and ways of coping with the loss of mediating structures in society.[8]

The psychiatrist Saul Levine (1984), who interviewed and observed hundreds of young members of various NRMs, presents a similar profile. He insists that he found 'no more sign of pathology among [the members and ex-members of NRMs that he studied] than ... in any youthful population.' He also notes that the joiners he met were largely children of privilege; they were 'good kids from good backgrounds' (1984: 4). Yet they engaged in the kind of 'radical departures', as he calls them, that are highly disturbing to their families and friends. These radical departures are extraordinary, but seen from the right perspective, he argues, they make sense. 'They are desperate attempts to grow up in a society that places obstacles in the way of the normal yearnings of youth' (1984: 11). The young people who join NRMs, he believes, are distinguished by their curious inability to effect the kind of separation from their families consonant with passage into young adulthood (see 1984: 31–8, 46–7, 61). They are psychological 'children' trapped in a predicament that our fragmented and indulgent society may have induced. They wish to sever the parental bond and achieve independence, but they lack a sufficient sense of self to do so. On the one hand, the prospect of relinquishing the overly close tie they do have, in 'reality or fantasy', with their mothers and fathers is terrifying; it instills a great fear of personal 'depletion'. On the other hand, the self they display, whether seemingly normal or rebellious, feels 'fraudulent'. Such young people feel trapped: they can live neither with nor without their parents. All the while, though, as the children mature, their parents' foibles are becoming apparent, turning them into 'fallen idols'.

It is symptomatic, Levine says, that joiners have usually not experienced any mature romantic relationships and that they lack the kind of intimate peer relationships in which teenagers 'probe, analyze, confess, explore, and lay bare their very souls to one another' (1984: 35). But the social supports their parents had been able to call upon in their youth for guidance—churches, ethnic communities, patriotic activities, and a liberal arts education—have either disappeared or now appear unreal. Enduring this kind of acutely felt tension, these young people yearn for a quick cure for their sense of isolation and confusion (Lofland and Stark, 1965). They seek a sense of full belonging and purpose in life, independent of their families, but without engaging in the struggle to achieve true 'mutual understanding' between individuals or the serious 'analysis' of their situation required to find and shape their own identity. With so little real self-esteem, they are seeking to avoid, for a time at least, the responsibility of making choices. Then at a moment of crisis, a 'turning point', in Lofland and Stark's terminology (1965), they encounter the missionaries of one or another NRM offering just such an alternative path to (or temporary detour from) maturity.

If there is plausibility to Levine's theory, then the radical departure in question is perhaps not a departure at all (Barker, 1984: 210–11). Moonies, for instance, 'do not appear to be rejecting the values that were instilled into them during their childhood; they appear, on the contrary, to have imbibed these so successfully that they are prepared to respond to the opportunity (which society does not seem to be offering them) to live according to those very standards.' Similar conclusions have been drawn by others studying the Moonies (Parsons, 1986; Palmer, 1994: 92, 100) and the recruits to the Children of God/The Family (Chancellor, 2000: 35–57) as well. The pattern may well vary for other NRMs, but Palmer found elements of it in each of the seven NRMs she studied, and her findings are reminiscent of the views Tipton expresses in *Getting Saved from the Sixties* (1982: Chap. 3). This perspective certainly accords with the consistent finding that most of the people who join NRMs leave voluntarily within about two years (Barker, 1984; Levine, 1984; Stark and Bainbridge, 1985; Wright, 1987; Jacobs, 1989; Galanter, 1989; Palmer, 1994).

These profiles are less helpful, however, for understanding those groups that attract older followers to begin with and are less exclusive in their demands for commitment and less communal in organization, such as Scientology, Sōka Gakkai, Eckankar, and the Neo-Pagans. For example, the descriptions offered by Gussner and Berkowitz on the basis of their survey of 327 members of ten Asian-based meditational groups in North America, show some important differences (1988: 164–5):

> There is little evidence from our data that [respondents] were needier than others with comparable background characteristics. [Respondents] were generally integrated into a secular world, well-educated, and successful in primarily professional careers. While [respondents] were more closely identified with religious denominations while growing up than the U.S. population, generally, there is little evidence in their backgrounds of chronic religious seekership. The majority had simply switched from their original religion to the present group. . . . Although a larger proportion of [respondents] had been divorced than in the population, there is little evidence that this played a role in the decision to affiliate with Asian-based groups. . . . While many have argued that persons who become affiliated with NRMs did so out of immaturity during their high school or college years, out of failure to make important life-transitions, or to pursue real world careers, our data clearly indicates that those who affiliate with these groups tend to do so later in life and have been successful in most maturational tasks. . . . There is strong evidence, moreover, that affiliation constitutes a long-term commitment for most respondents.

THE RATIONALITY OF CONVERSIONS

There is little evidence that the decision to join an NRM differs significantly from other kinds of decisions in life, such as what university to attend or what occupation to pursue. As Stark and Bainbridge (1985, 1987) insist, given enough information on the background of converts and the social circumstances of their conversion, we can go a long way towards formulating a plausible explanation of their conversion in terms of their relatively rational calculation of their best interests at the time. Neitz (1987) certainly found this to be the case, quite independently, in her exacting and empathetic ethnography of a Catholic Charismatic community. External observers, with hindsight or broader knowledge, may wish to question the decisions of converts on one ground or another. But this possibility does not discount the relatively rational character of the converting process as converts try to assess their needs and determine the balance of rewards and costs associated with accepting a particular religious package of specific and general compensators. We all have occasion to think that we may have behaved irrationally or less rationally than we could have at various points in our past. But that does not mean we did not act rationally, with the information available under the circumstances, in making these past choices. All judgements of the rationality of all acts are ultimately contingent on our present state of affairs and frame of mind. We are trapped in an infinite process of re-evaluating our decisions in the light of new information. What sociologists (and others) need to agree on are some more independent criteria for determining if an act, like a conversion, was more or less rational given the circumstances at the time. But scholars have only begun to think about the complicated things that must be taken into consideration in assessing the relative rationality of conversions (e.g. Dawson, 1990, 1994b; Neitz, 1987; Stark and Bainbridge, 1987; Sherkat, 1997).

THE ROLE OF RELIGIOUS EXPERIENCE

All these speculations are just that, speculations. The empirical data provided is more reliable than the anecdotal evidence used in popular writing. We must remember, however, that while this information helps us to define who is more likely to join an NRM, the delimitation is still insufficient, given the small numbers of actual converts. Certainly the evidence runs counter to many of the assertions and stereotypes of the public and the anti-cult movement, but from a social-scientific perspective there is still a crucial and easily overlooked element of mystery about why people choose to be religious, especially in so radical a manner. So a full explanation of why people choose to convert still eludes our grasp. In these circumstances we must duly appreciate that people may well convert for precisely the reasons the religions themselves say they do: because they have achieved some form of enlightenment or insight into their salvation. At the very least they have had a very positive experience (mystical or otherwise) that they wish to pursue further through membership in a group.[9] This conclusion may seem sophomoric to some, but in the face of such relatively reductionistic theories as that proposed by Levine, I think this point must be explicitly made to help ensure that we continue to respect the religious choices people make, no matter how foreign they may be to our sensibilities.

Chapter Five

Are Converts to New Religious Movements 'Brainwashed'?

The Issue and Its Significance

The followers of NRMs are brainwashed! How else can one account for the seemingly sudden and unexpected conversion of ordinary middle-class young people to such outlandish new religions? How else can one explain the sweeping changes in their beliefs, attitudes, and behaviour? With this oft-repeated yet little-understood accusation we move to the heart of the contemporary controversy about cults, beyond the public lectures, books, and newspaper articles and into the courts of law. The brainwashing claim has been pivotal to numerous criminal cases and civil suits. Hoping to override the legal right of their adult children to choose whatever religious practices or world-view they wish, parents have sought to invoke the spectre of brainwashing to convince judges that their children are incompetent and in need of rescue. Deprogrammers,[1] having 'rescued' many cult members by force, have called on theories of brainwashing to defend themselves against charges of kidnapping and assault, arguing that their actions were the lesser of two evils (Bromley, 1988). Meanwhile former members of cults have sued various NRMs for damages, arguing that they have been harmed by their alleged experience of brainwashing while in a cult.

But are the charges of brainwashing true? In some cases, judges and juries have been convinced; in others they have not. (See Anthony, 1990; Anthony and Robbins, 1992, 1995; Richardson, 1991, 1995b, 1996b, 1997, 2004a; and Young and Griffiths, 1992 for excellent overviews of the issues and specific legal cases.) If true, then the NRMs in question do pose a serious public risk. If the charges are not true, then the primary risk to the public is posed by those who try to use this claim to suppress the civil liberties and religious freedoms entrenched in the US and Canadian constitutions and characteristic of most modern democratic societies (Bromley and Robbins, 1993; Richardson, 2004b).

It is understandably difficult for the parents of converts to see their dreams of worldly success for their children thwarted by the other-worldly demands of life in some unknown and exotic new religion. Recast as 'brainwashing', the unconventional religious choices of these young people can be seen as a medically definable deviance, subject to the same state scrutiny and intervention as other public health and social problems, such as gang violence, drug abuse, and AIDS (see Singer, 1995: 5, 84; Robbins and Anthony, 1982b). Do NRMs indeed use sophisticated techniques of 'mind-control', 'thought reform', or 'coercive persuasion' to entice and hold their devotees? Or does the brainwashing scenario simply allow parents and other opponents of NRMs to avoid facing other unwelcome possibilities? Perhaps the NRMs are actually offering the children something that they need or desire? Or perhaps the world the parents have created for their children is unsatisfactory in some crucial regard?

Most scholars associated with the academic study of NRMs have concluded that the charge of mind control has not been substantiated and is theoretically implausible. Most also tend to discount the admissibility of brainwashing claims made by expert witnesses in court cases. Rather, the vast majority of the scholars studying NRMs, with a few notable exceptions (e.g. Kent, 2001b), are of the opinion that accusations of brainwashing significantly distort the realities of cult life as revealed by years of systematic empirical study.[2] Such accusations are considered primarily to be tools of propaganda designed to persuade the public and politicians to act against the interests of NRMs. Nevertheless, despite the legal reversals suffered by the anti-cult movement, media reports indicate that there is still a nearly complete faith in the accuracy of the brainwashing supposition.[3]

American courts will no longer accept expert testimony on 'cult brainwashing' as scientifically credible (Young and Griffiths, 1992; Anthony and Robbins, 1995). But the same accusation has played an important role in the public reaction against 'cults' in Europe, Russia, China, and elsewhere, with very detrimental consequences for many NRMs (see, for instance, Richardson and Introvigne, 2001 and various essays in Richardson, 2004b and Lucas and Robbins, 2004). Thus the public debate over 'mind control' or 'mental manipulation' in the new religions is far from over.

I cannot pretend to be impartial here because I long ago dismissed the brainwashing scenario based on my own studies and the scholarly record, but there are many who still think otherwise, including some judges, lawyers, government officials, psychiatrists, psychologists, and even sociologists. So, having declared my bias, let me summarize the arguments for and against as even-handedly as I can, drawing first on the views of such anti-cultist writers as the psychologist Margaret Singer (1995), the sociologist Ronald Enroth (1977), who writes from an evangelical Christian perspective, and Steven Hassan (1988), an ex-Moonie and exit counsellor for people who have left NRMs. Their comments display the remarkable consistency of the argument made against the recruitment activities of NRMs, an argument that has changed little in over thirty years.

THE CASE Against tHE Cults

Early in the public debate about 'cults', the threat supposedly posed by these new religions was described as a 'very frightening form of thought control or brainwashing', a 'syndrome of seduction and mental subversion' (Enroth, 1977: 156). On the basis of anecdotal accounts of life in the cults, a comparison was made to the experience of the political thought-reform of some American prisoners of war during the Korean War (1950–3). In that war, for purposes of propaganda, the Communist Chinese had attempted systematically to break the will of some American prisoners in order to make them confess publicly to war crimes or betray their allegiance to the United States.[4] With repetition, the analogy drawn between the fate of these POWs and converts to NRMs soon took on an aura of factuality, and some people, like John Clark (MD) of Harvard University, even warned the American people of the extreme 'health hazards' posed by 'destructive cults' (cited by Enroth, 1977: 156). But the early analyses offered by Enroth (1977) and others were clearly speculative and based on a handful of stories of cult participation. The stories in question were presented as 'atrocity tales', designed to galvanize anti-cult sentiment, though many of these stories were in fact ambiguous. Soon the concepts of brainwashing and cults became synonymous in the minds of a naïve and fearful public. Anti-cultists like Singer and Hassan incorporate the concept of mind control into their very definition of 'cults' (Hassan, 1988: 55; Singer, 1995: 7; Langone, 1993: 5), which interprets all NRMs as destructive of individual integrity and autonomy; it is merely a matter of degree how bad (in this regard) they are. Some cults, the anti-cultists admit, are less harmful than others. But the use of some measure of brainwashing is necessitated in almost every case, they argue, by the hidden and true agenda of these organizations:

> Cults basically have only two purposes: recruiting new members and fund-raising. Established religions and altruistic movements may also recruit and raise funds. Their sole purpose, however, is not simply to grow

larger and wealthier; such groups have as goals bettering the lives of their members or humankind in general, either in this world or in a world to come. A cult may claim to make social contributions, but in actuality these remain mere claims or gestures. In the end, all work and all funds, even token gestures of altruism, serve the cult. (Singer, 1995: 11)

Of course, the cults place a near total emphasis on growth, it is assert- ed, to enhance the wealth, pleasure, and power of the cult leaders. The groups are essentially exploitive. In Singer's words (1995: 6): 'Cults seem to have no end to their peculiar practices. Cult leaders seem to have no end to their unconscionable behaviours and their capacity to abuse their follow- ers.' The statements of Enroth, Hassan, Singer, and many other anti-cultists (e.g. Conway and Siegelman, 1978; Delgado, 1980) tend to be extreme and absolute on these points. Yet Singer insists that her use of the term 'cult' is 'merely descriptive, [and] not pejorative' (Singer, 1995: 11).[5]

Cults, as a class of things, are to be indiscriminately feared and dis- credited because their recruitment practices run contrary to the primary value that Americans place on individual freedom. The success of the anti- cult movement rests, in other words, on the supposition that all, or at least most, cults employ brainwashing. Let me illustrate this point with a passage from Hassan (1988: 51–2):

The casualties of mind control include not only the millions of cult mem- bers themselves, their children, and their friends and loved ones, but also our society as well. Our nation is being robbed of our greatest resource: bright, idealistic, ambitious people who are capable of making an enor- mous contribution to mankind. Many of the former members I know have become doctors, teachers, counsellors, inventors, artists. Imagine what cult members could accomplish if they were all set free to develop their God-given talents and abilities! What if they channelled their energies into problem solving, rather than trying to undermine America's freedoms with some warped totalitarian vision?

Here we have the standard objections to the cults: they are redirecting talented people into useless, wrong, or even subversive causes, and these people are not free to return to more useful, right, and (in the US) proper- ly American ways of life. Whether NRMs are right or wrong in their goals and activities, or whether the pursuit of spiritual, as opposed to more worldly, goals is valuable or not is an ideological issue and not susceptible to any clear empirical determination. The best that social scientists can do is document and clarify the actual doctrines and doings of specific NRMs and let the readers of their studies draw their own conclusions. But whether or not people join or leave NRMs 'freely' is a topic open (with some qualification) to an important measure of empirical investigation.[6]

THE THREE PHASES OF BRAINWASHING

What do the anti-cultists have in mind when they say NRMs recruit and maintain their members through 'mind control'? Though the details differ, there is a remarkable uniformity to the arguments advanced. As classically delineated by Edward Hunter (1951), Joost Meerloo (1956), William Sargent (1957), Robert Lifton (1961), Edgar Schein et al. (1961), and many others, processes of 'brainwashing' roughly conform to a three-stage model of radical resocialization by which an old identity is stripped away and a new one is created. Both Hassan (1988: 67–72) and Singer (1995: 74–7) use Schein's terminology to characterize these stages as 'unfreezing', 'changing', and 'refreezing'. Other terms used include 'stimuli control', 'response control', and 'normative control'.

In the first stage or phase, the 'unfreezing', the victims are subjected to various incapacitating physical, psychological, and social conditions designed to induce a nearly complete cognitive, emotional, and social breakdown. The two primary means used are various forms of either sensory deprivation or sensory overload. Solitary confinement, as used regularly in our prisons to punish unruly inmates, is a standard way of causing sensory deprivation. With few exceptions, completely isolating someone from normal social contact, let alone light, sounds, and proper warmth or food, is an extremely effective way of bringing about at least temporary behavioural reform. The opposite technique, sensory overload, was (rather ironically) used by the FBI against the inhabitants of the Branch Davidian compound in Waco, Texas, during their fifty-one-day siege in 1994. The compound was flooded with bright spotlights, while loud and harsh music and other sounds blared from loudspeakers around the clock. The object of sensory overload is to disrupt and constantly change the daily routines and behavioural expectations of those being brainwashed. Physically weakened and psychologically disoriented by such practices, these people lose their sense of reality and their sense of self—the stable personality characteristics that anchor a person's behaviour. In this confused state the victims of brainwashing are susceptible, it is believed, to suggestions for alternative ways of ordering their lives. With NRMs in mind, Singer expresses this state of affairs as follows (1995: 75):

Successful behavioral change programs are designed to upset you to the point that your self-confidence is undermined. This makes you more open to suggestion and also more dependent on the environment for cues about 'right thinking' and 'right conduct'. Your resistance to new ideas lessens when you feel yourself teetering on the edge with massive anxiety about the right choices in life on the one side, and the group ideas that offer the way out of this distress on the other side.

In the second stage or phase of brainwashing, the 'changing', this openness to suggestion is used to impose a new identity—a new set of thoughts, feelings, and behaviours. Those being brainwashed are systematically and ever more intensely introduced to new daily routines, expectations, group activities, and rewards and punishments. Carefully monitoring and controlling all activity and social interaction, the brainwashers try to fashion a new environment with which those being brainwashed will identify out of their extreme need for predictable order and meaning in their lives.

The third and final stage or phase, the 'refreezing', attempts to consolidate and reinforce those changes by immersing the subjects of brainwashing in a new, stable, and supportive social environment, suffused with ritualized activities. Working together and hard on a new set of group tasks will generate new bonds of loyalty, as well as new conceptions of happiness, purpose, and self-worth. It is assumed that by the repeated and relentless control and manipulation of the external behaviour of the subjects (their words and deeds), these people can be conditioned to continue to censor and refashion themselves. Ideally, the change effected should be permanent, short of another round of counter-brainwashing (like the 'deprogramming' attempted by the anti-cultists).

APPLYING THE BRAINWASHING SCENARIO TO CULTS

How is this process applied in NRMs? Most discussions advance the following claims (see e.g. Enroth, 1977: 157–64; Hassan, 1988: 53–67; Singer, 1995: 113–19 and 128–72; Loomis, 1997):

1. It is repeatedly asserted that many NRMs, notably the Moonies, the Church of Scientology, and the Family, are very systematic and sophisticated in their recruitment activities. They research and apply social-psychological techniques of influence and prepare responses for many eventualities. Recruiters are carefully selected, trained, and supervised.

2. The training that the recruiters receive includes instructions on how to target and approach likely candidates for conversion. Recruiters are to

look for evidence that the person is alone, in a period of transition in life, or otherwise 'vulnerable' in some way (for example, young, wearing a backpack, seemingly not in a hurry to get somewhere, or looking distressed in some way).

3. Another part of the training is learning how to be deceptive, at least initially, in approaching potential recruits. New recruits, it is charged, are rarely told about the true or full nature of the group and its objectives. The identity of the group and the demands it places on its members are revealed only gradually as the recruit becomes more interested and involved. By the time of full disclosure, however, the processes of mind-control or brainwashing have taken hold, preventing the informed consent of the convert.

4. After the acceptance of one or more relatively innocuous invitations to dinner, a lecture, workshop, entertainment, or other social event, persons that have shown some interest in the group are pressured into signing up for a rapidly escalating series of lectures, study groups, retreats, training sessions, and other activities.

5. In these sessions and activities, new recruits are never allowed to be alone or to discuss what they are doing with each other. They are always in the presence of members, and all challenging inquires are directed to senior members of the organizations for a response. On the whole, however, negative comments or questions from the potential recruits are evaded or discounted as much as possible. Troublemakers and sceptics are weeded out of the pool of recruits (Galanter, 1980) or subjected to strong group pressure to stay quiet and wait for answers to their questions once a greater understanding of the beliefs and practices of the group has been achieved. Attention is focused on maintaining an uplifting sense of group harmony and an immediate and rather superficial aura of individual happiness.

6. At retreats and other events, potential recruits are kept abnormally busy. They are cajoled and coerced into participating in a frenzied round of daily activities: lectures, games, plays, sing-alongs, therapy groups, charity work, and so on. The object, it is presumed, is to stop the recruits from having the opportunity to reflect seriously on the new ideas and practices to which they are being exposed.

7. As much as possible these recruitment events take place in isolated environments, in the countryside perhaps, or in special facilities where the group can control the recruits' access to information and other people. The recruits are encouraged to begin the process of cutting themselves off from their aimless or evil past and, hence, from their friends and family.

8. Techniques like 'love-bombing' will be used to ensnare the candidates for conversion and to lessen their natural scepticism. In love-bomb-

ing the new recruit is surrounded with praise, compliments, flattery, affection, hugs, and other forms of emotional support, much as parents attempt to reassure and bolster the confidence of a young child trying something new (like skating or swimming). This 'love' is presumed to be insincere.

9. Simultaneously, recruits will be drawn into various types of 'confessional' activities, by which the group can learn something of the past, fears, and self-conceptions of potential converts. This information will be used to play upon their natural feelings of guilt and anxiety about past experiences and future uncertainties. Enroth, Hassan, and Singer all place particular stress on the supposed manipulation of the feelings of inadequacy so common amongst young people.

10. Having thus implemented a kind of sensory overload, the cult leaders mix in a most basic form of sensory deprivation. Recruits are fed inadequately, often on vegetarian diets, and prevented from sleeping enough. Thus their ability to think clearly or offer emotional resistance is physiologically undermined.

11. Even more perniciously, cults, it is charged, use sophisticated yet low-key methods of hypnosis to induce trance states in recruits so that their psychological defences can be systematically stripped away and suggestions implanted for a new way of life. The methods vary from lengthy, droning, repetitive, and rhythmical lectures, to guided-imagery sessions and the practice of meditation. The latter two techniques, in various forms, have an ancient religious lineage in both the East and the West, and they are commonly used in psychotherapies of all types. Cult leaders, however, allegedly abuse these techniques to serve their own selfish ends. Singer (e.g. 1995: 139) in particular argues that these and other means are used to induce altered states of consciousness and other physiological affects that the group can 'reframe' for the recruit as experiences of partial enlightenment or spiritual progress or regression. As the interpretations proffered by the groups are often less than scientifically accurate, it is assumed that the groups must have some deceptive purpose in mind in religiously 'reframing' the recruits' experiences.

12. Last, NRMs often seek to effect a complete transformation of identity by giving the converts new names, changing their clothes, hairstyle, diet, and other personal habits. Often, people are asked to abandon or donate all of their material possessions to the group and to live communally and very simply, forgoing their own needs and aspirations in favour of those of the group. This is said to create a condition of direct material dependency that binds the convert to the group and further inhibits thoughts of leaving.

Each of these claims is supported by Enroth, Hassan, Singer, and others with reports of interviews with ex-members of cults or the written accounts of ex-members (often those who, like Hassan himself, have been deprogrammed). Some of these stories stem from the authors' own research, others come from other sources. One must read the accounts to get an adequate sense of the specifics and to decide if the stories recounted warrant the generalizations drawn. But the stories cited are usually presented with little development of the broader context, and traceable references to specific NRMs or incidents are rarely provided. They are 'stories', collected in different ways by different people for different purposes, but they do not constitute systematically secured data.

The net result of cult involvement, we are told repeatedly, is that the recruits experience and display a marked impairment, even a regression, in their capacity to think logically and independently. In fact, it is often more or less suggested that converts to NRMs have altogether lost the capacity to think for themselves in any sustained way. In some cases, Enroth (1977: 164) goes so far as to propose that there is evidence (unspecified) of a loss of basic cognitive skills, like the ability to read and write at normal levels. Certainly, the recruits are thought to have mortgaged their futures by interrupting their educations, losing their possessions, and damaging their health, in return for shoddy spiritual goods. Converts characteristically display a long-term emotional flatness, we are told, and become deeply alienated from their families and past friends. In some cases, the destabilizing recruitment milieu has supposedly induced true states of psychopathology, ranging from blackouts and phobias through schizophrenic episodes to severe depression and even suicide. Despite many seeming qualifications, in the literature and the presentations of the anti-cult movement, the bottom line is stereotypically clear: with few exceptions, cult recruiters use deception along with sophisticated and powerful techniques of influence to find and exploit the personal vulnerabilities, deficiencies, or just desires of potential converts, with results that are always socially and psychologically damaging.

The Case Against Brainwashing

The reasons for being doubtful of the brainwashing charge made against NRMs are many. Here I will formulate a critique based on twelve of the most telling criticisms made by academic students of NRMs.

Before doing that, however, I want to reiterate that our concern is with the charge of brainwashing, not with the clear fact that some NRMs, at some times, have clearly engaged in objectionable or suspect practices. For example, it is well known that for a time the so-called Oakland Family of the Unification Church in California did practise 'heavenly deception' while recruiting. They introduced themselves to prospective recruits under false guises (for example, as a conventional Christian youth group, or spiritually inclined environmentalist commune) and postponed revealing their true identity and connections with the Reverend Sun Myung Moon for as long as possible (see Barker, 1984: 94–120, especially 100–3, and 176–8). They also used high-pressure social tactics to persuade recruits to make a commitment. The Unification Church, like many other NRMs, such as Scientology, was also in the habit of issuing wildly exaggerated membership figures (e.g. Galanter, 1989: 110) in order to promote recruitment and secure respectability. Likewise, for a time in the mid-1970s the International Society for Krishna Consciousness became preoccupied with securing funds for its activities and employed some deception (for example, by wearing conventional street clothes and even wigs) in their aggressive campaigns to sell literature, flowers, incense, and other items in airports, on the streets, and in other public places (see Rochford, 1985: 171–89; Rochford, 1988). Even more notorious was the practice by the Children of God/The Family of encouraging their young female members to use sexual flirtation and favours to attract new male members. This practice of 'flirty fishing', which lasted from about 1977 to 1987, was eventually repudiated, but the reputation of the group has been permanently damaged (see Richardson and Davis, 1983: 406–20; Van Zandt, 1991: 46–8 and 169–70; Lewis and Melton, 1994; Chancellor, 2000). Whatever the failings of religions, new and old, this chapter is not intended as an apologia for NRMs. The question at issue is solely whether the claims of brainwashing made by the anti-cult movement enhance or inhibit our understanding of NRMs.

QUESTIONING THE SCIENTIFIC CREDIBILITY OF THE BRAINWASHING CHARGE

Moving roughly from general to specific, twelve criticisms can be made about the adequacy of the brainwashing scenario:

1. With few exceptions the literature of the anti-cult movement displays a persistent tendency to lump all NRMs together. By repeated implication, if not stated as fact, accusations made against any one group are generalized to almost all other new religions (and many similar organizations), ignoring their marked differences in origins, doctrines, practices, objectives, and organizational structures. Illustrations, in the form of 'atrocity stories', are opportunistically drawn from an indiscriminate array of NRMs and used to 'prove' the accusations levelled with little regard for the varied nature and circumstances of the groups cited. No systematic means of comparison is even attempted, because it is assumed in advance that all cults are essen-

tially the same. To recognize the inadequacy of this assumption requires some familiarity with the very real differences between NRMs, something most members of the public lack. But with only a passing knowledge of the obvious differences in the origins, doctrines, practices, objectives, and organizational structures of Scientology and Krishna Consciousness, for instance, it is hard to see how we can assume that these and other groups practise some uniform mode of recruitment.

2. One cannot help but detect a consistent ideological bias in the attempts made to apply brainwashing theories to NRMs. Apart from the obvious and admitted Christian polemic of much of this literature (see Cowan; 2003), it is clear that the collectivist sentiments and practices of many NRMs clash with the markedly individualistic orientations of contemporary Western, and particularly American, culture. Moreover, elements of ethnocentricism and even racism can be detected: 'The fact that a number of new religions are from outside Western culture and were founded and led by foreigners should not be ignored in understanding the propensity to apply simplistic brainwashing theories to explain participation and justify efforts at social control' (Richardson, 1993b: 79). Remember that the sudden visibility of NRMs in the 1960s stems, in part, from the repeal of the Asian exclusion laws in 1965 (see Chapter 3). These immigration laws had systematically prevented Asian gurus and their followers from settling in the United States.

3. As Eileen Barker (1984: 126–7) and dozens of other commentators on the cult controversy have observed, there are neither logical nor empirical reasons for the repeated anti-cult assertion that only someone who is brainwashed could believe some of the incredible doctrines of most NRMs. As the historical and anthropological record amply documents, there are few limits to the exotic character of the beliefs different people have held over the years. The strangeness of the beliefs adopted does not, in and of itself, demonstrate or necessarily even imply that the process by which they were adopted was coercive. There are few if any universal criteria of reasonable belief, and all conclusions about the religious beliefs of others are a matter of perspective. A similar lack of cause-and-effect afflicts the assumption that the seeming suddenness of many conversions to NRMs proves that brainwashing was used. 'Suddenness' is not proof of 'brainwashing'. There is considerable reason to believe, in any event, that the supposed 'suddenness' of these conversions is more apparent than real (see Box 5).

4. A close study of the original theories of brainwashing cited as authorities by the anti-cultists poses problems for their case. The theories of Hunter (1951), Meerloo (1956), Sargent (1957), Lifton (1961), and Schein et al. (1961) are based on contradictory ideas of human nature and psy-

chology that are used so superficially by the anti-cult movement that the inconsistencies in their explanatory frameworks are barely noted, let alone thought to matter.

There are also problems with the lineage and foundation of these original theories of thought reform and control. The journalist Hunter, who first popularized the term 'brainwashing', was a CIA operative, and his book was written for propagandistic purposes (Richardson and Bromley, 1983; Anthony and Robbins, 1994: 459). Moreover, all of the theories are based on extremely small samples of people subjected to various programs of thought reform, and they rely on largely anecdotal and retrospective accounts. We have little information about the prior lives of these victims of brainwashing or about their lives after these episodes. Of the almost 350 American POWs systematically subjected to brainwashing during the Korean War, only 21 ever chose to betray their country (Anthony and Robbins, 1994: 460).

In 1956, the psychiatrists Lawrence Hinkle and Harold Wolff, of Cornell University, undertook an exhaustive study of brainwashing, with the support of the government and full access to the secret files of the CIA as well as some former Communist interrogators and their prisoners. Their long-overlooked report refutes the effectiveness of all efforts to brainwash anyone—especially through inducing altered states of consciousness. Where thought-reform techniques do seem to have produced results, they argue, we are merely witnessing behavioural compliance brought on by threats and the experience of physical abuse (Hinkle and Wolff, 1956; Anthony and Robbins, 1994: 460–1).

5. Even a slightly sceptical reading of the books of Enroth, Hassan, Singer, and others will quickly reveal the tendency of these authors to make dramatic claims based largely on anecdotal evidence, which cannot be disproven by empirical test. Members of NRMs constantly reiterate, for example, that they are perfectly free to come and go as they please and that they made a conscious and free choice to join these new religions. Yet the anti-cult movement simply argues that these beliefs are held only because the members have been brainwashed to believe and say they are free (Barker, 1984: 122–3). How is one ever to know this, and how can one ever argue against such a self-validating point of view? No counter-arguments are possible in the face of such a claim (Richardson, 1992b).

The practice of 'love-bombing' is another case in point:

> The display of affection toward new and potential converts ('love bombing'), which might be interpreted as a kindness or an idealistic manifestation of devotees' belief that their relationship to spiritual truth and divine

love enables them to radiate love and win others to truth, is also commonly interpreted as a sinister 'coercive' technique. . . . . Yet successfully deprogrammed ex-devotees have enthused over the warmly supportive and
'familial' milieu at post-deprogramming 'rehabilitation' centers such as the
Freedom of Thought Foundation (e.g. Underwood and Underwood,
1979). Could this also be 'love bombing'? (Robbins, 1984: 245)

Many of the complaints made by the anti-cult movement are in line
with their misgivings about love-bombing. Without some preconceptions,
it is often not immediately apparent that we are dealing with a truly objectionable practice. In fact, Barker notes (1984: 186–7):

Most Moonies would be genuinely shocked at the suggestion that they are
being deceptive when they offer their guests affection. They would not
only protest that they ought to love them as people (and many undoubtedly do develop a genuine affection for some of their guests), they would
also be convinced that it is in the guest's own interests (as well as the interests of the world) for him to become a Moonie.

For the impartial observer, there is often no decisive way to choose
between the perspectives of the cult members and those of their critics.

Contrary to the thinking of the anti-cultists, however, common sense
combined with some knowledge of other religious traditions can go a long
way towards defusing many of the more naïve yet fervent criticisms of
NRMs. Let me illustrate my point with the following passage from Margaret
Singer. In discussing how cults induce trance states to seduce their victims,
Singer says (1995: 155–6):

Sometimes the induction method is speech filled with paradox and discrepancy—that is, the message is not logical and you are unable to follow
it, but it is presented as though it were logical. Trying to follow what is
being said can actually detach the listener from reality. A good example of
this technique comes from the cult leader Bhagwan Shree Rajneesh's comments at an initiation ceremony in which he gave each disciple a new
name along with . . . . a necklace with his picture on it. Reading what
Rajneesh said can give you a feeling for what words can do to cause a person to enter a light trance, or space out.

'First, the picture is not mine. The picture only appears to be mine. No
picture of me is really possible. The moment one knows oneself, one
knows something that cannot be depicted, described, framed. I exist as an

emptiness that cannot be pictured, that cannot be photographed. That is why I could put the picture there. . . . The more you know the picture— the more you concentrate on it, the more you come in tune with it—the more you will feel what I am saying. The more you concentrate on it, the more there will not be a picture there.' (Quotation marks added)

Is this nonsense or, even worse, a sinister attempt intended to detach the followers of Rajneesh from reality? With a bit of understanding of traditional Eastern religious philosophy, Singer could say that in line with a long tradition of mystical thought, present in the West as well, Bhagwan Rajneesh is using paradoxical language and the focal symbol of his picture to serve a number of ends: (1) to highlight the folly of identifying our true selves with our physical bodies, or, even worse, our physical appearance; (2) to highlight the spiritual (that is, non-material) character of our true selves; (3) to highlight the bewitchment of language and the inadequacy of ordinary concepts in the face of the ineffable character of the truth. Rajneesh may also be alluding to the basic Buddhist doctrine of 'not-self' (an-attā in Pali, an-ātman in Sanskrit)—the claim that there is no permanent self or eternal soul. His picture and the words he uses in the initiation ceremony are analogous to a Zen Buddhist *koan*. Like the well-known puzzle 'What is the sound of one-hand clapping?', these seemingly nonsensical questions and claims are used as foci of concentration in meditation to break the hold of conventional patterns of thought (i.e. Singer's logical thought), opening the consciousness to a higher sensibility ('satori' in Zen). From a knowledge of these things one may still ultimately wish to question or reject these and other teachings, but to hold them up to ridicule as Singer does is counter-productive.

6. In all the original reports of the brainwashing of prisoners of war and political prisoners, the victims were forcibly confined and physically tortured. Yet no academic or legal evidence has ever been presented that any NRM has ever held potential recruits or members against their will, let alone physically abused them (e.g. Barker, 1984: 141). Cults are what sociologists call 'voluntary associations', and that is why their opponents have had to go to such extremes to establish a psychological justification for the intervention of the state and professional deprogrammers. But, as the original studies of thought control suggest, the evidence is weak for assuming that the full and involuntary transformation of identity signified by 'brainwashing' can occur in the absence of physical restraint and abuse. The process of deprogramming, on the other hand, is defined by the fact that people are kidnapped from the NRMs, physically held against their will, and subjected to a hostile and intimidating interrogation for days or even weeks.

7. The literature of the anti-cult movement is, as already indicated, distorted by sampling bias (Barker, 1984: 128–31). The brainwashing scenario of NRMs relies heavily on the testimony of individuals who have undergone deprogramming or 'exit counselling'. The latter is the noncoercive equivalent of the former. In her initial popular discussion of the brainwashing accusation, for example, Singer (1979) notes that 75 per cent of her subjects had been deprogrammed. These people are under great pressure to account for their aberrant behaviour (that is, joining a cult) and to direct the blame away from themselves, their families, and the community (Richardson, van der Lans, and Derks, 1986). This may be necessary in order to make peace with their families and regain entry into other community groups (for example, when returning to school or a job), or simply to resolve the cognitive dissonance they are experiencing from the contrast of their present and past behaviour. The brainwashing scenario, to which they are 'programmed', provides a non-stigmatizing way to absolve everyone, most importantly themselves, of responsibility and actually secure the sympathy of others. Furthermore, as discussed, the books and articles of the anti-cultists tend to employ small and non-random samples of stories drawn from sources that are identified either inadequately or not at all. Several academic studies, on the other hand, have revealed a marked and consistent discrepancy between the post-involvement attitudes of converts who leave these groups voluntarily and those who are deprogrammed. Only the latter show a strong statistical correlation with negative views of their cult experience (e.g. Solomon, 1981; Wright, 1984; Lewis, 1986; Lewis and Bromley, 1987; Galanter, 1989; Introvigne and Melton, 1997). Most people who leave an NRM voluntarily (and most of those who leave do so voluntarily) continue to express very positive feelings about their involvement. Wright found that 67 per cent of voluntary defectors said they were 'wiser for the experience' of membership, and only 9 per cent invoked the brainwashing explanation for joining in the first place (Wright and Ebaugh, 1993: 127; see also Levine, 1984: 188). From his study of the Unification Church, Galanter (1989: 116) reports 'a striking contrast' in attitudes between voluntary defectors and those who were deprogrammed:

> The first group had mixed feelings about their experience but expressed a relatively benign view of both their own involvement and the ongoing participation of their remaining compatriots. Most (62 per cent) still felt strongly that they 'cared for the ten members they knew best,' and the large majority (89%) believed that they 'got some positive things' out of membership. On the other hand, those who were deprogrammed had a much

more negative attitude toward the sect and . . . eight out of ten deprogrammed ex-members had participated in attempts to coerce other members to leave, whereas none of those who left voluntarily had done so.

In fact, Wright (1984) and Jacobs (1989) found that half to three-quar-
ters of those who deconvert voluntarily from one NRM eventually join
another similar group.

8. The issue of sampling bias, however, raises a related and more complicated problem, that of accounts (Turner, 1978; Beckford, 1978; Wallis
and Bruce, 1983; Dawson, 1994b; Zablocki, 1996; Kent, 2001b; Dawson,
2001b). The study of conversions in general is largely dependent on the
'accounts' provided by converts, whether still members of groups or former members. The problem is to what extent we can trust people's descriptions of their own actions, especially their past actions. Everyday life, history, the social sciences, and the law demonstrate that there is much potential for inaccuracy and deception (including self-deception). But conversion accounts have proved to be especially problematic because converts
often take the opportunity to witness or proselytize for their faith. In fact,
some scholars have argued that the best indicator that a religious conversion has occurred is evidence of 'biographic reconstruction' (Snow and
Machalek, 1984; Staples and Mauss, 1987). Religions expect converts to
reinterpret their pasts in ways commensurate with their new identities.
Converts to all religions, new and old, are strongly inclined to exaggerate
the sinfulness or distress of their pre-conversion lives and the rewards of
their post-conversion lives. The reverse surely holds true for those who
have been deprogrammed.

In her research on NRMs, Barker (1984: 170–1) found that respondents
often change their interpretations of experiences at some later point. Many
who have left NRMs

> admitted that they had believed at the time that they were having a reli-
> gious experience, but had subsequently come to the conclusion that it had
> been their imagination or the result of some mundane trigger. Conversely,
> those who had since become part of a religious community were more
> likely to say that they had dismissed the experience at the time, but now
> realized that God had been talking to them.

So we must be very cautious in accepting conversion accounts at face
value, far more cautious than the anti-cultists have thought to be, but also
more than even most other scholars studying NRMs have been. As
Richardson, Balch, and Melton (1993: 217) recommend, when studying

any NRM every researcher should seek to use 'a number of data sources simultaneously . . . data should be gathered from members and ex-members, from apologists and detractors, from leaders and followers within the group, from parents and from sons and daughters who are members, and so on.' The inevitable clash of claims will have to be weighed against the presumably more neutral and exacting observations of the researcher.

9. The entire credibility of the brainwashing explanation of cult conversions is called into question by the information now available on the low rates of recruitment and high rates of defection experienced by most NRMs. Contrary to the impression created by the anti-cult movement, only a very small number of the many thousands of people approached by NRMs ever agree to attend a lecture, dinner, workshop, or other recruitment event. An even smaller number choose to join, and most of these soon leave voluntarily. In her detailed study of the Unification Church, one of the prime targets of the brainwashing rhetoric, Barker (1984: 144–8, 259) found that only about 10 per cent of the small number of participants in a workshop chose to join the group. One-third of these left of their own accord after four months, and few lasted more than two years. In fact Barker calculates that no more than 0.5 per cent of prospective converts who visit a Unification Church centre will be associated with the movement two years later (see Levine, 1984: 65–6 and James Beckford, cited in Wright, 1987: 2, for similar estimates). Sampling a more diverse array of groups, Bird and Reimer (1982) found that two-thirds of the most highly involved members eventually left, while for the twenty or more NRMs he studied, Saul Levine (1984: 15) concludes, 'Over ninety per cent [of radical departures] end in a return home within two years.'

In the face of these bleak figures does talk of brainwashing have any credibility? If the cults use sophisticated techniques to turn their followers into psychological captives, then why are the results of their recruiting so poor and how is it that so many defect voluntarily?

10. In her award-winning study of conversion to the Moonies, Barker (1984: 194) speaks of a 'checklist' she found herself drawing up of the 'characteristics and experiences . . . frequently taken to indicate that [a] person will be particularly vulnerable . . . to the "lure of the cults".' This checklist, she explains,

> included things like the immaturity of youth; a history of mental disturbances, drug abuse and/or alcoholism; poor and/or erratic performances in school; divorced parents and/or an unhappy childhood; lack of ability to keep friends; being in a transitory state and/or having no clear prospects or direction in life; and a tendency to be indecisive, and/or to drift from one job and/or girl/boyfriend to another.

These are presumably the kind of characteristics and experiences that mark someone as particularly prone to the 'suggestibility' exploited by mind-control techniques. The trouble is, the data she collected did not conform to the checklist:

> The Moonies did score slightly higher than the control group on some of the characteristics on the checklist, but on others they scored slightly lower, and on yet others there were more similarities between the British Moonies and the (British) control group than there were between the British and European or American Moonies. In other words, national or cultural differences were often more obvious than Moonie/non-Moonie differences. (Barker, 1984: 196)

Pressing on, Barker made an even more startling and complex discovery (1984: 198, 203). Only a small portion of the Moonies seem to display the characteristics indicative of being more prone to 'passive suggestibility' than her control group of ordinary people. What is more, it was the people most at risk amongst the attenders of Moonie workshops 'who did not join, or, if they did, were among those who would leave pretty quickly'. Barker showed that while the experiences of some Moonies might make the 'refuge from society' explanation plausible, on the whole their experiences were not markedly worse than those of the control group. And again, those with the more traumatic experiences tended either not to join the church or to leave shortly after joining. So whatever may draw people to the Unification Church, and perhaps to other NRMs as well, it would not appear to be their susceptibility to being brainwashed, at least not as normally understood and argued by the anti-cult movement.

11. There have been a reasonably large number of psychological and psychiatric studies of people who still are or recently have been members of NRMs (see the summary analyses provided by Rochford et al., 1989; Saliba, 1993, 2004; Richardson, 1995c; Aronoff, Lynn, Malinoski, 2000). Using various combinations of clinical interviews and/or standard psychological tests, researchers have examined the psychological well-being of people involved with such diverse groups as the Unification Church, Hare Krishnas, the Children of God/The Family, Scientology, Zen Buddhism, the Divine Light Mission, the followers of Bhagwan Shree Rajneesh, and various Pentecostal and Jesus movements. The results, which are very diverse and often divergent, do not support the brainwashing scenario.

Problems stem from the tendency of the studies undertaken so far to divide into two camps: studies of current members of NRMs, and studies of deprogrammed or disgruntled ex-members. 'More than 75 per cent of studies of the former type tend to show that the psychological profiles of individuals tested fall well within "normal" bounds' (Saliba, 1993: 106). In fact, many of these studies suggest there is evidence for the therapeutic effect of cult involvements. As discussed in point 8, though, the testimonials of cult members hardly constitutes a sound source of information on this point. Certainly some people experience a 'relief effect' from their cult involvements (e.g. Galanter, 1989: 35; Rochford et al., 1989), but this could well be temporary or superficial. 'Studies of the latter type generally conclude that ex-members suffer from serious mental and emotional dysfunctions that have been directly caused by cultic beliefs and practices' (Saliba, 1993: 106). But this is speculation. No logical way exists for causally linking the distress noted and the instructional programs and lifestyles of the new religions (see Rochford et al., 1989: 69–71). 'It is equally plausible and consistent with the data that the impaired mental and psychological condition of these ex-members existed prior to entry into the cult or is the result of the deprogramming methods themselves' (Saliba, 1993: 107). Moreover, as already noted, too many of these studies fail to employ such fundamental methodological safeguards as random samples and control groups. We know little, that is, about how the results obtained by the anti-cultists compare with data for other groups of people, especially young people. The psychiatrist Saul Levine (1984: 4) says that the hundreds of converts and ex-converts he interviewed 'showed no more sign of pathology . . . than is found in any youthful population.' From the discoveries of Barker discussed in point 10 above, the importance of making such comparisons with control groups is readily seen (see also Barker, 1984: 131–4).

In fact, the strong correlation found by sociologists between people with negative views of their cult involvements and the experience of deprogramming or exit counselling (e.g. Solomon, 1981; Wright, 1984; Lewis, 1986; Lewis and Bromley, 1987) supports the counter-charge that the only deleterious brainwashing, and hence psychological impairment, occurs with deprogramming. It is not difficult to understand why deprogrammed ex-members report far more psychological problems adapting to life after their cult experiences than those who have left of their own volition. As both Stuart Wright (1987) and Helen Rose Fuchs Ebaugh (1988) have established, the process by which anyone gives up any role in life, whether an occupation, a marriage, or a religious identity, tends to follow a fairly set pattern of stages by which the person psychologically and socially anticipates and prepares for the impending change (see Wright and Ebaugh, 1993: 124–8). That process is short-circuited by deprogramming, which leaves involuntary ex-members ill-prepared to assume a new identity. In place of gradually forging new grounds of self-worth and purpose in life, those who are deprogrammed are assigned, and often assume, the identity of a victim. But this passive identity causes them to feel vulnerable and in need of completing the process of 'role exiting'. The resultant quest for some more secure identity may explain why so many of the deprogrammed have become deprogrammers themselves.

To clarify the psychological picture, we need reliable profiles of converts before they joined NRMs and of the large number of converts who have left voluntarily. We are not likely ever to obtain the former, since by the time a person becomes a convert we might want to study, it is obviously too late to profile their pre-cult mind, but more studies of the latter type could and should be done. The existing literature does clarify one thing: 'The brainwashing model begs the questions it purports to ask and has generated little productive research' (Saliba, 1993: 107).

In general, the diagnoses provided by modern Western psychology have not proved well suited to dealing with the cult controversy, partly because they display a consistent bias in favour of the modern Western pursuit of individual independence. When applied to a more collectivist life and absolutist moral agenda, they tend to produce negatively skewed results: 'Individuals, who for ideological reasons and emotional satisfaction prefer an arranged marriage and/or communal style of living in which their individuality is subordinated, are not necessarily suffering from a personality disorder, as the psychiatric diagnostic manuals infer or assert' (Saliba, 1993: 108). Richardson (1993c) has specifically documented and criticized the negative religious stereotyping and ambivalent attitudes towards religion, especially NRMs, found in *The Diagnostic and Statistical Manual of Mental Disorders* (third edition), the bible of the American psychiatrists, psychologists, and social counsellors.

Saliba (2004: 318–320) points out that the text of that book has improved since the mid-nineties with the publication of the fourth edition of *The Diagnostic and Statistical Manual of Mental Disorders* (1994), in which the American Psychiatric Association is more careful about telling researchers and therapists to treat 'religion as an independent variable that can have positive as well as negative effects on human personality' (2004: 319). The book also advises its readers to exercise much greater caution in their approach to the relationship between any religious practices and possible psychopathologies. But in the conclusion to his latest survey of the psychological literature on NRMs, Saliba suggests that (2004: 327) problems persist:

> Unfortunately many of the negative conclusions of the effects of cult membership give little indication that the researchers had explored, much less understood, the belief system of the individuals they were studying. The

training of mental health care providers to recognize and deal with religious or spiritual problems needs to be addressed.

In the end, the inconclusive results of the psychological study of members and ex-members of NRMs cannot conceivably be used to support either the case for or against brainwashing. In the face of the quite specific and dramatic claims of psychologists like Singer, however, it seems odd that the reliable psychological data available so far are so inconclusive, if not largely contrary to the expectations of the anti-cult movement.

12. Are the followers of NRMs brainwashed? There is not much reason for believing so. Are many recruits to NRMs subjected to strong social pressures to join and rapidly introduced to systematic programs of indoctrination? Sometimes, undoubtedly. Barker (1984: 174) comments that there 'can be little doubt that the Moonies are successful in controlling the environment of their workshops.' All is carefully planned, activities are not optional, guests are seldom out of the presence of enthusiastic Moonies, there is little opportunity for the recruits to discuss seriously the teachings being presented amongst themselves, and the lectures and other activities are received with so much enthusiasm by the surrounding Moonie 'cheerleaders', as Barker (1984: 174) calls them, that it can be most difficult to resist the urge to conform. But as she also comments, these practices are 'by no means . . . unique'. Religions have been in the business, throughout the ages, of emotionally prompting and physically and socially supporting the abandonment of old habits of thought, word, and deed and inducing new ones. The American psychiatrist Marc Galanter specifically notes the parallels between the practices of some NRMs and the sponsorship system employed by Alcoholics Anonymous, as well as the kind of group-based induction techniques pioneered by earlier Christian sects (Galanter, 1980; cited in Barker, 1984: 286). Conversions, in religions new and old, occur by way of processes of deconditioning and resocialization, processes readily delineated by established theories of social psychology (e.g. Kanter, 1972; Preston, 1981; Wilson, 1984; Richardson, 1993b).

By the late 1980s and early 1990s, American courts began to consistently exclude expert testimony on brainwashing in cults. This was done for two reasons: (1) the evidence presented by Singer and others failed to meet the minimum standards of scientific credibility set by the courts (the Frye and later the Daubert standards; see Young and Griffiths, 1992; Ginsburg and Richardson, 1988; Anthony 1990, 1999); (2) the courts concluded that 'the acts in question do not differ significantly from those by established churches that are never seriously accused of coercive persuasion' (Young and Griffiths, 1992: 99), so admission of such testimony would put the constitutional guarantees of all religions in jeopardy.

In response to this opposition, the anti-cult movement has increasingly dissociated itself from true deprogramming in favour of less coercive forms of 'exit counselling' and 'strategic intervention therapy', expanded the types of organizations targeted as 'destructive cults', and shifted its legal focus to questions of deception and child abuse (e.g. Shupe and Bromley, 1994; Coates, 1994; Hassan, 1994; Singer, 1995; Bradney, 1999; Richardson, 1999). Formally, anti-cult organizations deny that they are still in favour of the forcible removal of members of NRMs. In part this is due to the increased professionalization of the movement, as the leadership has acquired more psychological and legal expertise (see Shupe and Bromley, 1994). Nevertheless, the largest such organization, the Cult Awareness Network, was forced into bankruptcy by the courts in June 1996 when its legal liability for facilitating the failed deprogramming of a young Pentecostalist was demonstrated in a civil suit. As this case shows, the category of destructive cults has also been expanded to include such other new threats to public health as 'therapy cults, political cults, or commercial cults' (Coates, 1994: 93), as well as more traditional Christian groups like fundamentalist and Pentecostal or charismatic sects (e.g. Coates, 1994: 97). This larger number of targets, of course, expands the field of opportunities for the more professionalized anti-cult organizations in the face of the shrinking audience for critiques of the Moonies, Hare Krishna, and so on.

Finally, it is clear that issues of deception have acquired a new strategic significance in the anti-cult literature. Once again, using a wholly inappropriate and unrealistic medical definition of 'informed consent', Hassan, Singer, and others claim that acceptable religions should fully disclose all information about themselves, their past, and their practices, as well as any possible negative consequences of joining, to all recruits upon first meeting them (e.g. Singer, 1995: 79–80). As Singer herself comments, under such legal restraints it is unlikely that anyone would ever join another cult. Of course, it is equally unlikely that anyone would ever join the vast majority of voluntary associations operating in the United States, including most of the established religions, if they were compelled to operate under the same guidelines. Outside of strictly experimental circumstances (in medical or psychological research), these kinds of ethical dictates for complete disclosure are completely unrealistic, inappropriate, and unenforceable.

BOX 5 THE ACTIVE VERSUS PASSIVE CONVERT

It is ironic that, in carrying to an extreme the assumptions of human pas-
sivity underlying most social scientists' ideas about conversion,[7] the anti-
cult movement's brainwashing scenario actually helped foster a new image
of converts. The research prompted by the anti-cult claims has suggested
that converts are less passive than once thought. Roger Straus (1976,
1979), for instance, uses the testimony of converts to various evangelical
and charismatic Christian groups, Nichiren Soshu/Sōka Gakkai, Divine
Light Mission, Transcendental Meditation, Kundalini Yoga, Eckankar, and
Scientology to suggest that religious seekers, far from being manipulated
by cults, are often creatively exploiting religious groups in order to experiment with new roles and meanings in their lives. And on the basis of the
cumulative empirical record, Bromley and Shupe (1979b, 1986) argue that
the processes of affiliation with and disaffiliation from the Unification
Church, Hare Krishna, and the Children of God/The Family, are best
thought of as rather ordinary transitions in people's social roles. These affiliations and disaffiliations are the result of various ad hoc processes of
negotiation between those converting or deconverting and the NRMs, and
as such are subject to their mutual influence.

The Old Pauline Paradigm

The prototypical conversion experience in Western culture is that of St
Paul, the great Christian evangelist and founder of the Church (Acts 9:
1–19). We are told that Paul, a Palestinian Jew, was on the road to Damascus
to persecute Christians when he was suddenly smitten blind by a brilliant
flash of light from which Jesus spoke to him. Three days later his blindness
was healed by a pious Christian from Damascus sent to restore his sight by
Jesus. Paul then converted and was baptized into the new faith.

Much like Paul's experience, conversions are traditionally thought (1) to
be sudden and often dramatic, (2) to be emotional and even irrational, (3) to
be single events, (4) to create total life changes that last a lifetime, (5) to be
individual experiences, and not a collective phenomenon, and (6) to be something the convert passively receives as a result of the actions of some seemingly external agency. For centuries, of course, the external agency was
thought to be supernatural (for example, God). From the psychological and/or
sociological perspectives of today, the external agency is often conceived to

be some compelling set of unconscious processes or cultural and social expectations and pressures. The pattern of change in question is usually understood in terms of a sequence of changes in beliefs, followed by changes in attitudes, that produces congruent changes in the behaviour of converts.

The New Active Paradigm

The new view emerging from the study of NRMs and from other developments in the social sciences postulates a much more 'active' involvement of converts (see Richardson, 1985; Dawson, 1990). This more active interpretation is based on a number of observations:

1. Sudden conversions are actually rare. More commonly, conversion experiences, even those that seem sudden, are rooted in long-term, though partially cloaked, struggles of conscience and identity. Mounting tension and discontent, combined with the anticipation of starting a new life, may trigger a moment of self-surrender that becomes identified as the conversion.

2. Many converts engage in some measure of 'seekership' before converting. They have been actively searching for information and opportunities. Moreover, they often have what has come to be called 'conversion careers' (Richardson, 1980). That is, many have been affiliated with other groups before converting to their current faith.

3. Processes of conversion appear to be largely social (that is, collective). They are the result of interactions between specific individuals and groups where an exchange of rewards is negotiated. Contact itself is most commonly the result of social networks, and involvement depends on the development of close interpersonal bonds between converts and members of the group.

4. Interviews with converts and observations of those participating in NRMs have revealed more rational calculation and conscious lifestyle experimentation than expected. Converts are more aware of their situation than social scientists expected—assessing circumstances, weighing the advantages and disadvantages of affiliation. In fact, they often display latent reservations, when pressed, about their actions long after converting. In some instances, they even have begun to plan their post-cult lives while still being actively involved, even as leaders, in their religions (Wright, 1987).

5. Consequently, it appears that many conversions entail more role-playing than actual transformation of the personalities or self-conceptions of

converts. Converts learn how to pass for a member of the group they have joined. They learn the 'convert role' in order to explore possibilities within the group (Balch, 1980). Behavioural changes, that is, precede any real changes in attitudes and then finally beliefs. In fact, the latter changes may or may not follow at all.

The growing evidence that conversion is a more active than passive process points the way to a rational-choice approach to the study of religion, as discussed in Chapter 1. Within the limits of the convert's own definition of the situation, social scientists have no a priori reason for assuming that religious activities, like conversions, are any more irrational and hence inexplicable than other kinds of social actions. As Gartrell and Shannon (1985), Stark and Bainbridge (1985, 1987), Neitz (1987), Dawson (1990), Stark and Finke (1993), and Stark and Iannaccone (1993) have argued, principles of exchange apply in this context as well as elsewhere. Individuals and groups satisfy each other's demands and needs in an exchange of goods and services. The dissolution of group bonds rather logically follows from declining returns and diminished or changed needs. It is difficult, however, to decipher from data the nature of the exchange and the needs at stake; this requires first-hand familiarity with the individuals and groups in question, something academics and anti-cultists alike rarely have the opportunity to acquire.

Reformulating the Issues in the Brainwashing Debate

But that is not the end of the story. Two sociologists of religion have made efforts to rehabilitate the concept of 'brainwashing' as applied to NRMs. Stephen Kent (2001b) and Benjamin Zablocki (2001) have controversially sought to revive the fortunes of this idea by switching the focus of attention from the analyzis of how NRMs acquire new members to what some groups do to retain them.

Zablocki admirably seeks to reframe the brainwashing theory in terms of a carefully formulated set of definitions and testable hypotheses (2001: 181–194). He is convinced from his years of experience studying NRMs that something like the process of brainwashing is occurring in some instances, with evident negative consequences for the individuals involved. He makes a cogent plea for setting aside the skewed and contentious treatments of this topic induced by years of legal disputes and exaggerated fears. If we are ever going to understand the processes giving rise to the undesirable authority and obedience displayed in the violence associated with groups such as Aum Shinrikyo or Heaven's Gate (see Chapter 7), Zablocki asserts, we need to return to the study of the patterns of interaction that the anti-cult movement sought to identify with the concept of brainwashing. To this end we must recognize that, contrary to the popular notions under debate, 'brainwashing has absolutely nothing to do with the overthrow of "free will" or any other such mystical or nonscientific concept. People who have been brainwashed are "not free" only in the sense that all of us, hemmed in on all sides as we are by social and cultural constraints, are not free' (2001: 204). Brainwashing represents a more extreme manifestation of conventional and scientifically accepted processes of influence and authority in totalistic groups centred on the teachings and authority of charismatic leaders.

This is how the concept was framed in the foundational studies of Lifton (1961) and Schein et al. (1961), Zablocki argues, before being mis-interpreted by both the proponents and the opponents of the brainwashing scenario in contemporary cults. Lifton and Schein are addressing the inten-sive resocialization programs to which already committed members of groups are subjected. Their theories have no bearing on how followers of groups are 'obtained'; they are about how members are 'retained.' More specifically, it is a label for certain types of systematic efforts made to turn selected ordinary members into 'deployable agents'. This term designates individuals that the group can trust to perform their assigned duties, no matter how mundane, personally costly, or morally suspect, with a mini-mum of continued surveillance by the group. These individuals have been pressured and manipulated into a state of such complete identification with their religious leaders and groups that it is no longer possible for them to rationally reflect on the nature of their commitments and to end them, once they have become psychologically injurious or immoral. The 'exit costs' are too high, the deployable agents believe, because they are no longer capable of envisioning any worthwhile alternatives.

Characteristically, Zablocki stipulates (2001: 176):

> . . . nothing in the brainwashing model predicts that it will be attempted with all members, let alone successfully attempted. In fact, the efficiency of brainwashing, operationalized as the expected yield of deployable agents per 100 members, is an unknown (but discoverable) parameter of any particular cultic system and may often be quite low. For the system to be able to perpetuate itself . . . the yield need only produce enough value for the system to compensate it for the resources required to maintain the brainwashing process.

The process itself is fully 'interactive.' It is not simply about the imposition of a new identity on someone, as the popular discourse implies. Instead, it is contingent on at least three sets of variables: individual predispositions, the existence of certain social conditions, and specific types of resocialization practices. Existing studies show elements of all three of these at work, and future studies must refine these insights. In the meantime, the sweeping generalizations of the past must be avoided for scientific progress to be made. Brainwashing, Zablocki concludes (2001: 204):

> . . . is an administratively costly and not always effective procedure that some cults use on some of their members. A few cults rely heavily on brainwashing and put all their members through it. Other cults do not use the procedure at all. During periods of stressful confrontation, either with external enemies or among internal factions, or in attempts to cope with failed apocalyptic prophecies, it is not uncommon for brainwashing suddenly to come to play a central role in the cult's attempts to achieve order and social control. At such times, risk of uncritically obedient violent-aggression or mass suicide may be heightened.

Kent (2001b) pursues a more straightforward line of argument to exonerate the idea of brainwashing. He argues that the systems of internal discipline instituted in such groups as The Children of God/The Family and Scientology are too severe and reminiscent of the regimes of thought reform (i.e. brainwashing) run by Communist regimes in the Soviet Union, China, Korea, and elsewhere. These programs are abusive, he asserts, and violate the human rights of their participants. He supports his case with material drawn from the documents and literature of these organizations and the accounts of aggrieved ex-members.

At present neither of these efforts has proved persuasive and each has been subject to telling criticisms from other scholars in the field (e.g. Bromley, 1998; Anthony 2001; Dawson, 2001b; Anthony and Robbins, 2004). In fact the debate has become so fractious and obscure that most scholars have refused to engage the issue any further. There is much to recommend Zablocki's analysis of the issues at stake, but the popular prejudices invoked by the mere word 'brainwashing' prevents me from feeling much enthusiasm for even his more moderate conception of the process.

In many respects, as Thomas Robbins (1984) and David Bromley (2001) argue, the debate over brainwashing represents a clash of perspectives rooted in irreconcilable political differences. The dispute over cult brainwashing persists because it is really about a broader conflict of values masquerading as a scientific debate. As Bromley deftly delineates, the controversy may be intractable because it is really about 'morally advantaging and disadvantaging certain kinds of individual-group relationships by designating them as [either the product of a legitimate process of] conversion or [an illegitimate process of] brainwashing' (2001: 326). As he observes (2001: 329–30):

> There are numerous institutional arenas through the social order in which high control, encapsulation, and identity transformation occur that do no evoke a brainwashing designation. These settings are considered 'functional' to the social order, and assessments of individual participation range from rehabilitative [(e.g. mental hospitals, prisons)] to honorific [(e.g. military training, convents and monasteries)]. . . . By contrast, where the form of organization is contested and deemed illegitimate, organizational settings receive brainwashing designations.

In this regard, he also observes (2001: 332):

> The difference in linguistic patterns between the two camps, in terms of both observational and theoretical accounts, is informative. Where the brainwashing theorists see individuals being disciplined, conversion theorists observe disciples. What the former regard as captivity, the latter perceive as captivation. What is humiliation to brainwashing theorists is humility from the perspective of the conversion theorists. Brainwashing theorists describe religious movements as coercive communities, penitentiaries, while conversion theorists describe communities of penitents. Whether affiliates of these movements are assessed as thralls or enthralled is a function of the political location from which the narratives are constructed. The theories serve as political narratives in the sense that they are working from conclusions to data.[8]

Using slightly different terms of reference, Robbins (1984) agrees. What is evidence of abuse and manipulation from a 'critical external perspective' can be interpreted as evidence of intense religious commitment and authentic spiritual development from an 'empathetic internal perspective.'[9] Under these circumstances no amount of additional evidence is going to shake people free of their convictions and talk of brainwashing is likely to persist because it serves the interests of certain people:

> The medicalized 'mind-control' claim articulates a critique of deviant new religions which not only obviates civil libertarian objections of social control but also meets the needs of the various groups which are threatened

by or antagonistic to cults: *mental health professionals*, whose role in the rehabilitation of victims of 'destructive cultism' is highlighted; *parents*, whose opposition to cults and willingness to forcibly 'rescue' cultists progeny are legitimated; *ex-converts*, who may find it meaningful and rewarding to reinterpret their prior involvement with stigmatized groups as basically passive and unmotivated; and *clerics*, who are concerned to avoid appearing to persecute religious competitors. An anti-cult coalition of these groups is possible only *if medical and mental health issues are kept in the fore-front* . . . and if the medical model is employed in such a way as to disavow the intent to persecute minority beliefs and to stress the psychiatric healing of involuntary pathology. (Robbins, 1984: 253; see also Richardson, van der Lans, and Derks, 1986)

Zablocki's new approach may appear to obviate some of these concerns; certainly it is designed to do so. But it is dependent on problematic and unanalyzed value judgements. What ultimately distinguishes brainwashing in his model from other more conventional forms of influence and social control is the inducement of a condition of 'hyper-credulity.' This 'is defined as a disposition to accept uncritically all charismatically ordained beliefs' (2001: 184). The hallmark of brainwashing, then, is the presence of uncritical obedience (e.g. 2001: 185), which presumably is rare. This is why a new and separate term is needed. But how are we to determine when the behaviour in question is sufficiently 'uncritical'? Such judgements are culturally relative, context-dependent, and notoriously difficult and subjective. In some other contexts, moreover, such as soldiers at war, conventional society demands and honours acts of unquestioning obedience. One cannot help but suspect that Zablocki is also in some ways working backwards from conclusions to data. His further reliance on the supposedly 'traumatic' effects of brainwashing to justify its study, while acknowledging the wholly inadequate nature of all current psychological studies of converts to NRMs, supports this suspicion (2001: 177–179).

As Barker comments, 'what is one man's meat is another man's poison.' Intuitively, I suspect everyone involved in the public debate over whether converts to NRMs are brainwashed knows this to be the case.[10] So the 'cult bashers,' to use Zablocki's terms, seek to disguise their real objectives by donning the cloak of scientific legitimacy, while the 'cult apologists' content themselves with debunking this pretense of scientific credibility in defence of the established legal and moral safe-guards of religious liberty. Regrettably this means that some of the important questions Zablocki raises about the processes of social control exercised in many NRMs may continue to be neglected. But talk of 'brainwashing' will inevitably conjure up naive and false images of zombie-like cult devotees who have been system-atically stripped of the capacity to make free and rational decisions about their religious behaviour. The consequences of perpetuating this public myth outweigh the merits of reformulating the concept (see Pfeifer, 1992, 1999; Richardson and Introvigne, 2001).

In the end, though, all parties to this dispute must guard against indulging too readily in reductionistic analyses. We are often quick to ques-tion the motives or causes of other people's behaviour, even though we expect others to accept our motives at face value. We may deny others this courtesy just because we dislike or fail to understand their point of view. Yet because everyone's thoughts and actions are socially conditioned, all that we say or do may bear the marks of rationalization, self-deception, or simply ignorance. For that reason, social scientists are cautious in attributing motives, especially if they are contrary to those given by the persons in ques-tion. This is particularly the case with reasons given for religious beliefs. Special care must be taken in the face of the irresolvable metaphysical ques-tions raised by claims to knowledge of the transcendent, and the exercise of free will (Dawson, 1986, 1988). We cannot simply discount the claims of converts to be acting in accord with some divine plan and to be acting freely. We have no conclusive way either to verify or to refute such claims.

Chapter Six

Why Are New Religious Movements So Often Accused of Sexual Deviance?

Through the centuries, defenders of orthodoxy have sought to undermine the credibility of heretical ideas and new religions by suggesting that their beliefs lead to immoral and dangerous behavior.[1] Charges of sexual impropriety and debauchery have been used to turn the public and the authorities against groups outside the mainstream. In nineteenth-century America, for example, even the Catholic Church was attacked. For most Americans then the Catholic Church was a minority religion closely associated with strange new immigrants from Ireland and, later, from eastern and southern Europe. Fearful of the changes the immigrants were bringing to America, many members of the Anglo-Protestant majority believed the charges of sexual deviance brought against Catholics in widely disseminated books and pamphlets. These anti-Catholic tracts alleged that, within the shrouded confines of the convent, priests and nuns were indulging in illicit orgies and producing babies that were killed and buried in the cellars (e.g. O'Gorman, 1871; Monk, 1876). Today such charges seem preposterous, yet they reflect the general distrust of a large segment of the public. Similar claims of sexual deviance are used today to discredit unconventional religions. In fact, as several scholars have documented,[2] there is an uncanny resemblance between the criticisms leveled at groups such as the Unification Church, the Children of God/The Family, and the Branch Davidians, and those made in the past against the Quakers, Mormons, and Shakers. This does not mean that some new religious movements are not engaged in unconventional sexual practices—many are—but scholars have learned to treat popular discussions with suspicion. To sway public opinion or to win court cases, opponents and competitors of new religious movements are inclined to exaggerate their claims, and the media are often less than sufficiently skeptical in reporting these accusations.

No systematic analysis of the sexual orientations and deviations of new religious movements has been published. Helpful information is provided, however, by studies of gender relations in the groups (e.g. Jacobs, 1984, 1989; Aidala,1985; Bednarowski, 1992; Palmer, 1994; Puttick, 1997), as well as the work of scholars describing more generally the history, beliefs, and practices of prominent movements (Miller, 1995; Goldman, 1999; Palmer, 2004). There is, for example, a growing body of reliable information on the Children of God/The Family, a group commonly criticized for its unusual sexual practices (e.g. Melton, 1994; Chancellor, 2000; Bainbridge, 2002).

This all calls attention to a related set of issues of concern to sociologists: Does the experience of men and women in these groups differ, and how are gender relations conceived? Are most new religions patriarchical or experimental, or something else, when it comes to the regulation of the sexes? The charges of sexual deviance leveled at contemporary cults are often rooted in a deeper social anxiety about the abusive or subversive potentialities of the patterns of gender relations modeled. The groups that reinforce and extend the traditional subjugation of women may be seen as regressive, while those that place women in charge of men may be seen as threatening to the rest of society. As Puttick (1997) observes, the sexual beliefs and behaviours of religions correlate with their ideas about the nature of femininity, and hence about women's proper place in the hierarchy of social control. These questions first came to the fore, in a less contentious way, when scholars began to wonder if men and women were attracted to NRMs for different reasons, a question to be addressed in the second part of this chapter.

Sexual Deviance and the Cults

'Free Love' or Asceticism

In dealing with the sexual deviance of cults, academics often talk about the 'antinomianism' of new religions. Antinomian individuals or groups no longer believe they are bound by the moral conventions or laws of humanity because they have achieved, through their faith or other spiritual means, a higher state of being and salvation. In 1534, for example, during the Protestant Reformation, the radical Anabaptist followers of Jan Matthys and John Bockelson seized control of the German city of Münster. Enraptured by visions of the impending apocalypse and the final triumph of good over evil, they declared Münster to be the New Jerusalem and instituted an order of Christian communism and free love. Based on a literal restoration of Old

Testament times, polygamy was introduced to the city, and in the domestic confusion that followed something close to total promiscuity reigned for a time (Lewy, 1974: 116–129). This attempt to usher in the kingdom of heaven on earth soon degenerated into a reign of terror at the hands of the Anabaptists, and they were eventually slaughtered by the besieging army of the German princes.

In nineteenth-century America, the religious visionary John Humphrey Noyes created the highly successful Oneida Community (1849–1881) in upstate New York. This free-love community instituted a policy of 'complex marriage' in which all the men and women of the group were available for sexual relations with each other. The intention of this practice was to overcome the selfishness and unnaturalness of romantic love and monogamous relationships. In the sexual life of the community a committee of elders decided who would be allowed to make love to whom on any given night— physical love only, that is, since romance was strictly forbidden. Also, the men were not allowed to ejaculate during sex because Noyes believed that this had debilitating effects on their physical and spiritual well-being (Kephart and Zellner, 1991: 45–87).

More recently in America one might think of other communities like The Farm (Greenfield, 1975, pp. 103–126; Traugot, 1998, pp. 41–62), Rajneeshpuram (Carter, 1990; Goldman, 1999; Puttick, 1997), and the Children of God/The Family (van Zandt, 1991; Chancellor, 2000). Inspired by the sexual revolution of the counter-culture of the 1960s, these and other groups identified sexual liberation with spiritual enlightenment. Drawing on the new therapeutic ethic of the human potential movement in psychology and rooted in the theories of Sigmund Freud, Wilhelm Reich, and others, these groups believed that the personal and social distress caused by the sexual repression of the dominant Christian culture was preventing people from realizing their true natures, the purpose of life, and a proper relationship with God. To foster a new and fuller understanding of their spiritual potential, these groups instituted ways of life designed to challenge the 'uptight' sexual habits of their contemporaries.

In the early seventies, for example, David Berg, the founder of the Children of God, condemned the distorted and 'unbiblical' conception of sex as sin. He called upon his many youthful followers to practice 'Revolutionary Sex' (Melton, 1994). Sex was a natural and God-given good, and people should live free of guilt and false modesty. This attitude soon developed into the controversial 'Law of Love' whereby the tenets of the Old Testament were declared null and void. Adultery, for instance, no longer existed if the sharing of sex was undertaken in the spirit of true love and to spread the word of God. Partners were encouraged to share themselves with others in the movement and to use 'flirty fishing' to attract others to the cause. Women were asked to use their feminine wiles, and if need be sexual contact, to convert lonely men to Christ and the Children of God. This practice along with controversial claims about the sexuality of children soon invoked strident opposition to the movement, and in the 1980s their communities in Spain, Australia, and Argentina were subjected to midnight raids by the police (Richardson, 1996b, 1999; Bainbridge, 2002). In the end all charges brought against the group were dismissed, but the reaction of the public leading to necessitated changes, the movement's transformation into the much more conventional evangelical group, The Family.

An ethic of free love has been manifested in many ways in the proliferating new religions of North America. In most instances the seeming acts of sexual deviance are part of a structured set of beliefs and practices that are carefully regulated by the group and directed to specific ends. In their authentic form they do not constitute a mere excuse for hedonism. In fact their ultimate end is often the reverse. The movement founded by the Indian 'sex guru' Bhagwan Shree Rajneesh (later known as Osho), for example, openly encouraged sexual experimentation. Rajneesh's stated objective was to overcome the western obsession with sex to lay a sounder foundation for the life of celibacy required for true spiritual enlightenment. Rather typically his teachings offered an amalgam of insights from the ancient Tantric teachings about sexual mysticism in Hinduism and Buddhism and various contemporary forms of psychotherapy. The practice of these somewhat esoteric teachings is open to abuse and misunderstanding (Puttick, 1997; Chancellor, 2000: 94–150), and the sexual liberation advocated by Rajneesh, and by David Berg as well, was also not complete. Male homosexuality, for instance, was sharply condemned by both religious leaders as unnatural (Melton, 1994; Goldman ,1995; Puttick, 1997; Chancellor, 2000). In other words, while the notion of sexual deviance is commonly redefined by these so-called free love groups, it is not eliminated altogether.

Some new religions are taken to task by their critics for their liberal attitudes to sex. But by the standards of contemporary western society it is as likely for new religions to be criticized for their asceticism. Members of the Unification Church are strictly forbidden from engaging in premarital sex and are expected to remain celibate for many years before marrying. Once married the husband and wife are to remain celibate for several more months or even years, a further demonstration of their dedication and spiritual purity. In the Unification Church marriages are arranged by the church, must be formally blessed by the Reverend Moon and his wife, and usually take place in large mass services. Marriage is the key sacrament and sex is primarily understood as a means to produce 'godly children' for re-establishing the foundation of the Kingdom of God on earth. Divorce, adultery, and homosexuality are harshly repudiated as contrary to the will of God. Many other groups, like the International Society for Krishna Consciousness or the Brahma Kumaris (see Puttick, 1997: 109–111), are equally rigorous in their ascetic beliefs and practices. For the Moonies, it must be understood, the evils of this world stem from the failure of Adam and Eve to refrain from sexual intercourse until they were sufficiently mature spiritually. The Moonies are seeking to reverse this original disruption of God's plan and to restore the divinely intended harmony of matter and spirit, heart and mind, male and female, and parent and child (Galanter, 1989). In our society, suffuse with the commercial imagery of sex and the ideology of romantic love, the sexual restraint of the Moonies appears deviant.

DILEMMAS OF MORAL RELATIVITY

It is difficult to discuss the sexual deviance of religious cults when both sexual indulgence and abstention have been the object of public scorn. What is deviant to some members of our society, or to one or another of the religions, is not deviant to others. In the pluralistic context of life today there is no satisfactory way to identify the relevant standards of normalcy for determining the deviancy of any religiously justified sexual practice without running the risk of arbitrarily favouring one religious tradition over another. Reason alone cannot guide us to some objective morality that can be applied to all places and times. A charge of sexual deviance must be supported with some evidence of harm. Sexual deviance, in and of itself, is not enough. In Canada and the United States, the principle of religious freedom is guaranteed by constitutional law. As James Spickard stipulates (1994: 253): 'To the extent that a religion's practices follow its teachings, there is in principle no way to judge it to be abusive without violating that religion's freedom'. In the quest to save souls, moreover, religious leaders have long advocated that strong means may be required to overcome the seductive bonds of pleasure and egocentrism that are said to rule in this world. In the face of such claims, how can one say that the value we place in the inviolability of the person must necessarily take precedence over the salvation of the soul? Cognizant of these and other dilemmas, scholars of religion have tended to err on the side of tolerance and shy away from talking in terms of 'sexual deviance'. But what about instances when the members or leaders of a religion fail to abide by even their own standards of conduct? Are matters not more straightforward then? Not necessarily, since there always is room for debate about the nature and application of even these internal standards.

To illustrate the point, let us briefly consider the grounds for deeming sexual relations between a religious leader and a follower deviant. In recent years there have been many sexual scandals involving religious leaders in America, from the televangelists Jim Bakker and Jimmy Swaggart to the Zen master Richard Baker or the Tibetan lamas Chögyam Trungpa and Sogyal Rinpoche. In the Christian context, where sex outside of the confines of holy matrimony is clearly a sin, the deviance of such sexual liaisons is apparent. But things are not as clear in the guru-disciple relationship of many eastern religions. Here the objective of instruction is often to wrench the disciple free of his or her preoccupation with the self and to stimulate the growth of their spiritual insight by moving against the currents of ordinary life. To that end the guru may deem that sexual therapy is in order. Sex may be viewed as the means of enhancing the follower's self-esteem or overcoming some childhood fixation preventing proper meditation. In these religious contexts there are often no rigid restrictions against the use of sex, like anything else, to open new and necessary horizons of self-understanding (Feuerstein, 1990). Elaborate and ancient rites exist in the Tantric traditions of Hinduism and Buddhism for the acceleration of spiritual growth through the controlled release of sexual energy. But as can be imagined, the disciple may still confuse the emotions of devotion with those of romantic love, or seek to curry the favour of the guru through the provision of sexual services. In doing so the disciple may be entering into a religious 'economy of love' (Jacobs, 1984) that is inherently exploitive or demeaning because the exchange is founded on an extreme imbalance of power. Disciples may not be adequately prepared to handle the strong emotions released by intimacy with the object of their adoration. They may eventually be hurt to discover, for instance, that they are only one of many such lovers. They also may feel compelled to engage in sexual practices they find disconcerting. They may experience all manner of psychological wounds in a relationship where they lack control, wounds that heighten their self-doubts and lead to spiritual disillusionment. These things may happen no matter how carefully the guru has sought to prepare the disciple and to control the conditions of contact. In some cases women may come to the painful realization that they have been victimized by a religious leader who is a misogynist or by a tradition of misogynist thought (Jacobs, 1989).

It must be realized that these same women may have complained that their spiritual progress was being blocked because their gurus had not picked them to be their consorts. Many women have left religious cults because the guru would not have such a relationship with them (Jacobs, 1984; Puttick, 1997). So we must keep the complexity of the situation in mind; the complaint of the follower against the guru, after a falling out, may be interpreted as stemming from a failure to achieve the true self-surrender and loss of ego demanded by Eastern paths of enlightenment. Nonetheless, as Elizabeth Puttick (1997: 47) comments in one of the most detailed discussions of these issues: 'There seems to [be] an innate paradox, if not contradiction, between the goal of therapy (responsible maturity) and the path of Eastern mysticism (childlike innocence and trust). This may be an endemic, insoluble problem at the heart of the master-disciple relationship.'

RELIGIOUS SIGNIFICANCE OF SEX

But why do questions of sex and sexual regulation figure so prominently in religious cults in the first place? There are both ideological and organizational reasons for why new religions so often experiment with alternative sexual relations. Sexuality is a profoundly personal matter closely associated with our deepest self-understanding. In groups seeking to refashion the self to save the world it is logical that sexuality should be a focal concern. The power relations in society are commonly reflected in its sexual customs, while the intimacy and ecstasy of sexual life itself has long been used to symbolically express human relations with the divine (e.g. from the arrows of Christ's love penetrating the heart of the great Spanish mystic Teresa of Avila to the erotic tales of the young Krishna in Hinduism). In controlling people's sexual activity, new religions are seeking to challenge conceptions of social power and relations with the divine. Sexuality provides a means of access to the human psyche, a means of redirecting attention from the limited rewards and worries of this world to the greater promise of another.

In the utopian view of most new religious communities, 'everything should be shared, affection as well as material possessions' (Kanter, 1972: 86). By limiting or expanding sexual activities in certain ways, attention is focused on the charismatic leader, the needs of the group, and its religious goals (see Bainbridge, 2002: 122–123 as well). 'Exclusive two-person bonds within a larger group, particularly sexual attachments, represent competition for members' emotional energy and loyalty' (Kanter, 1972: 86). In interviews with James Chancellor, the practitioners of sexual sharing and flirty-fishing in the Children of God/The Family characteristically justified their actions through reference to an early message from their leader. In this so-called 'One Wife!' letter Berg says (Chancellor, 2000: 110):

> . . . The Family marriage, the spiritual reality behind so-called group marriage, is that of putting the larger Family, the whole Family, first, even before the last remaining vestige of private property, your husband or your wife!

We do not minimize the marriage ties, as such. We just consider our ties to the Lord and the larger Family greater and more important. — And when the private marriage ties interfere with Our Family and God ties, they can be readily abandoned for the glory of God and the good of the Family! . . .

God's in the business of breaking up little selfish private worldly families to make of their yielded broken pieces a larger unit — One Family! He's in the business of destroying the relationship of many wives in order to make them One Wife — God's Wife — The Bride of Christ! . . .

As the empirical work of Stuart Wright (1986) confirms, the success of a new religious movement may be threatened by the problem of 'dyadic withdrawals'. When one member of a couple wishes to leave, it is highly likely that their partner will be lost as well, even if he or she is still a true believer.

In the end, then, it must be realized that there are good reasons why sexual and spiritual deviance have gone hand-in-hand for centuries. The links between spiritual and sexual experimentation, however, are often costly. The abuses that can creep in when taboos are lifted have alienated many members from the groups in question and provided ammunition for their enemies (see Box 6). Religious revolutionaries rarely seem to realize adequately the care with which such issues must be handled.

BOX 6 CHILD ABUSE AND THE SOCIAL CONTROL OF NRMs

Certainly one of the most difficult issues to address in the study of NRMs is the repeated accusations of child abuse, especially sexual abuse. To date the historical and legal record has demonstrated that most of these allegations are unfounded. They are leveled at groups by authorities under the influence of 'cult experts' associated with the anti-cult movement, with the intent of suppressing supposedly deviant religions. This is not to say that the religions are always blameless, but in the high profile cases of the 1990s it is clear that the public response to such accusations was grossly disproportionate and biased. The members of religious groups were wrongfully stripped of their most basic legal rights, while innocent parents and their children were traumatized on the basis of scant evidence. A cluster of incidents around the world suggests, as Richardson (1999) observes, that the moral entrepreneurs of the anti-cult movement turned to issues of child welfare as a new pretext for justifying the persecution of 'cults' when accusations of brainwashing were rejected by the courts (see Chapter 5).

Throughout the last few decades individual parents and religious leaders have been accused and sometimes convicted of the neglect, manslaughter, and even murder of children in their care. While rare, these cases are extremely serious and often the result of misguided efforts at corporal punishment, spiritual healing, or exorcisms. Many of the accusations of sexual abuse involving NRMs stem from contentious custody disputes. When one parent has left an NRM and is seeking custody of the children who remain in the group with the other parent, claims of possible sexual abuse can be raised to influence the decisions of judges (see Homer, 1999). These kinds of disputes played a prominent role in the mounting tensions that precipitated the violent confrontations with the authorities of the Peoples Temple in 1978 and the Branch Davidians in 1993 (Hall, 1987; Ellison and Bartkowski, 1995; Homer, 1999: 199). Beginning in the early 1980s, however, the accusations took on a new and disturbing generality. The claim was made that all the children in certain new religions were in harm's way simply because they were in groups with objectionable beliefs and practices (Richardson, 1999: 175–176). On this basis mass actions were taken by law enforcement agencies against several new religions in Argentina, Australia, France, Spain, and the United States. The surprise police raids resulted in the wrongful and harsh imprisonment of the entire adult populations of the accused communities and the removal of their children to state institutions, often for several months. In each instance the groups were eventually exonerated. The courts dropped all the charges, and in several cases rebuked the authorities for subverting the law to serve their own prejudices.

At 2 a.m. on 1 September 1993, for example, heavily armed police, accompanied by social workers and the news media, raided five communal homes of The Children of God/The Family, in Argentina. Nearly 140 children and dozens of adults were taken into custody. The children were rushed off without their belongings or a chance to speak to their parents, who were arrested but denied any information on the charges they faced. They were denied the right to make a phone call and access to legal council. Parents and teenagers were imprisoned under harsh conditions. Their homes and possessions were ransacked for evidence, then left unprotected while the NRM members were detained. The children were subjected to extensive psychological and physical examinations, and the parents faced weeks of strenuous and intimidating interrogations. At press conferences the authorities claimed the group was guilty of raping and sodomizing their children.

The claims made front-page news around the world.

In the end these widely publicized claims could not be supported. Repeated examinations of the children by their own experts produced no physical evidence of abuse. As more objective authorities became involved, the miscarriage of justice became clear. On 13 December 1993, the Argentine Court of Appeals of San Martin ordered the release of the adults and the return of the group's children. In its three-hundred-page decision, the court declared the magistrate spearheading the raid to be incompetent, and lamented the influence of 'the career apostates from outside the country who had initially promoted the charges' (Richardson, 1999: 179). Eventually an appeal of this judgement to the Argentine Supreme Court was unsuccessful and damages were awarded to the Children of God/The Family.

Much the same happened in each of the other mass raids made on the homes of The Children of God/The Family in Australia, France, and Spain. The raids were launched with no prior serious investigation of the credibility of the accusations or discussions with the members of the religion. The authorities acted on the word of a handful of aggrieved ex-members and anti-cult 'experts' alone. News of the dismissal of the charges received little publicity, buried in the back pages of newspapers.

The Children of God/The Family have since opened their homes to assessment by the appropriate child welfare authorities in the many countries where they live, without further incident. They have introduced even more stringent safeguards for the welfare of their children. But these events have scarred the group and many of its individual members deeply (see the testimony provided by members in Chancellor, 2000: 195–202). With their 'free love' ethic and prohibition against birth control, many children were born into the group, beginning in the late 1970s. By the mid-1980s the group began to make child-care and home-education a priority. The future of their mission, they realized, lay with the many children swelling their ranks.

But the group cannot absolve itself of some of the blame for its fate. The leader David Berg had ominously and carelessly stretched the bounds of acceptable behavior in his pursuit of the revolutionary implications of his understanding of the biblically enjoined 'Law of Love.' He had made pronouncements in writing that appeared to condone or even advocate sexual relations between children and adults (see Chancellor, 2000: 132–138). It seems that few followers ever acted on his lurid and flamboyant suggestions. But many admit they knew of some abuses and some of the children who later left the movement complained they had been sexually molested. The group strongly associates the pleasures of bodily love with God's blessings. At one time its literature was replete with graphic sexual images. Nudity and sexual sharing were widely practiced by the adults in their communal homes. At the height of the group's antinomian rebellion against what they called 'the system', they had produced videos of young and scantily clad or nude women and children dancing, and they were openly engaged in 'flirty fishing' to save souls and win recruits. There is no doubt that some children were cajoled or pressured into sexual relations with some adult members of this community well before they could understand or deal with the consequences of these acts (see the testimony in Chancellor, 2000: 223–229).

Ironically, by 1987 all these practices had been abandoned and new guidelines enacted to protect children. The offending tapes and literature were supposed to be destroyed. But inevitably some of the material found its way into the hands of the anti-cult movement, greatly facilitating their efforts to instigate the police actions of the 1990s.

In the world inhabited by contemporary NRMs, the objectives of the anti-cult movement can be served by merely drawing attention to the emotionally powerful accusations of child abuse. As Richardson concludes (1999: 181):

> The effect on the targeted group can be devastating. Once children are removed by the state and their parents arrested, the group has little recourse but to allocate all available resources to fighting the charges ... And the group may have few resources to allocate, a situation with significant consequences ... The group must also cope with the accompanying media barrage of negative publicity. Regardless of whether the charges have any substance, the impact can be profound. The group must adjust its priorities and alter its very shape, a short-term process that may well have long-lasting repercussions. In this way, the group's organizational life becomes 'deformed' by the necessity of dealing with such pervasive external pressures ....

The Children of God/The Family has apologized to any members hurt by their past experiences in the group, refuting and suppressing the earlier teachings and behaviours. In this regard they have been compelled by both the law (Bradney, 1999; Chancellor, 2000) and the practical requirements of organizational survival to correct their ways. Even the near scriptural legacy of their charismatic and beloved spiritual father, David Berg, has been expunged of its most offensive material. But no amount of vigilance can ultimately protect such countercultural religious groups from future persecution brought on by their sexual deviation from the conventional norms of the larger societies in which they live.

Gender Matters

Gender, the socially constructed identity (masculine or feminine) ascribed to us by virtue of our sex (male or female), is what sociologists call a 'master status'. That is, it is one of the crucial determinants of our sense of self and of how others will interact with us. Not surprisingly, then, many sociologists of religion have investigated the role, if any, of this great differentiating factor in explaining the emergence of NRMs and why people join them. Do men and women join NRMs for different reasons?

To the extent that theorists are correct in linking the emergence of NRMs to disruptions and deficiencies in the private sphere of life, it is likely that women, who were traditionally identified with that sphere as lovers, wives, mothers, and housekeepers, should be strongly affected. The accepted patterns of courtship, sexuality, marriage, reproduction, and child-rearing have changed with the rise of the feminist movement, coinciding with the rise of the NRMs. While liberating and beneficial for many, this has also been disruptive (see, for example, Davidman, 1990: 405; Goldman, 1999). By helping to fracture the consensus on traditional gender roles, it has created a heightened sense of anomie for many women. This is especially the case in combination with the growing economic necessity for families to have two incomes. Women in particular are under stress from the growing fragility of the marriage bond, the weakening of the parent-child bond, and the increased penetration of all aspects of life by the impersonal and instrumental social relations of the contemporary workplace (Palmer, 1994: 5–8). Feeling the weight of their quadruple burden as wives or lovers, housekeepers, workers, and mothers, the absence of an adequate normative order can produce in some women a nostalgia or utopian yearning for a simpler society and more social support for the nuclear family. Under such circumstances, as Berger's theory of religion predicts, it is not surprising that individuals seek out a new 'sacred canopy' under which to reorder and legitimate their lives. Indeed, in study after study, sociologists have found that the delineation of new and clear guidelines for the nuclear family and corresponding gender and sex roles is pivotal to the construction of reality and the appeal of new religions, sects and cults alike (e.g. Richardson, Stewart, and Simmonds, 1979; Aidala, 1985; Rochford, 1985; Ammerman, 1987; Neitz, 1987; Rose, 1987; Warner, 1988; Davidman, 1990; Palmer, 1994; Puttick, 1999; for a fuller set of references consult Davidman and Jacobs, 1993). Like the Shakers, Mormons, Oneida Society, and others before them in the nineteenth century, 'modern prophets exhibit a profound concern for what they deplore as the increasingly secular and materialistic approach to sex and marriage in American society', and they 'hope to achieve harmonious relations between the sexes based on new models of gender that reflect the divine cosmos' (Palmer, 1994: 4).

In a path-breaking study of religious and non-religious communes founded since the 1960s, Angela Aidala (1985) found a common preoccupation with issues of sexuality and gender. But whereas the non-religious communes adopted an experimental orientation guided by the constant negotiation and renegotiation of gender norms and functions, the religious communes were oriented to the consistent implementation of a particular, well defined, and usually conservative vision of male-female relations. Investigating the backgrounds of members of the religious communes, Aidala (1985) unearthed evidence of a 'low tolerance for ambiguity' in their lives. Palmer (1994: 236) similarly says that the women in NRMs that she interviewed displayed a marked 'intolerance for the perceived chaos in [contemporary] social relations'. Given the crucial role of gender identities in the development of our self-conceptions, it is not surprising then that religious communes should emerge out of the flux of the counterculture and the contemporary world in general. These groups often seem to reinstate and reinforce the patriarchal patterns of authority and responsibility characteristic of the idealized family life of a baby boomer's youth. Good Christian or Jewish or Krishna wives are to be submissive to their husbands and confine their influence and activity to the domestic sphere. Their primary role is to support and nurture their husbands and children, materially, emotionally, and spiritually. Governance of the movements and the responsibilities of public leadership are a male preserve.

·Meanwhile, men in these new religions face both greater and lesser expectaions regarding the traditional male role (Aidala, 1985; Rose, 1987; Stacey, 1990; Palmer, 1994). On the one hand, the men are expected to be more actively and intimately involved in family life and caring for children than their fathers (as a generation) ever were. On the other hand, because of the communal system of mutual support and the ideological clarity of these groups, young men are relieved of some of the anxiety born of being the breadwinner, protector, and primary authority in the family. All members of the group must care for each other as one family, and within the couples a corresponding pattern of mutual respect, open discussion, and decision-making tends to prevail. It appears that the 'women within these groups negotiated and willingly made compromises in order to "build-up" their men into responsible, and responsive partners who would cooperate in the maintenance of a stable family unit' (Davidman and Jacobs, 1993: 180). The men in question, it must be remembered, were often the rather anarchistic and perhaps disillusioned ex-leaders of the counterculture and the student protests of the 1960s.

Gender Role Diversity in NRMs

In her excellent study of women in seven quite diverse NRMs, Palmer (1994) adds some interesting twists to this picture. In the first place she discounts the tendency to group NRMs by gender issues into such simple dichotomies as Robbins and Bromley's (1992) differentiation between patriarchal (for example, the Unification Church, Krishna Consciousness, and most Christian-based communes) and feminist-empowerment groups (for example, Rajneesh movement, many forms of neo-pagan goddess-worship, and witchcraft groups) or even Aidala's distinction between religious and secular communes. Instead, as Palmer demonstrates, there is a surprising diversity of complex gender relations available to women in NRMs. For analytical purposes, she sorts the possibilities into a three-part typology of sexual ideologies: 'sex-polarity', 'sex-complementarity', and 'sex-unity'. As I will illustrate, however, Palmer alone highlights the real diversity of new religious beliefs, practices, and organizational forms through which each of these sexual ideologies may be expressed.

Sex-polarity groups (such as Krishna Consciousness, 3HO, the Rajneesh movement, and many kinds of feminist and lesbian goddess-worship) view 'the sexes as spiritually distinct, separate, and unessential or irrelevant to the other's salvation'. The spiritual superiority of one sex is asserted, and the sexes are usually only 'permitted to engage in limited, highly controlled relationships'. Sex-complementarity groups, like the Unification Church, the Church Universal and Triumphant, and the Mormons, regard 'each sex as endowed with different spiritual qualities and emphasize the importance of marriage for uniting two halves of the same soul to form one, complete androgynous being.' It is often thought that the right marriage and procreation will help 'usher in the millennium' (Palmer, 1994: 10). In the case of sex-unity groups, the body and gender are seen 'as a superficial layer of false identity obscuring the immortal, sexless spirit', and such groups often believe in 'letting go of sex identification'. For the Raëlians, the followers of Bo and Peep, and Scientologists, one's sex is open to choice and change by various means (such as elective surgery, theories of cloning, or reincarnation).

No matter how the links between gender and salvation are envisioned, many different paths to enlightenment exist within each type. For instance, the sex-polarity category encompasses such seemingly antithetical groups as Krishna Consciousness and the Rajneesh movement. The International Society for Krishna Consciousness is a communal organization that allows the development of families but seeks largely to segregate the sexes, even after marriage. In spiritual matters the male quest for salvation takes priority, and male householders are ultimately expected to abandon their families and return to the celibate life in their quest for spiritual purity. For women the spiritual ideal is the obedient, devoted, and supportive wife. The movement founded by Bhagwan Shree Rajneesh, on the other hand, is libertarian in its sexual relations. Following the Tantric tradition in Indian religious philosophy, brief and intense sexual experimentation between the sexes within a communal policy of free love is the primary means of securing the inner knowledge and detachment from conventionality that is essential to psychological well-being and spiritual enlightenment. The inspirational messages and spiritual exercises of Rajneesh place a priority on the superior spiritual energy and wisdom of the feminine. Accordingly, traditional female gender roles are rejected in favour of a spiritualization of the role of 'lover', and the leadership of the group tends to be dominated by women.

As might be expected given these differences, Palmer found that the two NRMs attract markedly different kinds of women. Note the many ways in which her observations resonate with things said in the two preceding chapters:

> Women joining the Krishna Consciousness movement tend to be young— in their late teens to early twenties—and tend to be from middle to upper-middle-class families. Judging from the interviews, they remember their family life as materially privileged but dysfunctional, and themselves as abused or neglected children. Many of them appear to be exchanging the uncontrolled, arbitrary patriarchy of their fathers' rule for what they consider a benevolent system of male protection based on the authority of an ancient lineage of guru succession. The ISKCON community, therefore, beckons to these women as a safe haven where masculine tyranny and passion has no place; where they will find protection and will not be sexually exploited (Palmer, 1994: 42).[3]

> . . . I would argue that [the Rajneesh] movement attracts a type of woman: the middle-aged, upper-middle-class woman who is accustomed to independence and a lucrative employment, and who tends to be childless, unmarried, and highly educated. Moreover, this type of woman chooses to participate in this NRM because it offers an alternative philosophy of sexuality that is consistent with her previous lifestyle, and that validates her life choices. Finally, it will be argued on the basis of data found in the interviews that the role of 'lover', as defined by Rajneesh, is perceived by these women as offering religious solutions to problems of intimacy and family life that they have encountered in their previous life. (Palmer, 1994: 45)[4]

In the face of such diversity, Palmer insists nevertheless that, in line with the insights of Aidala, Davidman, and others, the seven NRMs she studied share common features that display an abiding concern with problems of gender ambiguity and sexual abuse experienced by contemporary women (1994: 209–10):

1. 'Each group rejects the courting phase in favor of arranged marriage or instant intimacy';

2. 'Each group emphasizes one (or at most two) role(s) for their women,' defining them as sacred and rejecting all other roles as profane;

3. 'Each group rejects the model of the child-centered family by providing cooperative day care, and . . . either delaying parenthood, shortening its term (ISKCON), or . . . [abandoning] parenthood altogether.'

It is these common features, she suggests, that have led women to join NRMs in pursuit of a '*safe and sacred environment* where they can explore their sexual identity and pursue their relationships with men' (Palmer, 1994: 232). The women are seeking an environment free of the anxieties stemming from such problems as high divorce rates, the unjust burden of working mothers, the weakening of the bond between parents and their children, child abuse, sexual harassment, homosexuality, AIDS, wife-beating, abortion, and the heartbreaks of romantic love (Palmer, 1994: 210, 219).

Two twists emerge from Palmer's rich interview data and observations. First, women are drawn to various movements not just because they provide a way to escape gender abuses and ambiguities in society or moral accountability, but also because the 'theologies of love' of the various charismatic leaders and the behaviour of their followers promise a sacred haven. 'Rather than insisting that women join NRMs to pursue particular kinds of relationships,' she states (Palmer, 1994: 235–6), 'it might be more accurate to suggest that they join to find a hidden, sacred meaning or spiritual dimension to their interpersonal relationships—a dimension that appears to be lacking in secular, contractual relationships.' In other words, the declarations of the women she met convinced her of the need to be particularly leery of falling too readily into a fully reductive interpretation. These women could have had recourse to other solutions to their problems (for example, through careers, therapy, or various secular movements and causes), but they preferred to find spiritual solutions to the negative consequences of social change. They were after a spiritualized sense of their sexuality (1994: 236–7).

These new devotees are quite different, then, from the secular women joining a large Orthodox synagogue studied by Davidman (1990: 389).

Nearly every woman I interviewed specifically mentioned a longing for family and a committed relationship as an important factor in her attraction to Orthodox Judaism. The dominant theme that comes through in my interviews is not the search for God or metaphysical truth or spiritual experience. In fact, half of the women at Metropolitan Synagogue were not even sure they believe in God! Yet every woman I spoke with spontaneously highlighted the salience of her desire for a family.

Is the difference between Palmer's and Davidman's findings simply a function of their different samples—true cults versus a more conventional sectarian form of religious expression? Or do the differences strictly lie in the interpretive proclivities of the two authors? Davidman (1990: 388) notes that the women in her sample are older (in their thirties), well educated, and tend to work in well-paid positions in business or the professions. Could there, in fact, be more similarities between these women and the kinds of women Palmer found to be attracted to the Rajneesh movement than the surface clash of the authors' interpretations suggests? As ever, there are no clear and easy answers, and the perspectives point to the need for more detailed comparative studies.

Second, and contrary once again to the thrust of the argument of Aidala, Davidman, and others, Palmer concludes (1994: 262):

> Our data suggest that the innovations in sex roles and sexual mores presently developing in NRMs, far from representing a conservative reaction against mainstream experimentation and feminism, might more accurately be characterized as offering even more extreme, intensified, and diverse versions of the ongoing experimentation already occurring outside these utopias. The highly organized and strictly supervised group experiments occurring in NRMs appeal to prospective members as safe havens in which they might engage in more radical forms of experimentation than are possible in the secular sphere. Our informants appear to be responding not so much to gender ambiguity per se (Aidala 1985, 287), but to the disorganized and haphazard ways in which 'sexual experiments' were being conducted in the larger society.

Palmer (1994) believes these findings – with the discovery of different sexual ideologies in NRMs, the diversity of women attracted to different NRMs, and the sex ratios of different NRMs – 'challenge prevailing notions that "cult women" are the passive victims of the ineluctable forces of charisma and "brainwashing"' (p. 240). Just as the evidence discrediting brainwashing seems to be wilfully ignored by certain seasoned exponents, so deviancy lives on in public debate despite the descriptions offered by Palmer and others. The more typical cult experience is one of sexual and gender experimentation that people engage in to suit their particular needs. While we must be vigilant regarding the rights and safety of children, to dismiss alternative ideologies and gender roles as deviant is too simplistic a judgement of other people's constitutionally defended freedoms.

Chapter Seven

Why Do Some New Religious Movements Become Violent?

I began this book by remarking on the inadequacy and hostility of the public response to the mass murder-suicide of the Solar Temple (l'Order du Temple solaire) in 1994. Like the Jonestown massacre of 1978 and the Waco debacle of 1993, the unexpected deaths of the Solar Temple galvanized public alarm about NRMs. In the minds of a public that is rarely directly affected by cult activities, these and other mass suicides and murders have heightened the exaggerated fears spread by the anti-cult movement (see Table 1).

Responding to the Recent 'Cult' Tragedies

These tragedies are fuel for the fire of cult controversy,[1] but the anti-cult movement's reliance on the brainwashing scenario does not help us understand them. The explanations offered in so many documentaries are no better. Purporting to tell the 'whole' or 'true' story, these journalistic accounts describe the events immediately preceding the disaster, mentioning the benefits enjoyed by the group leaders as an imputation of who is to blame. Exploiting the lurid appeal of these tragedies, popular investigators speculate too readily about what happened and why, raising the spectres of criminality and insanity. The images in our memory of the sun-bloated bodies of Jonestown, the Davidian compound in Waco burning to the ground, the charred remains of the Solar Temple members, and the neatly arranged and cloaked bodies of Heaven's Gate, defy such easy treatment. We are just beginning to discern some of the complex conditions that may have led these people to collectively sacrifice themselves for their religious visions of the future.

Detailed studies have been undertaken of many of the major cult tragedies (see Table 1); can we now say something more about the forces that precipitate cult violence? Are there some common factors that might help us to discern if and why such tragedies may happen again? Others have already reconstructed what happened to the Peoples Temple, the Branch Davidians, the Solar Temple, Heaven's Gate, and Aum Shinrikyō; my focus is on the more generic question of why such events happen at all.[2]

TABLE I – CULT TRAGEDIES

NRM	Location and Year	Number of Deaths	Research Literature
Peoples Temple	Jonestown, Guyana; November 1978	914 (mostly suicide)[3]	Hall (1987, 1990, 2000) Chidester (1988) Maaga (1998) Wessinger (2000) Walliss (2004)
Branch Davidians	Waco, Texas; April 1993	80 (murder-suicide)	Tabor and Gallagher (1995) Wright (1995b) Hall (2000, 2002) Wessinger (2000) Docherty (2001) Walliss (2004)
Solar Temple	Switzerland, Quebec, and France; October 1994, December 1995, March 1997	53 (murder-suicide) 16 (suicide) 5 (suicide)[4]	Introvigne (1995) Mayer (1999) Hall and Schuyler (2000) Wessinger (2000) Inrovigne and Mayer (2002) Walliss (2004)
Aum Shinrikō	Tokyo, Japan; May 1995	12 (murdered [and thousands injured]) 23 (previous murders)	Lifton (1999) Hall and Trinh (2000) Wessinger (2000) Reader (2000, 2002) Walliss (2004)
Heaven's Gate	San Diego, California; March 1997	39 (suicide)	Hall (2000) Wessinger (2000) Balch and Taylor (2002) Walliss (2004
Movement for the Restoration of the Ten Commandments	Uganda; March 2000	780 (murder-suicide)	Mayer (2001) Melton and Bromley (2002) Walliss (2004)

In answering this question, I will not attempt to psychoanalyze the individuals involved. In my opinion it is far too difficult, and probably unnecessary, to determine if the followers and leaders of the Peoples Temple, Branch Davidians, Solar Temple, Aum Shinrikō, and Heaven's Gate fit some problematic 'personality type' (narcissistic, authoritarian, or whatever), and to conclude how this psychological type may be prone to violence under certain circumstances. In each case we simply do not know enough about the psychology of the actual members of these groups. However, the behaviour of these sacrificed souls can be at least partially explained by calling on some simpler, well-known, and more empirically substantiated principles of social psychology—principles that seem to apply to all of us.

NRMs and Violence

In a media environment fraught with emotion and suspicion, dubious claims are made and accepted, minor wrongdoings exaggerated, and exonerating reports downplayed or ignored (see Melton, 1992b; Melton and Bromley, 2002). As mentioned in the previous chapter, the police raids in which children were taken from their cult-following parents in Spain, Australia, Argentina, and England followed widely circulated yet often anonymous reports of child abuse (see Box 6). To find the reports of how the courts dismissed the charges, however, one had to search the back pages of the newspapers (see Richardson, 1996a: 894–9).

Violence can occur in new or marginal religions. As Melton (1992b; and Melton and Bromley, 2002) carefully documents, groups like the Black Muslims, Synanon, Hare Krishna, Scientology, House of Judah, the Children of God, Church Universal and Triumphant, and various fringe Mormon and Christian groups have been involved in incidents of assault, the harassment of opponents or defectors, the stockpiling of weapons, interference with or resistance to civil authorities, abuse of children, death threats, and even, in a few instances, murder. Three points must be kept in mind. First, in all but a few cases the incidents in question have not been systematically linked to any specific policies of the religious groups.[5] Rather, they appear to be the aberrant acts of overzealous or unstable individuals. In some cases, the defensive or paranoid attitudes of religious leaders helped to motivate some members to commit illegal and dangerous acts (although the circumstances differ). Second, when one considers the claims made by the anti-cult movement itself about the number of NRMs in existence (stated to be 3,000 or more), and the number of people ever involved (often stated to be about ten million in the United States alone), then the number of incidents of cult violence is not exceptional, especially compared to the high levels of violent crime in America. Third, one need only think of the cases of child molestation that have recently scandalized the Catholic Church to appreciate that NRMs have no monopoly on deviant behaviour. Few people would condemn the Catholic Church as a whole for the errant ways of some of its members. Placed in proper cultural context, then, the crimes of most NRMs are rather ordinary, though regrettable and worthy of condemnation. The tragedies of Jonestown, Waco, the Solar Temple, Aum Shinrikō, Heaven's Gate, and the Movement for the Restoration of the Ten Commandments call out for special attention precisely because they are extraordinary, even within the context of other known incidents of cult violence.

As the historical reconstruction of these events has demonstrated, each tragedy is the result of the confluence of a rather idiosyncratic set of factors, so it is not easy to draw general conclusions. In fact, as Robbins and Anthony (1995: 237) point out, the eruption of violence stems from the interaction of a diverse array of external circumstances, which they call 'exogenous factors', and internal processes, which they call 'endogenous factors', and 'the relative weight or significance of the contributions of exogenous and endogenous factors may vary from one . . . event to another.' Robbins and Anthony (1995: 237–8) use a comparison of Jonestown and Waco to illustrate their point:

> To elicit a fatal violent response from Jim Jones's Peoples Temple required only that a congressman and a press entourage visit Jonestown and attempt to return to the United States with a handful of defectors. In contrast, to set off the immolations in Waco (assuming that the Davidians were responsible for setting the fire), what had to transpire was not only the initial military-style raid on the 'cult compound' by the Bureau of Alcohol, Tobacco, and Firearms (BATF) but also the subsequent breaking down of the walls of the compound by armoured vehicles and the insertion of CS gas. It may therefore be a viable thesis that the role or weight of exogenous factors was smaller at Jonestown compared to Waco. Or to put it another way, the Branch Davidian community at Waco was less internally volatile or violence-prone than the Peoples Temple settlement in Guyana.

The exogenous factors that condition cult-related violence (for example, the nature and levels of the hostility, stigmatization, and persecution experienced by a group) vary widely and are difficult to compare. With the endogenous features, however, at least three have been repeatedly linked to violence: (1) apocalyptic beliefs, or at least world-rejecting beliefs; (2) unusually strong psychological and emotional investments in charismatic leadership; and (3) processes of social encapsulation that set in place ever stronger symbolic and physical barriers between the members of some NRMs and the rest of society (see Smith, 1982; Mills, 1982; Wallis and Bruce, 1986; Galanter, 1989; Hall, 1990; Robbins and Anthony, 1995; Palmer, 1996; Robbins, 2002). No single factor will generate violent behaviour, nor will the simple combination of these three. Instead, they constitute some of the prime conditions 'necessary' for the eruption of major incidents of cult-related violence, although they are not 'sufficient' to predict this violence.

Apocalyptic Beliefs

In each of the recent instances of mass religious violence involving NRMs, apocalyptic beliefs—prophecies about the ultimate end of human history—have played a crucial role. Such prophecies date back to antiquity and are present in almost all cultures, but they have been particularly strong in the West, especially in the Christian tradition. Biblical sources have stimulated speculation about and preparation for the time when 'time shall be no more', prompting many violent episodes over the centuries. In 1525, for example, during the Protestant Reformation, visions of a new age and the final triumph of good over evil inspired the radical and charismatic Protestant theologian Thomas Münster to lead a mass revolt, known as the Peasants' War. This ill-conceived venture resulted in his own execution and the death of tens of thousands of his followers (see Lewy, 1974: 110–16; Boyer, 1992: 58). A similar gruesome fate befell the Anabaptist followers of Jan Matthys, as mentioned in Chapter 6.[6]

These well-known incidents from European history are far from unique. The Middle Ages were marked by hundreds of apocalyptic uprisings, all with disastrous results (Cohn, 1961). Similar beliefs have persisted into the modern world, playing a prominent role in the cultural history of the United States. The scholar Paul Boyer writes: 'From the early seventeenth century through to the late eighteenth century, the entire span of American colonial history was marked by speculation about America's role in God's plan. That the colonizing venture began at a time of intense apocalyptic awareness in England meant that it, like everything else in these years, took on an aura of eschatological [i.e. involving doom and judgment] meaning' (1992: 68). Though less prevalent in the nineteenth century, prophecies of the imminent end of the world inspired many uniquely American religious groups, like the Millerite movement of the 1830s and 40s, which gave rise to the Seventh Day Adventists; the new apocalyptic vision of Joseph Smith, which laid the foundations of the

Church of Latter Day Saints (that is, the Mormons); and the apocalyptic claims of Charles Taze Russell, which undergird the teachings of the Jehovah's Witnesses. In fact, talk of the apocalypse permeated the revivalistic culture of the Methodist and Baptist churches throughout the nineteenth century and continues to this day. One need only listen to a Billy Graham crusade to hear the familiar apocalyptic refrains and admonitions repeated over and over again.

THE BASIS OF APOCALYPTIC BELIEFS

But what is the basis of this apocalyptic fervour? God's plan for the end of human history is laid out, in rather cryptic form, in four main texts of the Bible: in the Old Testament the important passages are chapters 37–9 of the Book of Ezekiel and the Book of Daniel; in the New Testament, the relevant sources are the thirteenth chapter of the Gospel of Mark and the Book of Revelation. The latter text, the last book of the Bible, is the best known, most influential, and most extensive account of the apocalypse. The Book of Revelation presents a narrative of the 'end times' of staggering symbolic complexity, ambiguity, and detail. The account takes the form of the prophetic vision of John of Patmos, a Christian being persecuted by the Romans. In nineteen chapters, the Book of Revelation gives a detailed and truly bizarre description of the miraculous events that will precede and accompany the return of Christ to earth and the beginning of a millennium of peace. The early Christians eagerly awaited the events foretold, for John's vision states that 'the time is at hand' (Revelation 1:3). Throughout the centuries, however, countless people have believed that the events of their own times conformed to the events prophesied by John, and so they have prepared themselves to meet their Maker and to suffer the terrible tribulations that they have been told will first afflict humanity. For the time just before the end, the time of apocalypse, is to be bloody indeed, as numerous wars and natural disasters, such as plagues, earthquakes, and fires from heaven, are destined to ravage the earth and its people. All is to culminate in a final colossal battle—Armageddon—between the forces of evil, led by Satan's representative on earth—a world ruler called the anti-Christ—and the forces of good, led by a warrior Christ.

The fate awaiting us is so horrific in scope and kind that, as the Bible says, 'in those days men shall seek death, and shall not find it; and shall desire to die, and death shall flee from them' (Revelation 9:6). Calamity after calamity is described by John, with an imagery that is strange to our modern minds, as exemplified by the following passage:

And I saw the seven angels which stood before God; and to them were given seven trumpets.

And another angel came and stood at the altar, having a golden censer; and there was given unto him much incense, that he should offer it with the prayers of all saints upon the golden altar which was before the throne. . . .

And the angel took the censer, and filled it with fire of the altar, and cast it into the earth: and there were voices, and thunderings, and lightnings, and an earthquake.

And the seven angels which had the seven trumpets prepared themselves to sound.

The first angel sounded, and there followed hail and fire mingled with blood, and they were cast upon the earth: and the third part of trees was burnt up, and all the green grass was burnt up.

And the second angel sounded, and as it were a great mountain burning with fire was cast into the sea: and a third of the sea became blood....

And the fifth angel sounded, and I saw a star fall from heaven unto the earth: and to him was given the key of the bottomless pit.

And he opened the bottomless pit; and there arose a smoke out of the pit, as the smoke of a great furnace; and the sun and the air were darkened. . . .

And there came out of the smoke locusts upon the earth: and unto them was given power, as the scorpions of the earth have power.

And it was commanded them that they should not hurt the grass of the earth, neither any green thing . . . but only those men which have not the seal of god in their foreheads.

And to them it was given that they should not kill them, but that they should be tormented five months: and their torment was as the torment of a scorpion, when he striketh a man....
(Revelation 8:2–8, 9:1–5; Authorized Version)

This passage, though typical, is also one of the milder and most comprehensible in the Book of Revelation, and the disasters it foretells are only a small part of a series of repeated assaults upon the earth. Since the eighteenth century some have believed that a small population of the elect— 144,000 faithful souls—are to be spared and taken up into heaven, in what is called 'the rapture'. Countless others, redeemed by their prolonged struggle with these calamities and the forces of the anti-Christ, will also eventually be blessed with eternal bliss here on earth. In the end, after many clashes, Satan and his earthly and spiritual minions are to be consigned to an eternity of torment in 'the lake of fire'.

The details of John's revelation, barely suggested here, have baffled, per-
plexed, and fascinated scholars and lay people alike for centuries. The
obscure yet graphic imagery of John's apocalyptic vision has given rise to
countless interpretations. For David Koresh and the Branch Davidians, the
decoding of the Book of Revelation was a pivotal concern. It obsessed
Koresh while he struggled to resist the BATF and FBI agents that had laid
siege to his home. He tried to speak with the FBI negotiators for hours about
the need to understand the ways of God, as given in the Book of Revelation
and elsewhere, in order to understand his community and his own future
course of action. At his death he was working on a manuscript in which he
was deciphering the revelation and his own role in the cosmic drama. He
said he would surrender to the authorities upon its completion, and as best
we can tell it was almost complete. But the FBI agents had run out of
patience. They had already cast Koresh as a crazy man or a terrorist. They
were not particularly interested in nor very sympathetic to his religious
monologues, which they dismissed as 'Bible babble' (Tabor, 1995: 266;
Sullivan, 1996: 221; Docherty, 2001). Unable to turn him from his endless
preoccupation with religious concerns, they soon stopped listening and
decided to apply the tactics of 'psychological warfare' to the Davidian compound. The power and water were cut off, communication with the outside
world was blocked, and the men, women, and children in the compound
were bombarded with bright lights and loud noises such as Tibetan chants,
sounds of rabbits and lambs dying, and rock music, while helicopters hov-
ered overhead throughout the day and night.

No effort was made to grasp the dynamics of biblical apocalypticism by
calling on the help of religious scholars to address Koresh in the language
with which he understood his situation. From the perspective of the
Davidians, then, surely the anti-Christ and his minions were at the door,
dressed in the tactical combat gear of the BATF and FBI. The prophecies of
the apocalypse were coming true! Perhaps a knowledgeable dialogue about
the texts with which he interpreted his world could have led Koresh to
think otherwise? We will never know, because the FBI chose to ignore the
advice of its own behavioural scientists, who urged greater patience, tactical withdrawal, and the opening of more channels of religious dialogue
(Wright, 1995a; Ammerman, 1995: 290–1; Sullivan, 1996: 219–20;
Docherty, 2001). The police chose instead to launch the final assault. Four
tanks spraying CS gas[7] were used to crash holes in the walls of the compound, and though the FBI could see that the Davidians were using
kerosene lanterns to light their home, no fire trucks were on hand when a
blazing fire soon engulfed the fragile wooden structure, killing Koresh and
almost all of his followers, including sixteen children under the age of five.[8]

An apocalyptic world view may, of course, stem from or largely incorporate materials from elsewhere than the Bible. The Solar Temple, for example, grew out of a very long and very complicated tradition of secret neo-Christian mystical organizations based on ancient and medieval lore about the quest for the Holy Grail and the teachings and tragic fate of a powerful twelfth-century ascetic order of warrior monks called the Knights Templar (Introvigne, 1995). To this already eclectic mixture of beliefs and practices the Solar Temple added a variety of occult notions 'ranging from Rosicrucianism to Egyptian thanatology to Luc Jouret's oriental folk medicine and ecological apocalypticism' (Palmer, 1996: 305). Through a complex manipulation of these diverse ideas, the core members of the Temple were prompted to believe that the time was right to protect the group from what appeared to be imminent collapse. This final act of self-defence took the form of a radical and final 'transit' of the membership, through the ritual orchestration of their physical deaths, to a higher level of spiritual existence in another part of the galaxy. The apocalyptic beliefs in question, in other words, were significantly different from those guiding the Branch Davidians or the Peoples Temple, but the consequences were much the same (as carefully reconstructed in the accounts of the events surrounding the tragedy provided by, Introvigne, 1995; Palmer, 1996; Mayer, 1999; Hall et al., 2000).

Much the same can be said about Heaven's Gate, the California cult that committed suicide when the comet Hale-Bopp came into view in 1997 (see Balch and Taylor, 2002). One need only read the advertisement that the group ran in *USA Today* in 1993, or the website they later created. In both places, Do (the leader previously known as Peep) issues the same warning: 'The earth's present "civilization" is about to be recycled—spaded under. Its inhabitants are refusing to evolve. The "weeds" have taken over the garden and disturbed its usefulness beyond repair' (Steiger and Hewes, 1997: 179, 196). In the days immediately preceding their suicide, the group's website declared: 'Red Alert. Hale-Bopp Brings Closure.' Here and elsewhere, in line with their own synthesis of traditional religious themes and contemporary UFO mythology, they frankly announced their plans to leave their earthly 'containers' (that is, their bodies), to be carried to their new home in 'The Evolutionary Level Beyond Human (the "Kingdom of Heaven")' by a UFO thought to be accompanying the comet Hale-Bopp as it approached close to earth (Steiger and Hewes, 1997: 207).

THE BEHAVIOURAL CONSEQUENCES OF APOCALYPTIC BELIEFS

There can be little doubt, then, that the Branch Davidians were prepared to die for their beliefs, whether in fact they were ultimately responsible for their own deaths or not. And the members of the Solar Temple and Heaven's Gate acted with clear premeditation. So in what ways are these apocalyptic beliefs related to the potential for violence?

A number of behavioural consequences follow from the belief that we may be living in the last days (see Robbins and Anthony, 1995: 239–41). First, for a person anticipating the millennium of peace following Christ's return, conventional rules and norms, even the law itself, become relative. Of what good are the laws of humans, who are steeped in evil, in the face of the ultimate acts of divine justice and retribution? The righteous will not need the force of law to live in peace and joy, and the evil are destined to perish. Second, serious anticipation of the apocalypse entails preparing to deal with violent times and the persecution of the righteous by the Antichrist (before the return of Christ). Many of the saved will be forced to struggle long and hard with the forces of evil before their salvation; to that end, weapons must be secured and defences prepared, for example, by building shelters, storing supplies, and generally training to be self-suffi-cient. This anticipation of violence sets the stage for its actual occurrence, as people look for evidence to confirm their fears and legitimate their prepa-rations. In the process they will try to identify their enemies in advance. This leads to a third consequence: demonizing. Opponents are portrayed as capable of the most heinous acts; they can thus be fairly resisted with the most extreme force. Fourth, the language and symbolism of Christian apoc-alypticism are steeped in what has been called 'exemplary-dualism' (Robbins and Anthony, 1979a, 1987; Anthony and Robbins, 1997). All is either good or evil, of God or of Satan, and this sharply dichotomized view of the world 'confers deep eschatological significance on the social and political conflicts of the day, thereby raising the stakes of victory or defeat in immediate worldly struggles. Thus communism, radical feminism, the papacy, and exotic cults have all been identified by some Protestant mil-lenarians with the biblical Beast or the "Whore of Babylon"', other names for the Antichrist in the Book of Revelation (Robbins and Anthony, 1995: 243). From such a perspective, great importance can be attributed to rela-tively small events, precipitating a disproportionate response. Fifth and last-ly, a life lived in serious expectation of the apocalypse tends to instill an enthusiasm for the cause that can blind a person's judgement on matters both great and small.

The role of apocalyptic ideas in fostering extreme behaviour is readily documented. What is less easily realized is the depth of conviction and com-mitment that such ideas can inspire. This requires an act of considerable per-sonal and sociological imagination. One might keep in mind, however, that more than a year after the original death of fifty-three members of the Solar

Temple, sixteen more members chose to ritually kill themselves (21 December 1995). Then, even more surprisingly, five more members took their own lives on 22 March 1997. Exploring precisely why and how apocalyptic beliefs can have such a grip on people's consciousnesses goes well beyond the scope of what we can sensibly hope to address here (see Strozier, 1994; Lifton, 1999). Robbins and Anthony (1995: 249) call our attention, though, to one obviously important factor: 'Millenarian-apocalyptic worldviews are most likely to be associated with volatility and violence when they are embodied in charismatic "messianic" leaders who identify the millennial destiny of humankind with their own personal vicissitudes.' Charismatic leadership is itself problematic; combined with an apocalyptic conception of the world it can be lethal—but only if the charismatic pattern of authority enacted in an apocalyptic group takes on a specific character.

In saying all this, however, we must recognize that even though there have been many world-rejecting apocalyptic groups, few of them have been implicated in any acts of violence, towards themselves or others (Hall, 1990; Robbins and Anthony, 1995: 243). At present, many millions of Americans take the apocalyptic prophecies of the Bible seriously.[9] But before those beliefs can lead to dangerous actions, many other things, including the charismatic leadership we are going to examine next, must come into play.

Charismatic Leadership

'Prophecies', Robbins and Anthony dryly observe, 'presuppose prophets' (1995: 245), and most apocalyptic movements presuppose belief in at least two kinds of prophets: the original founders of the apocalyptic vision and contemporary figures who expound this vision to a new age. It is the destiny of the contemporary prophet to prepare the way for and to herald the completion of the original prophecy. Throughout history the relevance of apocalyptic lore to this world has been tied to the appearance of such a religious leader with charismatic authority.

Following Max Weber (1964: 324–92), sociologists have traditionally distinguished between three 'ideal types' of legitimate authority in society: traditional authority, charismatic authority, and rational-legal authority. Leaders are said to govern by tradition when their right to exercise authority over others is granted by the governed because it has simply always been so. Custom dictates that the nobility or others have the divine or natural right to rule. With rational-legal authority, however, the right to rule is identified with certain legally constituted offices, no matter who may occupy those public positions. The authority is invested in the position, not the person. For most of human history traditional authority has held sway, whereas the modern world is marked by the ascendency of different regimes of rational-legal authority, like those established by the English, American, French, Russian, and Chinese revolutions. History has also repeatedly witnessed, however, the rise to power of those who are granted the right to rule by virtue of their 'supernatural, superhuman, or at least specifically exceptional powers or qualities' (Weber, 1964: 358–9). This is charismatic authority, rooted in the display of seemingly divine gifts. One need only think of such powerful military and political figures as Alexander the Great, Julius Caesar, Napoleon, Hitler, Stalin, and Mao. But of course one also thinks of the founders of the world's great religions, the Buddha, Moses, Jesus, Mohammed, and many other prophets, sages, and saints from Saint Francis to Madame Blavatsky.

THE NATURE OF CHARISMA

True charisma, however, is not so much an attribute of someone's personality as it is a quality attributed by other people. No charisma exists without the recognition of a group, which then grants authority to the person on that basis; it is phenomenon born of social interaction. Moreover, as social analyses reveal, even the 'imputation of extraordinary qualities to the leader is a consequence of charismatic activities, not their foundation' (Couch, 1989: 274). Accordingly, many sociologists have begun to explore the ways in which charisma is acquired or 'socially constructed', how it operates, and how it can be lost (e.g. Wilson, 1975; Johnson, 1979; Wallis, 1982, 1984; Palmer, 1988; Couch, 1989; Bird, 1993; Gardner and Avolio, 1998). Being a charismatic leader need not be correlated with any virtues, intelligence, or even competence. It undoubtedly entails special talents—but of a diverse kind difficult to specify. Bryan Wilson complains (1975: 6–7) that the modern tendency to equate charisma simply with the attractiveness or appeal of politicians, entertainers, and other media personalities unduly dilutes the magic and religious quality of charismatic leadership. The sort of charisma shown by the prophets of the Old Testament, or indeed by Hitler, David Koresh (Branch Davidians), or Do (Heaven's Gate), may be less attractive,[10] yet they are able mysteriously to galvanize the commitment of followers in ways unparalleled by other forms of authority. As Weber (1964), Wilson (1975), Wallis (1982), and many others commentators have stressed, the authority of the charismatic leader is founded in a deeply personal relationship with his or her followers, a relationship of extraordinary faith and trust. We can say that the demand for such relationships stems, at least partially, from a simple origin: 'It is the easiest and perhaps the most natural recourse for [people] … in distress to believe that a father [or mother] will come and save them' (Wilson, 1975: 96).

THE PRECARIOUSNESS OF CHARISMATIC AUTHORITY

A crucial feature of charismatic leadership is that it is non-institutional or even anti-institutional. Charismatic leaders, Wilson asserts (1975: 9–10), in line with Weber (1964), are neither merely the admired begetters of a new order nor just gifted innovators (like President Abraham Lincoln or Bill Gates of Microsoft). As Weber classically presented them, charismatic leaders are romantic disrupters who abrogate and transcend social conventions. They tend to break the existing patterns of authority or harness even older ones to new circumstances. In the process they lift 'sanctions on previously proscribed behavior' (Wilson, 1975: 26). At the same time, of course, they impose new demands for obedience and new standards of service and sacrifice, but they do so within an emotionally charged framework of relationships and activities. The very personal style of leadership is intrinsically precarious, particularly in the modern context where rational-legal forms of social organization tend to dominate, and it can render this mode of leadership dangerous to the members of an NRM and to its opponents. The dynamics of a charismatically led group can produce a kind of feedback loop of 'deviance amplification', transforming the charismatic relationship into tyranny (Wallis, 1977: 208; Couch, 1989: 274–5). Claims to charismatic authority by a leader and their followers can bring persecution from outside the group and lead to power struggles within the group, and both processes tend to aggravate the tyranny and instability further.[11]

Outside their own groups, leaders of new religions in the contemporary West lack the conditions of social support that have traditionally existed for the prophets of old or that continue to exist for charismatic leaders in less industrially developed countries (for example, in much of India): 'In modern times, charismatic leadership persists only in the interstices between institutional orders, in the narrow social space that remains for collective behaviour, spontaneous faith and unconstrained obedience and adulation' (Wilson, 1975: 2). By default, charisma is now associated with such trivial phenomena as rock idols and movie stars. More authentic charismatic leaders are forced to struggle against the marginalization of their efforts by a society that neither understands nor respects the special deference granted to them. Through inevitable interactions with the larger society, charismatically led groups feel pressure to bring themselves into greater conformity with the dominant social values and systems of authority, but the constant struggle to resist this assimilation can infuse a dangerous paranoia into the dealings of charismatic leaders with outsiders. This seems to have been the case for Jim Jones and

Jonestown, the chief lieutenants of Bhagwan Shree Rajneesh during the struggle to establish Rajneeshpuram, and in the last months of the Solar Temple and Aum Shinrikyō.

The precariousness is compounded by the paradoxical problems caused by the very success of some charismatic leaders. A measure of bureaucracy inevitably accompanies the growth of these successful new religious organizations, and charismatic leaders display a marked inclination to resist this process.[12] It would seem that they fear the 'routinization' of their authority, to use Weber's well-known phrase. Past a certain point, leaders can no longer maintain the personal contact with all their followers that is the hallmark of charismatic authority. They cannot even personally supervise all the essential activities of their group. As in any organization, authority must be delegated to others, and associated with positions or offices rather than particular persons. The leaders often feel this shift to rational-legal modes of authority as an unacceptable weakening of their own power. In fact, with this shift 'some members will not be as emotionally dependent on the leader as others and thus will have less reason to grant total loyalty to the leader' (Johnson, 1979: 317).

Moreover, the delegation of authority may set in place the means for alternative sources of power to arise within these organizations. 'Large groups inevitably are more heterogeneous than small ones, and the effects of this heterogeneity compound the [leaders'] problem of maintaining firm or absolute control over all [their] followers' (Johnson, 1979: 317). Successful lieutenants may begin to usurp some of the prestige and power granted to the original charismatic leader.

Charismatic leaders are caught on the horns of a dilemma. They may wish to exercise ever greater control over an ever greater number of individuals and projects, but their continued charisma hinges on maintaining a delicate balance between exposure and secrecy. If too many people have too much contact with the leaders, their human frailties may show through, undermining the mystery and exaggeration essential to the aura of special authority.[13]

To maintain this crucial element of mystery as a group grows in size, many charismatic leaders deliberately begin to practise a measure of segregation from their followers. Access is restricted to those who are especially prepared, especially loyal, or very much in need of guidance, while occasions of mass exposure must be carefully managed to maximize their impact and minimize the chances of embarrassment. For the last twenty years of his life, for example, L. Ron Hubbard, the founder of Scientology, maintained a life of romantic secrecy and complete seclusion, sailing round the world on his yacht, accompanied by the elite Sea Org (mentioned in Chapter 2). Bhagwan Shree Rajneesh separated himself from his followers by taking a vow of silence. At occasional (and highly orchestrated) sessions, he used his eyes, actions, and thoughts alone to inspire and guide his devotees. One can often trace a pattern of concentric circles of delegated authority radiating out from the charismatic leader, with the real power in the hands of an inner cadre in close daily contact with the leader. These individuals act as gatekeepers to others clamouring for access to the leader.

In discussing the prophetic claims of Moses David (David Berg), the extravagant and mysterious leader of the Children of God/The Family, Roy Wallis (1982: 37) highlights some of the ramifications of this organizational tendency:

> Few things can be more precarious than a conception of oneself as a direct agency and voice of a God whose present doctrine and approved practice is so much at variance with tradition. So precarious a situation must be protected by considerable milieu control. Only those who are completely committed can be permitted to remain in contact with the source of everyone's self-conception. Considerable care must therefore be taken over the selection of those permitted access to the leader. If his standing is upset or denied, not only is the leader's self-conception jeopardized, but also that of everyone around him. Thus, the élite, the 'charismatic aristocracy' . . . have a substantial incentive to protect his environment. They will seek to exclude from interaction with the prophet all who might see him in terms of some earlier identity, or who—by the nature of their interaction with him—undermine or discredit his identity as a prophet. Not only will likely sceptics and critics be excluded, but also those who might primarily view him in terms other than his sacred status, for example, those who know and continue to treat him as father, husband, or mere expositor of the Bible.

But like the princes and viziers of old, 'the charismatic aristocracy' may itself come to pose a threat to the sovereignty of the king, sultan, or religious leader. These elite followers may gradually take control of the reins of power while conducting the daily business of the kingdom or religious empire. This is what appears to have happened to Bhagwan Shree Rajneesh, one of the most entrepreneurial and materially successful of the new gurus (see Milne, 1986; Palmer, 1988; Carter, 1990).

RESISTING THE ROUTINIZATION OF CHARISMA

Sociologists who have studied the likes of Moses David, Jim Jones, L. Ron Hubbard, and Bhagwan Shree Rajneesh have observed a tendency for these leaders to employ a common set of strategies to offset the external and internal pressures for change. On the one hand, they seek to resist the outside pressure to reduce the differences between an NRM and the rest of society. On the other hand, they wish to circumvent the pressures from inside the group for the 'routinization' of charisma just discussed. The strategies in question are presented as ways of maintaining the purity, intensity, and quality of the group's vision and commitment of these groups, in fact they may serve to do so. But they frequently have other deleterious consequences, ones that may jeopardize the members' safety.

What are these strategies? We can identify six conspicuous ones (as ever the distinctions between them are a bit theoretical and in real life they would appear as a messy state of affairs):

1. To keep followers off balance and their attention on the words and wishes of the charismatic leader, he or she may alter the doctrines and policies of the NRM, sometimes very suddenly. This may come about through the announcement of new visions or revelations or, more simply, with the claim that the group is ready to experience a deeper level of understanding of its beliefs and practices. Some leaders have proved to be most inventive in this regard, as two cases can illustrate.

Out of Dianetics, a psychological program of self-help, L. Ron Hubbard fashioned Scientology—a system of religious ideas and activities that kept expanding in scope and complexity for years. For example, 'to be Clear' was once the highest accomplishment for a Scientologist, but soon it was no more than an early, though foundational, qualification for progressing to a higher state of being, called the 'Operating Thetan' (see Wallis, 1977; Bainbridge and Stark, 1980; Bednarowski, 1989). Similarly, Chögyam Trungpa Rinpoche, the dynamic young leader of Vajradhatu/Shambhala, a new religion based on Tibetan Buddhism, attracted a large number of American adherents in the early 1970s with his highly approachable, casual, and Western style of presentation. In the mid-seventies, however, he sharply reversed course and imposed a much more austere, demanding, and traditional mode of Buddhist practice on his followers, chastising them for their laziness and countercultural appearance. Then, in the mid-1980s, just before his unexpected death, he suddenly switched gears again, initiating a plan to replace this tradition-bound and arduous path of enlightenment with a new system of meditative philosophy and practice called Shambhala Training. The new program was designed, once again, to present the truths of Tibetan Buddhism in a form more accessible to a wider Western audience (see Eldershaw and Dawson, 1995; Dawson and Eldershaw, 1998).

Shifts like these are intended to attract new members and tap new resources, but they are also used to force some of the old guard to the margins of the movements while elevating new people to the inner circle of devotees. The shifts have a levelling effect that reasserts the superiority of the leader to his or her followers. Meanwhile, the new structures of training, administration, and rewards that accompany the shifts fracture the patterns of influence and the personal and professional alliances that had been established within the organization. The change keeps the followers busy and diverted from challenging the leader, as they all become dependent on his or her guiding wisdom in the face of new ways of doing things.

2. Some charismatic leaders may need to seek constant reaffirmations of the loyalty from their followers, leading to an escalation in the demands they place on members for personal service and sacrifice to the group. This, too, is what many of the shifts in doctrine are about; often the new views, procedures, and administrative structures accompany new rituals or other acts of commitment. In the most notorious instance, Jim Jones asked his followers to undergo a series of 'White Nights' in which they rehearsed their final suicides. The members of the Peoples Temple never knew if the 'poison' they drank during these rituals was real. These nights prepared them to really sacrifice their lives when Jones eventually decided that only an act of 'revolutionary suicide' could protect the symbolic integrity of the group and its beliefs (see Chidester, 1988).

3. Like apocalyptic teachings, the precariousness of charismatic leadership reinforces the tendency of members to demonize their enemies (real or imagined). Charismatic leaders may play upon a group's fears of persecution by inventing new and ever greater enemies. By condemning the acts of others, the leaders can divert attention from their own failings and those of the group, providing a convenient excuse for any troubles. In the oldest political ploy known to humanity, the internal solidarity of the members is galvanized by the leader's call for unity in the face of new external threats.

The followers of Jim Jones, for example, lived in constant fear of a sudden midnight raid on their compound in Guyana by mercenaries hired by the CIA (Layton, 1998). The Japanese cult leader Ashara ironically claimed that American airplanes were trying to spray his compound with the very same Sarin nerve gas that Aum Shinrikyo⁻ eventually unleashed on the Tokyo subway. Do and Ti, the leaders of Heaven's Gate, invented a race of evil aliens, dark angels, intent on foiling their efforts to realize their true natures and escape a dying earth.

4. Charismatic leaders will often call into question the inspired messages of all competitors for authority, both external and internal to the group. As a rule dissent is stifled through the careful control of information and the public use of ridicule and other means of peer pressure. Any apparent source of alternative leadership arising within the group is marginalized or simply

ejected. Small and relatively inconsequential challenges to the authority of leaders are often seized upon as a pretext for fomenting a sense of crisis, effecting a shift in practices, justifying the movement of people in and out of the inner circle of the leader, and discrediting or expelling lieutenants who appear to be too popular or influential.

Jim Jones kept tight control over many of his lieutenants by granting or denying them the privilege of leaving their jungle outpost to see to the group's business in the United States and elsewhere. Loyalty was assured and delegated power held in check by the periodic and unpredictable recall of members to Jonestown (Layton, 1998). Do and Ti once removed complacent and nonconforming members of Heaven's Gate by rather ingeniously ordering them to establish a separate colony in Arizona, knowing that they would likely fail and defect from the group (Hall, 2000).

5. Similarly, many charismatic leaders test loyalty, heighten emotional dependence, and generally disrupt potential sources of alternative authority by criticizing or even physically separating couples and other close pairings within the religious groups. The bonds of romantic love, even those of good friendship, must not be allowed to take precedence over the tie to the charismatic leader (Wright, 1986). Of course, religious orders in almost all cultures have long recognized the need to regulate and suppress sexual attachments if higher spiritual ends are to be served; consider the monastic orders of the Catholic Church. But those devotees enter with a fuller knowledge of what they are sacrificing, as do members of prominent NRMs like the Unification Church and the Hare Krishna movement. (Both groups require celibacy of their members until the leaders decide who will marry whom, and even then they exercise a regulatory control over conjugal relations [see Galanter, 1989; Rochford, 1985].) Heaven's Gate insisted on strict celibacy and attempted to mask sexual differences by requiring everyone to wear the same loose-fitting clothing. Married couples were separated upon joining, and several people, emulating their leader Do, chose to have themselves surgically castrated.

In other instances, however, as with the Peoples Temple and with David Koresh at Waco (and sometimes in the Children of God/The Family, the Solar Temple, Synanon, and the Rajneesh movement), the leaders' control of their followers' sex lives is only introduced late in the history of the group. In an extreme instance, David Koresh eventually claimed a monopoly on sexual access to all the women in the Davidian compound. The commitment of the men to the apocalyptic world view of the group was tested by the requirement to surrender their wives, lovers, and daughters (often at quite a young age) to Koresh. The women involved supposedly considered it an honour to be with Koresh, the anointed messenger of God and the last of the prophets. Part of his task was to populate the world with his godly children, both spiritual and biological.

6. When all else fails, and sometimes earlier, some charismatic leaders have tried to consolidate their control and diminish countervailing influences by changing the location, and hence the operating environment, of their groups. Often these moves are to a more isolated spot. Jim Jones, for example, moved the Peoples Temple from Indianapolis to a secluded part of California, before eventually switching to the South American jungle (Chidester, 1988). Moses David removed the Children of God from southern California and for years the movement was scattered throughout Europe, South America, and the Far East (Davis and Richardson, 1976; Van Zandt, 1991; Chancellor, 2000). The Solar Temple began in Switzerland and France before attempting to establish itself in Quebec, with the hope of eventually fully relocating there (Palmer, 1988; Mayer, 1999). Over the protests of many of his followers, Chögyam Trungpa moved Vajradhatu/Shambhala from trendy Boulder, Colorado, to the (according to them) untrendy and provincial city of Halifax, Nova Scotia (Eldershaw and Dawson, 1995).

The implementation of these strategies, often done in an ad hoc and confusing manner, can have very deleterious effects for the stability of an NRM. The leader's choices can contribute to the group's social implosion, heightening the possibility of violence.

CRISES OF CHARISMATIC LEGITIMACY

These observations only capture part of the problem.

> Charismatic leaders, more so than traditional or rational-legal leaders, must sustain their own legitimacy. They exist largely without the external support of custom and established institutions. Any particular traditional leader is essentially just the temporary embodiment of a set of ingrained cultural expectations, while any particular rational-legal leader is only a representative of an abstract set of principles, rules and regulations. Alternatively, every charismatic leader is essentially a rule of custom or law unto themselves. Each of their actions either establishes, reinforces, or undermines their own authority. In fact, much of the authority of charismatic leaders stems from the very nature of the impressions they create in their daily interactions with others. As these patterns of interaction change, so does the very nature and viability of this authority.

> Charisma requires a kind of continuous legitimation work. Of course this is true to a lesser extent with the rule of custom or law as well.

Revolutions may happen when any particular manifestation of traditional or rational-legal authority is delegitimated by its own short-comings. But charismatic authority is far more dependent on an ongoing display of the prowess and virtues of the leader. This is why [Max] Weber considered charismatic leaders transitory historical figures and dedicated most of his [classic] analysis of charismatic authority to tracing the ways in which it will normally evolve into one of the other two types (Weber, 1964: 363-386). When this evolution fails to occur in a charismatically led group, it will either soon cease to be or it will implode and become unstable. It is the latter path of development that often leads to violent behaviour and confrontations. Fundamentally, the potential for violence in new religious movements stems, in part, from failing to cope with the more or less perpetual legitimation crisis experience by charismatic leaders (Dawson, 2002: 85).

To fully appreciate the social dynamics of the generation of violence in NRMs, we need to develop a much more elaborate appreciation of the cross-cutting management pressures that bedevil the charismatic leaders of controversial religious groups. I have identified at least three other interrelated and common legitimation problems: (1) maintaining the leader's image, (2) moderating the psychological identification of followers with the leader, and (3) achieving new successes. The details of each of these additional problems goes beyond the needs of this introductory discussion. But in each of the NRMs that became violent there is evidence that their leaders crucially mismanaged various crises of legitimacy born of these problems (see Dawson, 2002). It is these failures, when combined with the behavioural effects of holding strong apocalyptic beliefs and the processes of social encapsulation, that set the conditions that induced choices that resulted in violence.[14]

The groups that suffered from this descent into violence were drawn into the cycle of 'deviance amplification' mentioned earlier. The attempts made to perpetuate and intensify leaders' powers, and the increased homogenization and dependence of the followers, set the conditions for the charismatic leaders to indulge the 'darker desires of their subconscious' (a phrase used by Wallis and Bruce, 1986; cited in Robbins and Anthony, 1995: 247). This in turn heightened the negative response of the surrounding society, and the resultant hostility increased the fears, anxiety, and paranoia of the members of the NRM—a fear shared by the charismatic leader and also exploited. In the standard deviance amplification model, conflict with state authorities or other presumed enemies can have a catalytic effect, sending the group into a potentially fatal cycle of negative feedback with the rest of society.

Social Encapsulation

The last piece of the puzzle in explaining cult violence involves the processes of social encapsulation. New religious movements, Marc Galanter (1989) suggests, form small yet fairly complete social systems. To survive, all social systems must satisfy certain requirements. Amongst other things, they need to receive and respond to feedback (either in terms of comments and reactions from communities outside the system, or the criticisms of those within) and to maintain system boundaries. Interference with either of these can lead to dysfunction and violence. The increased isolation characteristic of many apocalyptic and charismatically led groups can have a disruptive effect on their functioning, preventing sufficient feedback and heightening the threat members perceive in any incursions on their boundaries.[15]

The isolation and the boundaries are both social and physical. The members of the Solar Temple, for example, never ceased to participate physically in the daily activities of life in Europe, Quebec, and elsewhere. They had regular jobs, families, and homes, and they frequently interacted with outsiders. But they also cultivated a profound sense of themselves as a distinct community, a spiritual elite that, while in this world, was symbolically set apart from it. Special knowledge and rites were used to establish and maintain a clear social boundary around the group. As the end drew near, the leaders and many of the core members of the Temple strove to tighten this boundary to resist the inquiries of the governments of Switzerland, Quebec, and Australia into their affairs (see Palmer, 1996; Mayer, 1999) and the potentially embarassing revelations of ex-members.

In the case of Koresh and his followers, the Davidians had built a compound in the rural area outside the city of Waco, Texas. They had chosen to segregate themselves physically, as well as socially and symbolically. Since the community was not fully self-sufficient, many members still had to travel out to work, buy groceries, see doctors, and so on, but the communal life within the compound, as well as regular participation in Koresh's lengthy and strenuous Bible study sessions (often lasting all day or all night), welded the group together and helped to separate the Davidians from their neighbours. This separation was partly a matter of the followers' sense of their own identities, shaped by their dedication to a transcendent cause (Tabor and Gallagher, 1995; Bromley and Silver, 1995; Docherty, 2001).

The initial situation of the Peoples Temple was similar as well, especially during the prosperous years the group spent in Ukiah in northern California, and then in San Francisco. When things began to sour, the threat of persecution prompted Jim Jones to raise the physical barriers round his group and to tighten his control. He hastened his departure for Jonestown, which he had already begun to build, and persuaded many of his most loyal followers to move there with him. In the jungle of Guyana, the community was almost totally cut off from outside influences (Chidester, 1988; Layton, 1998), and the feedback that all systems require began to dwindle.

In fact, each of these groups found itself in circumstances where feedback, especially of a negative sort, was suppressed. Negative feedback performs an important regulatory function in any social system, whether it comes from within the system or from outside. In NRMs, internal and external complaints and resistance exert a moderating effect on the pursuit of apocalyptic visions and the authoritarian proclivities of some charismatic leaders. Negative feedback is part of what helps a social system to maintain its equilibrium. Cut off from the outside world, socially and physically, it is quite possible that the Solar Temple, the Branch Davidians, the Peoples Temple, and, we might speculate, Heaven's Gate and the Movement for the Restoration of the Ten Commandments all lost an essential source of negative feedback. Without access to the reactions of outsiders, it may have become increasingly difficult for their members to gauge whether the behaviour of the group was becoming too bizarre and maladaptive. Turned in on themselves and feeling threatened, the members may have become preoccupied with hiding or destroying any signs of weakness, perhaps suppressing individuals with complaints or simply alternative views. In each instance the resultant homogenization and social encapsulation of the members may have made the groups paranoid about transgressions on their symbolic boundaries.

Ironically, in seeking to strengthen their boundaries against an apparent external threat, each group may have become too rigid in its internal functioning and increasingly unrealistic in its dealings with the rest of the world. By being tightened, the boundaries may have become brittle and even more susceptible to symbolic violation. In most cases, however, we have too little detailed evidence to know exactly what happened.

Thinking of Jonestown, the most extreme and best-documented case, Galanter notes (1989: 124) that the mere 'arrival of Congressman Ryan and his entourage', which included several hostile ex-members of the Peoples Temple, was sufficient to precipitate the final act of mass suicide. Why? Because it 'portended the imminent disruption of the group's *control over its boundary*' (emphasis in the original).

> Ryan's visit jeopardized the system's integrity. The fact that four cult members chose to leave with him posed a challenge to the group's monitoring of the membership. Moreover, an intrusion by the U.S. federal government

meant that suppression of negative feedback could no longer be absolute. On both counts, it was reasonable for Jones to fear that the cult could no longer operate in total identification with his will. In deciding to assault the Congressman, he realized that, 'They will try to destroy us.' Once it became apparent that his cult's boundary could no longer be secured, Jones chose to preserve its identity in spirit if not in living membership.

Did something similar happen to the members of Heaven's Gate, contributing to their unexpected deaths? We do not know enough about what happened; unlike Jonestown or Waco, there were no survivors to tell the tale.[16] But from the work of Robert Balch, the sociologist who studied this group in its earlier guise as the Bo and Peep UFO cult, it appears that a process of social encapsulation had begun twenty years earlier. In 1976, Bo and Peep (also known as The Two, and later as Ti and Do) decided to impose a systematic policy of social and sometimes physical isolation on their followers, combined with a comprehensive regime of daily activities designed to breach the social customs and routines we all have learned so thoroughly. With little advance notice, Bo and Peep regularly moved their followers from one place to another, and from one kind of environment to another. As they moved from state to state in the American West, they lived in rugged campsites, inner-city homes, suburban homes, large and small farms and ranches, and finally a three-million-dollar mansion. In every locale, elaborate schedules of daily activities and training exercises were introduced that were followed meticulously for a time, only to be either gradually modified or suddenly abandoned altogether. By these means, Bo and Peep sought to free their followers from their 'attachments to the human level' in preparation for moving to 'the level beyond human'.

By way of illustration, Balch offers some insights into the schedule prescribed for one woman who left the group in the early 1980s (1995a: 157–8):

Her first of four daily rest periods began at 3:36 p.m. and ended exactly two hours later. At 5:57 she bathed. Twenty-four minutes later she took a vitamin pill, one of thirty-two consumed every twenty-four hours. At 6:36 she drank a liquid protein formula, and one hour later she ate a cinnamon roll. By 9:54 she was back in bed for another two hours. During her waking moments she wore a uniform at all times. Free periods were devoted to 'fuel preparation' (i.e. cooking), classes on astrology or 'brain exercises' such as working on jigsaw puzzles. Because she never left the house, the only way she knew what the weather was like was by watching the sky through a clerestory window—the only window in the house that wasn't covered. She wasn't sure how long this phase lasted because she lost track of time.

Was life in the group much the same years later when the members methodically poisoned themselves in three shifts? We have only a very incomplete record of the group's activities in the intervening years (see Balch, 1995a: 163–4; Balch and Taylor, 2002). But the information provided by the news and police reports of their suicide is itself suggestive. Much also can be gleaned from the Heaven's Gate webpage (http://www.heavensgate.com) and the video they left behind with a member who had recently defected. The eerily neat, uniform, and orderly condition of the bodies of the followers when they were found, the carefully arranged, spotless, and spartan interior of their mansion, and the fact that the group had only recently rented their new palatial home after living for some time on an isolated compound, surrounded by a twenty-foot wall of dirt-filled tires (55 miles southeast of Albuquerque, New Mexico) all suggest that there had been little change in the basic beliefs and practices of the group. For the devoted core, however, some important symbolic threshold may have been crossed. Conditioned by decades of patient training for the next level, isolated from external feedback by their elaborate routines, and sparked to action by the spectacular arrival of the comet Hale-Bopp, the thirty-nine committed members of Heaven's Gate may well have felt a strong collective urge to finally act upon their beliefs.

After their deaths it was reported that the leader, Do (Marshall Herff Applewhite), had told some of his followers he was dying of cancer. He was not. On the group's website, however, the sixty-two-year-old Do ominously says: 'I'm in a vehicle that is already falling apart on me, and I'm desperate to try to help you have a last chance to go.' Go where? To the 'Evolutionary Level beyond Human', of course. In 1985, Do's partner Ti (Bonnie Lu Trusdale Nettles), to whom he was extremely close, had died of cancer, and the belief in his own illness may have helped to cultivate a 'now or never' attitude in Heaven's Gate.

For the Solar Temple, the final act was prompted by rising dissent and conflict within the group, combined with fears of persecution brought on by recent government investigations of the group's financial dealings. It is likely that Luc Jouret and Joseph Di Mambro, the leaders of the Solar Temple, thought there was a serious threat to the integrity of their group and to their personal authority (Palmer, 1996; Hall and Schulyer, 2000). In fact, Di Mambro, the true power behind the scenes, was dying of cancer.

Was the murder-suicide he planned for those he thought were betraying him, and for his most loyal followers too, the desperate act of a man intent on saving his reputation at all costs? We can never know.[17]

Helpful Insights from Social Psychology

Some rather straightforward insights from social psychology can supplement the discussion of social encapsulation. Here I will focus on three relevant empirical generalizations about people's behaviour in groups, applying the principles of 'normative dissonance', 'groupthink', and 'shift-to-risk' to the behaviour of members of NRMs that have become violent.

With specific reference to Jonestown, for example, Edgar Mills Jr (1982) argues that 'the reduction of normative dissonance' in many NRMs impairs the autonomy of individual people and sets the stage for more extreme behaviour. To succeed, most NRMs need high levels of commitment from their members, but unless a certain balance is struck, this intense commitment may actually prove detrimental. Why? The answer lies in the function of disagreement about fundamental values and norms—which is what 'normative dissonance' refers to—in moderating the actions of all groups in society.

In most social situations we live amidst somewhat inconsistent values, norms, and conceptions of reality. Even in a family there are inevitable disagreements about what should be done, by whom, when, why, and so on. These serve as a constant reminder that we must be flexible in our dealings with others. We must always be ready to seek and live by compromises and to segment our roles and activities accordingly. (That is, under different circumstances we have different loyalties—for example, to school, work, and home.) This state of affairs has a moderating effect on our own actions and those of the groups to which we belong. The continual need to negotiate a path amongst differences imposes a crucial moment of critical distance between the impulse to act and the actions actually taken. Of course, a reduction in the normative dissonance in any situation will not necessarily result in impulsive, extreme, or violent behaviour. But it facilitates movement in that direction, and many NRMs engage in practices that systematically bring about such a reduction.

Most of the practices I have in mind we have addressed already. In the first place, many NRMs seem to attract relatively deprived or idealistic people, with a low tolerance for moral ambiguity or ambivalence. They want a higher than normal level of normative clarity and consonance in their lives. Second, the NRMs these people join commonly suppress or even expel dissenting members who offer an alternative source of authority. Third, there is a common tendency for charismatic religious leaders to surround themselves with sycophants. Lastly, the reduction of normative dissonance is intensified by the social isolation and encapsulation so commonly sought by these groups. In fact it is a mark of social encapsulation.

We know that people under pressure are susceptible to defective patterns of decision making. One such pattern was identified by Irving Janis (1972), who called it 'groupthink'. Janis examined a number of important political fiascos as test cases of faulty decision-making, decisions like that made by President Kennedy's advisory group to support the Bay of Pigs invasion of Cuba in 1961. In these groups Janis detected a common scenario that he thought accounted for their poor judgement. In these usually highly cohesive groups:

> Each member wants the approval of all the others, and this produces a strong tendency toward uniformity. No one wants to raise controversial issues, question weak arguments, or puncture unrealistic hopes. They sustain an illusion of invulnerability, marked by excessive optimism. They rationalize away any warnings and decline to reconsider past policy commitments that have brought them to this predicament. They take their own group's morality for granted and do not look carefully at the ethical consequences of their decisions. They assume that their enemies are too evil to warrant negotiation efforts, and too stupid or weak to stop whatever plans the group may devise. Each person censors his or her own doubts instead of voicing them. (Spencer, 1985: 171–2)

If this can be true of the advisers to the President of the United States, how much more is it likely to the case for such isolated and highly introverted, or even besieged NRMs as the Peoples Temple, the Branch Davidians, the Solar Temple, Heaven's Gate, and Aum Shinrikyō? Here we have truly homogeneous groups that fervently believe that the fate of the world ultimately depends on the cohesive front they can present to their enemies.

As other social-psychological experiments have shown, some groups are more inclined to entertain risky behaviour than the individual members would entertain on their own. Conditioned, perhaps, by the realities of normative dissonance in society, individuals leaning in a particular direction may believe that their own opinion is more extreme than that of other people, so they will refrain from acting on their beliefs. But if the other members of a group happen to share the individual's outlook, discussion often serves to validate these views and encourages the individual to express even more extreme opinions. Speaking out may, in turn, have a snowballing effect, radicalizing the views and behaviour of others in the group (Spencer,

1985: 172–3). This 'shift-to-risk' in some groups is, again, very likely in the NRMs that have become violent. The fatal combination of apocalyptic beliefs, unstable charismatic leadership, and social encapsulation has worked for years in these cases to select the membership of the groups in ways that would foster the emergence of ever more extreme views. Again, the homogeneity and solidarity that are necessary for the group's survival in a hostile social environment can become, paradoxically, the Achilles' heel that assures their abrupt demise.

Box 7 Surviving the Failure of Apocalyptic Prophecies

In the classic study *When Prophecy Fails*, Leon Festinger, Henry W. Riecken, and Stanley Schachter (1956) offer an account of one very small occult group, dubbed the Seekers, whose leader, Mrs Marion Keech, predicted the destruction of much of the United States by a great flood. Her loyal followers were to be rescued from this apocalypse by aliens aboard flying saucers, who were communicating with her by telepathy. Several dates for the end are foretold by Mrs Keech, but each passed uneventfully. Contrary to common sense, though, in the face of the stark disconfirmation of these prophecies the group did not abandon its beliefs and disband. Rather a faithful core persisted, redoubling their efforts to convince others of the veracity of their ideas. From the study of this one group, Festinger and his colleagues developed the theory of cognitive dissonance: when people with strongly held beliefs are confronted by evidence clearly at odds with their beliefs, they will seek to resolve the discomfort caused by the discrepancy by convincing others to support their views, rather than abandon their commitments. They will seek some means of re-establishing cognitive consonance without sacrificing their religious convictions. With experimental confirmation, this theory has gone on to become a mainstay of social psychology, and in the sociology of religion there is something like an implicit consensus in support of this view as well. But does the record show that the response of the Seekers is consonant with that of other religious groups in the thrall of prophecy?

Over the years many other groups have been studied (see table below). The results of these studies are mixed, but on the whole the record shows that Festinger et al. were right to predict that many groups will survive the failure of prophecy. Why they survive is another matter. The reasons are much more complicated than *When Prophecy Fails* implies.

Group Studied	Studied by	Survival of Failure of Prophecy
Seekers	Festinger et al. (1956)	Yes, for a time
Church of the True Word	Hardyck and Braden (1962)	Yes, quite well
Ichigen no Miya	Takaaki (1979)	Yes, barely
Baha'is Under the Provision of the Convenant	Balch et al. (1983) and Balch et al. (1997)	Yes, but with difficulties
Millerites	Melton (1985)	Yes, for a time
Universal Link	Melton (1985)	Yes, for a time
Jehovah's Witnesses	Zygmunt (1970) Wilson (1978) Singelenberg (1988)	Yes, quite well
Rouxists	van Fossen (1988)	Yes, quite well
Mission de l'Esprit Saint	Palmer and Finn (1992)	No
Institute of Applied Metaphysics	Palmer and Finn (1992)	Yes, quite well
Lubavitch Hasidim	Shaffir (1993,1994,1995) Dein (1997)	Yes, very well
Unarians	Tumminia (1998)	Yes, fairly well
Chen Tao	Wright (1998)	Yes, but weakened

So what can we glean from the scholarly record so far? We can document an array of strategies used by these groups in the face of the disconfirmation of their prophecies. We can also describe a number of conditions that influence which strategies are used and what their effects might be.

Adaptational Strategies
Proselytization
The literature reveals that proselytizing is only one of several possible strategies used by religions whose prophecies did not come true. Later studies reveal that only a minority of groups sought to convert others to compensate for their disappointment. This was mostly clearly true, for example, of the UFO cult examined by Festinger et al., and the Lubavitch Hasidim examined by Shaffir and by Dein. This proselytizing was mostly used in conjunction with other strategies. So strictly speaking the 'law' of cognitive dissonance in the case of prophetic failures, as formulated by Festinger et al., is incorrect, or at any rate it is framed too narrowly. At least two additional strategies have been identified, which I will call 'rationalization' and 'reaffirmation'.

Rationalization
Several studies have emphasized the rationalization of seeming failure is an important adaptational strategy (e.g. Zygmunt, 1972). In fact, as J. Gordon Melton (1985: 21) comments: '. . . the denial of failure is not just another option, but the common mode of adaptation of millennial groups following the failure of a prophecy.' The case studies mentioned here support this. It is successful rationalization, and not proselytization, that is the most important factor contributing to the maintenance of beliefs and the survival of the group. Melton would agree with Bryan Wilson (1978: 184) when he observes:

> For people whose lives have become dominated by one powerful expectation, and whose activities are dictated by what that belief requires, abandonment of faith because of disappointment about a date would usually be too traumatic an experience to contemplate. Reinterpretation is demanded.

To some extent all of the groups that survived the disconfirmation of their prophecies did so because they were able to promptly provide their followers with a sufficiently plausible reinterpretation of events. The leader of the one group that failed to survive altogether, the Mission de l'Esprit Saint,

and the leaders of groups that experienced dramatic declines in their fortunes (e.g. the Ichigen no Miya and the Baha'is Under the Provision of the
Covenant, at least as first discussed by Balch et al., 1983), also provided rationalizations, but the leaders were too late in crafting them and they were
inadequately communicated to the membership.

More specifically, as several of the authors suggest in various ways, we
can distinguish between at least four kinds of rationalization: spiritualization,
a test of faith, human error, and blaming others. Some of the groups studied
favoured one of these modes of rationalization over the other, but they usually appear in various combinations.

Melton (1985: 21) clarifies what he has in mind in proposing the useful
term 'spiritualization' as follows:

> The prophesied event is reinterpreted in such a way that what was sup-
> posed to have been a visible, verifiable occurrence is seen to have been in
> reality an invisible, spiritual occurrence. The event occurred as predicted,
> only on a spiritual level.

In the case of the Institute for Applied Metaphysics, a New Age-like
group, Palmer and Finn (1992: 406) report the curious finding that several hundred followers of Winnifred Barton, scattered in three widely separated parts of Canada, more or less spontaneously transformed a predic-
tion of the end of the world 'as we know it' (at 6 p.m. on 13 June 1975)
into a subtle shift in consciousness. In the words of one of Palmer and
Finn's informants:

> At ten o'clock suddenly Win arrives. She just came in and went to the
> front and started meditating. There was music playing and we all meditat-
> ed. An hour passed, then suddenly, it was twelve o'clock. We were still
> here. What had happened? Then I heard people around me saying, 'Wow!
> Did you feel that?' A lot of people definitely felt something, that something
> spiritual had happened. Certainly, nothing physical had. It's lucky that Win
> always tacked on that phrase, 'as we know it.'

Not all the followers agreed, but enough did to transform the group
from what was essentially a client cult into a full cult movement that chose
to live communally for the first time.

Perhaps the most interesting illustration of an attempt to spiritualize a
seeming prophetic failure is provided by the leader of the Ichigen no Miya,

Motoki Isamu (Takaaki, 1979: 227). On the day when the apocalypse failed to arrive as predicted, Isamu attempted a ritualistic suicide. This seeming admission of defeat was later reinterpreted and transformed into a sign of triumph. Having cut open his abdomen, Isamu had a vision of his body as the islands of Japan in flames, causing him to realize that 'God had transferred the cataclysm to my own body'. In Christ-like manner, then, he eventually announced that he had taken on the pain of humanity, spiritually staving off the anticipated earthquake.

For the second kind of rationalization, the test of faith, much depends on the beliefs in question, the specific history and circumstances of the group, the resourcefulness of its leadership, and its cultural heritage and context. The Jehovah's Witnesses, the Church of the True Word, the Lubavitch, and the Baha'is Under the Provisions of the Covenant all relied significantly on this approach. But there are elements of it in most of the thirteen groups analyzed. After forty-two days in the bomb shelters waiting for the apocalypse that never came, the 103 faithful of the Church of the True Word emerged to celebrate in unison the victory that their leader assured them they had achieved. They had proven their faith to the Lord and set an example for the world, preparing for the true destruction that they knew was still imminent (Hardyck and Braden, 1962: 138–139).

The third rationalization, attributing the failure of prophecy to human error, usually referring to the misunderstanding, miscalculation, or moral inadequacy of followers, is very common, especially in groups stemming from more traditional religious backgrounds. In the case of the Lubavitch, many members told Shaffir (1995: 127) quite straightforwardly that the messiah 'would have come, but we didn't merit it . . . if we merited it, things would have worked out differently'(see also Dein, 1997: 203). In the eyes of many of the faithful the error was theirs in even thinking that they could discern the mysterious ways of God. Soon new interpretations of past events and the words of their leader were circulating widely in the movement, all showing how the followers had failed to read the signs correctly.

The responses of the leadership of the Jehovah's Witnesses to the failure of their 1975 prophecy and the response of the leader of the Ichigen no Miya were similar, though more harsh in nature. By a rather bizarre turn of logic, the leaders in each of these cases chose to place their followers in a kind of 'Catch-22' by blaming them, after the fact, for having brought on the failure of prophecy by having believed in it too literally in the first place. In a speech to his followers, Motoki Isamu, the founder of the Ichigen no Miya told his devotees:

On 18 June at 8:30 a.m. God accepted the founder's life. Some people would speak of him as a living corpse, but God will make use of his spirit for ever ... All of you are failures. Why? You thought that if God's prophecy did not materialize, you would be so scorned and slandered by people that you would fall into total ruin. So you looked with eagerness for a disaster to occur. That was your wish, but it was not the will of God. If you had the magnanimity to desire that everybody be saved, you could be content with slander or any treatment you received. Above all else you should have prayed to God that everybody be saved without adversity . . . (Takaaki, 1979: 224)

Here, of course, we see the limitations of any typological approach, for the leader is blending two of the rationalizations I have distinguished to defend himself against criticism. He is pointing to the role of human error, my third type of rationalization, as well as directing the blame at others, my fourth type of rationalization.

Judging by the thirteen groups considered in the literature, directly blaming others (whether natural or supernatural beings, or impersonal forces) for the obstruction of a prophecy, is relatively rare. A similar instance is reported by Balch et al. (1997: 79-80) when they note that one of the many subtle rationalizations used by the Baha'is Under the Provisions of the Covenant was to blame outsiders for misrepresenting their qualified and humanly fallible 'predictions,' based on Biblical interpretation, for absolute 'prophecies' given by God.

Reaffirmation

Almost all of the studied groups have used the third strategy, reaffirmation, as a defense against dissonance, though some researchers seem to be attuned more to this fact than others. Melton (1985: 25) suggests that in the face of the social disruption attendant on prophetic failure, many movements turn inward and 'engage in processes of group building'. To illustrate his point he cites the Millerites as they consolidated into the Adventist movement, and the Church of the True Word as described by Hardyck and Braden. The leadership of the latter group never missed a beat. On the morning the group emerged from the bomb shelters a rousing collective service was held in which the seeming failure of prophecy was immediately cast in a new light as the followers were praised heartily for keeping the faith and admonished to keep preparing for the real apocalypse to come. Likewise, from the accounts of Shaffir (1995) and Dein (1997), it is clear that the Lubavitch took the physical death of their leader as a challenge, somewhat surprisingly, to proceed all the more zealously with their program of spiritual renewal and proselytization. A week after his death, for example, a day-long public 'teach-in' was held at their headquarters in Brooklyn, New York. On this and other occasions, Shaffir (1995: 128) notes, speaker after speaker drove home the same message: despite the overwhelming grief felt by all, immediate action must be taken to obey the leader's directives. His emissaries must turn their attention back to the mission he had so promisingly begun. Similar patterns can be traced for the Jehovah's Witnesses, the Unarians, and Rouxism. But the fullest appreciation of the possible significance of these acts of reaffirmation is found in Palmer and Finn's discussion of the Institute for Applied Metaphysics (IAM). In the conclusion to their paper Palmer and Finn (1992: 419) make some welcome and insightful suggestions:

> When contemporary spiritual groups unexpectedly embark on the millenarian adventure, the leader appears to be responding to conflicts or 'growing pains' within her or his community that require a radical reorganization—or a rebirth. In such cases, the rite of apocalypse, ostensibly aimed at destroying the old order of the planet Earth, actually functions to bring about a new order within the cult or sect. When examined within the framework of the charismatic career of the leader-founder, or the group's changing relationship with its host society, the 'acting out' of Endtime often appears to function as a collective rite of passage into a new group identity.

These observations help to explain the survival and transformation of the IAM in particular, and they show how the analysis of failure should be recast so as to view it in the context of the broader organizational processes for all apocalyptic NRMs grappling with this issue.

Denial and the Management of Dissonance

The resilience displayed by religious groups in the face of prophetic failures suggests, as several commentators have argued, that the level of dissonance experienced by insiders is less than that imagined by outsiders, particularly social scientific researchers with their greater personal and professional commitment to logical consistency. In the words of Snow and Machalek (1982: 23): 'Unlike belief in science, many belief systems do not require consistent and frequent confirmatory evidence. Beliefs may withstand the pressure of disconfirming events not because of the effectiveness of dissonance-reducing strategies, but because disconfirming evidence may simply go unacknowledged.' In *When Prophecy Fails*, however, Festinger et al. (1956) argue that it is a condition of the theory of cognitive dissonance that the disconfirmation of a prophecy must be recognized forthrightly by believers. But how can we gauge if this kind of recognition really has happened? It is not simply that we can never know fully the thoughts of others; rather, we are returned to the basic question undergirding the debate about the failure of prophecy. In principle, if a group does fully recognize such failure, why would it persist in its beliefs? The very continuation of these groups, which in a sense provided the raison d'être for this formulation of the theory of cognitive dissonance, also implies the reverse state of affairs: real recognition has not occurred, and that is why the groups continue. As this analysis of a range of case studies reveals, it does in fact seem that in these groups we are dealing with a significantly lesser or different standard of evidence than that applied by researchers. From their perspective there is ample 'evidence' of impending doom in the abundant imperfections of this world, and every reason to keep seeking dramatic release from these imperfections in the ever-receding yet open-ended promise of the future.

Drawn from Lorne L. Dawson, 'When Prophecy Fails and Faith Persists: A Theoretical Overview.' *Nova Religio* 3 (1): 60–82. Used with permission of the University of California Press

Concluding Remarks

Do these kinds of social-psychological processes account for what happened at Jonestown and Waco and in the inner circles of the Solar Temple, Heaven's Gate, Aum Shinrikyō, and the Movement for the Restoration of the Ten Commandments? The analysis seems plausible, and even considering this possibility begins to dispel the needless mystery and fear created by talk of 'brainwashing' and 'mind control'. The argument for brainwashing, as we saw in Chapter 5, is intrinsically weak. Moreover, we do not really need it in order to understand what is really just normal human behaviour pushed by abnormal social circumstances to an extreme. In fact, the evidence compiled by the US Departments of Justice and the Treasury, as well as by two Congressional hearings into the Branch Davidian fiasco, suggests that it is equally likely that the consistently poor judgement exercised by the BATF and the FBI agents who laid siege to the Waco compound can be explained in the same terms (Barkun, 1994; Tabor and Gallagher, 1995; Ammerman, 1995; Wright, 1995a; Sullivan, 1996; Docherty, 2001). The police officers experienced the consequences of a reduction of normative dissonance in their deliberations and fell prey to the faulty reasoning born of groupthink and a shift-to-risk.[18] The obvious and fatal insensitivity of the BATF and the FBI to the world view of the Branch Davidians suggests that they were more interested in pursuing their own organizational agenda than achieving a peaceful end to the conflict. Why were the media, for example, invited to witness the original BATF assault? Once officers were killed and injured in that assault, the federal agents became preoccupied with defeating the challenge to their authority and power. Simply waiting for Koresh to surrender did not seem to be an acceptable option.

It is evident that the threat to life and limb from cult violence is not intrinsic to NRMs, but stems from processes of social interaction that would tend to foster extreme behaviour in all of us under the right circumstances. Admittedly, these tendencies are aggravated in important ways by the belief in apocalypticism, charismatic authority, and need for social segregation found in some NRMs. But each of these elements is perfectly understandable in its own right, and all have been common in other kinds of religious and secular organizations and movements throughout human history.

As the concept of deviance amplification implies, and David Bromley (2002) and other scholars (e.g. Docherty, 2001) have recently stressed, the tragic violence experienced by these NRMs is ultimately the product of an 'interactive' process. As the old saying goes, it takes two to tango. It is the degeneration of the relationship between the group and the surrounding society's agents of authority that spells danger, more than any intrinsic properties of the new religions themselves. The emergence of what Bromley calls a 'dramatic denouement' is extremely rare because it requires an elaborate set of conditions to fall into place. Bromley (2002: 11–12) has masterfully sought to delineate the developments characteristic of these tragedies in terms of a progression through four stages:

(1) Latent Tension, in which the foundational logic and organization of [the] movement and society stand in contradiction to one another, although there may not be direct engagement; (2) Nascent Conflict, in which emergent bilateral conflicts are not articulated in ideological terms, [the] future adversaries have not mobilized organizationally, and [the] parties therefore orient toward one another as 'troublesome'; (3) Intensified Conflict, in which there is heightened mobilization and radicalization of [the] movements and oppositional groups, [the] entry of third parties

[(e.g. elements of the government and/or the media)], and orientation by [the] parties toward one another as 'dangerous' . . . ; and (4) Dramatic Denouement, in which polarization and destabilization of dangerous relationships lead to orientation by parties as 'subversive' and to projects of final reckoning intended to reverse power and moral relationships . . .

The progression towards violence can be short-circuited, wittingly and unwittingly, by a wide variety of acts and happenings. This is amply demonstrated by the many less well known and studied instances of sharp conflict between apocalyptic NRMs and authorities that did not result in violence, such as the child welfare disputes experienced by The Children of God/The Family (see Box 6) or the tensions set off by The Church Universal and Triumphant's elaborate preparations for the end of the world (Whitsel, 2003). In some instances we know that the potential for violence was defused when the law enforcement agencies involved learned the lessons of the disastrous confrontation at Waco and exercised greater patience. Recognizing the need for a finer appreciation of the unique dynamics of crises involving apocalyptic religious groups (Kleiver, 1999; Rosenfeld, 2000; Wessinger, 1999; Szubin et al., 2000), the authorities sought to avoid becoming embroiled in the cycle of deviance amplification. Through unilateral action—really inaction—they prevented the incidents in question from crossing the threshold from 'intensified conflicts' to 'dramatic denouements'.

As cautioned at the end of Chapter 1, however, almost any generalization about NRMs is subject to important exceptions and qualifications. In other instances of mass violence, such as The Solar Temple and Aum Shinrikyō tragedies, it can be argued that a more decisive intervention by state authorities at specific earlier points of conflict might have curtailed the deadly cycle of deviance amplification. Such an intervention might have served as a wake-up call, preventing the inner circle of these groups from succumbing to an ever more fantastic conception of the conspiratorial forces arrayed against them. Certainly Aum Shinrikyō was emboldened to engage in increasingly reckless behaviour by the failure of the Japanese police to investigate early accusations of serious wrongdoing out of fear of violating the religion's constitutional rights (Lifton, 1999; Reader, 2000, 2002). This may apply to Jim Jones and The Peoples Temple as well. But in other instances, like Heaven's Gate, simply no one knew what was happening until too late.

Students of religion have begun to explore the ways in which the processes discussed in this chapter have influenced the tragic cases of cult-related violence that we have helplessly witnessed. We should really seek, however, to complement these kinds of social structural and social-psychological analyses with a sensitive exploration of the world view of the members of the cults who have engaged in violence.[19] What I have in mind are efforts like that of David Chidester (1988) in his remarkable book on the Peoples Temple and the Jonestown massacre, *Salvation and Suicide*. Drawing on interviews with former members and survivors of the Jonestown massacre, as well as the written record and over 900 hours of audiotapes of Jim Jones's sermons and other talks, Chidester takes us into the inner world of this group. He pieces together a picture of how these people had come to hold an alternative understanding of the time and space they occupied, as well as the distinctions they made between different kinds of people in this world. Giving us a glimpse into the distressing lot of the poor blacks that constituted the bulk of Jones's devoted following, Chidester allows us to grasp how suicide could appear to be a plausible response, perhaps the only acceptable response, to their plight as they saw it. By the end of *Salvation and Suicide* we realize that many of these people had come from a world that most of us can only vaguely imagine, of racial prejudice, social oppression, and moral bankruptcy. We have been allowed, at least partially, to see the simple but satisfying replacement they thought they had found with Jim Jones and their religious compatriots, a religio-socialist utopia that is equally foreign to the experience of most of us. We can appreciate how the souls that Jones had lifted to a new self-respect and vision of hope could decide that it was better to die for their beliefs, and with their community, than to stand by and witness the defeat of their dreams and the destruction of their new extended family. Operating with their definition of the situation in mind, the collective plunge into death becomes meaningful—though not necessarily acceptable.[20]

If possible, we need to acquire a similar grasp of the worlds occupied by the members of the Solar Temple, Aum Shinrikyō, and Heaven's Gate. Here the challenge is much greater, however, for most of these seekers left behind conventional and comfortable environments—they were middle-class, white, and safe. In these cases, the sociological imagination may be stretched thin, but as yet few have dared to stretch it in this way at all.

Chapter Eight

What Is the Cultural Significance of New Religious Movements?

Our Skewed Perspective

We study NRMs because they are intrinsically interesting. Their beliefs and practices are unusual or even fantastic. So we are curious about why people belong to these odd groups, who belongs to them, how they came to belong, and what the consequences of their involvement are. This natural curiosity became more urgent for the scholarly community when the anti-cult movement succeeded in turning the emergence of NRMs into a social problem. Many sociologists of religion (and others) recognized the need to replace the suppositions and rhetoric with more reliable information. Scholars also paid attention to NRMs because they offered a good opportunity to study many of the essential elements of religious life in smaller and more manageable forums, where a researcher might witness the processes by which new religious phenomena—doctrines, rituals, experiential practices, organizational structures, and so on—are born, live, and die. It would be difficult to claim, however, that the significance of NRMs is due to their direct statistical impact on the religious economies of Western societies. No one can put an accurate figure to the number of people involved in NRMs. As mentioned, estimates offered by the anti-cult movement are inflated, and there is good reason to believe that the real numbers are relatively small. Contrary to the speculations of Stark and Bainbridge (see Chapter 2), it is unlikely any NRM is going to achieve the status of a truly world religion in the foreseeable future. In fact, membership in the most successful and hence most notorious NRMs founded in the 1950s, 1960s, and 1970s, groups like the Unification Church, the International Society for Krishna Consciousness, and perhaps even Scientology, seems to have declined over the last fifteen years. There is also little reason to believe that the number of new religions is growing appreciably, at least in North America and Western Europe.

Yet, as I have tried to show throughout this book, scholars have turned to the study of NRMs to learn something about the larger society and culture from which these movements have sprung and to which they are reacting. Scholars in the field have been asserting for some time that the significance of NRMs is 'cultural', though they rarely specify what they mean. We are told that they have a 'symbolic' importance out of proportion to their small numbers. In most cases, NRMs are presented either as sites of spiritual, social, and cultural experimentation and innovation or as nodes of staunch resistance to certain changes overtaking our societies. These views are seen in theories about the origins of today's NRMs, as surveyed in Chapter 3. Tipton's insightful analysis of the hybrid moral solutions offered by various NRMs to the disillusioned members of the counterculture suggests the cultural experimentation model, whereas Hunter's analysis of NRMs as agents of de-modernization clearly calls to mind the resistance model. In either case, it is argued, NRMs may be studied as barometers of the larger social transformations occurring around us, to give us insight into what may lie ahead for us all (see Hammond, 1987; Robbins and Bromley, 1992; Dawson, 1998a, 2004).

This set of options may be more apparent than real, though, since a close reading of the literature reveals that the whole dialogue is skewed by the assumption that religion has become a largely reactionary phenomenon in the modern world. This assumption stems from the pervasive influence exerted by secularization theory on sociology as a whole. Social-scientific analyses, sometimes explicitly and more often implicitly, cast religious activity as intrinsically pre-modern, if not anti-modern. This tendency holds true even for Tipton's argument about the social functions fulfilled by NRMs. These groups strike innovative moral compromises between the expressive ideals of the sixties counterculture and the need for authority and stable social order in people's lives. In form these compromises are relatively new. But the new religions are presented primarily either as ways of endowing their followers' identities with sacred significance, with an eye to putting a brake on social changes that the followers think are too chaotic and destructive (Mol, 1976), or as alternative ways of successfully reintegrating members into the dominant society (Johnson, 1961; Parsons, 1989). As 'religious' responses to changing social circumstances, rather than political, social, or psychological responses, they tend to be viewed as conservative instead of revolutionary or experimental phenomena.

Let me explain further. At the most basic and important level, people have turned to NRMs, like all other religions, to live in a meaningful and orderly world. In line with Berger, and Stark and Bainbridge (and Stark and

Finke), we can still say that being religious is about constructing a *nomos* that is highly resistant to the corrosive effects of the anomic elements of our lives, from loneliness through bad dreams and illness to death. Religion does this by anchoring that *nomos* in claims about some transcendent or supernatural aspect of our existence. On the whole, in this regard, we have encountered little evidence to suggest that the basic motivation of converts to NRMs differs from that of other religious people in our midst. It is their social circumstances, including the pervasive failure of conventional religions to keep a vibrant sense of the transcendent or supernatural alive in our societies, that seem to account for why certain people have become practitioners of Sōka Gakkai rather than rejoining their parents' Methodist church. The people who join NRMs are much like anyone else, except that (as shown in Chapters 3, 4, and 6) they have a higher sensitivity to ambiguity. They have a greater desire to live in a more coherent or at least meaningful world, as well as a good world. That is how scholars like Berger have helped us to understand these matters, but Berger's pessimistic reading of the future of religion, as expounded in his theory of secularization, does not necessarily follow from his theory of religion's fundamental nature and purpose. In accepting the truth of the one, we need not accept the other.

Employing Berger's terms of reference, as discussed in Chapter 2, we could say that the increased privatization and pluralism of the social and religious environment today need not result in the full 'de-objectivation' of religious life. In a society in which many religions compete for our attention, including religions that literally come from around the world, the old and dominant religious certainties and monopolies must certainly give way. Religious ideas are being relativized as never before, and consequently religious life has increasingly become a matter of subjective conviction more than social consensus. But as Stark and Bainbridge propose, the passions of religious commitment may be stirred more deeply in this context as religious activity starts to be about individual expression rooted in personal experience and intellectual experimentation, rather than mere social conformity or an ignorance of alternatives. The groups in which religious life finds expression may each be much smaller, and their nature may be markedly more diverse, but the life expressed may be as real and strong as religious life has ever been. The organization and practices of these religions, however, have been transformed to suit the highly mobile and differentiated character of modern social life. This is achieved in part by making better use of the new means of communication (for example, glossy publications, audio- and video-tapes, satellite radio and television, relatively cheap air fares, and the Internet), as well as modern systems of management, marketing, and so on.

Sociologists have tended to overlook this possibility because they have been theoretically captivated by at least one fundamental element of the dominant secularization thesis: the belief that the growing modernization (that is, rationalization) of our society is intrinsically antithetical to all kinds of religious activity. Like Berger, many sociologists of religion have tended to limit the options for all religions to one of two: they can accommodate themselves to the modern, rationalized social order and achieve a stable but extremely modest existence as a component in the growing leisure or service economy. Or they can 'entrench themselves behind whatever socio-religious structures they can maintain or construct, and continue to profess the old objectivities as much as possible as if nothing had happened' (Berger, 1967: 153; Wallis, 1984; Bruce, 2002). In other words, they can either survive, yet more or less disappear as distinctive social entities with a unique purpose, or they can remain distinct but more or less disappear, surviving only at the very margins of society, where they will become more and more difficult to sustain, both economically and symbolically.

In the face of this diagnosis, the prospects for attributing much in the way of real cultural significance to the continued emergence of NRMs is not very promising. At present it is too soon to tell whether the two limited options delineated by Berger, Wilson (1976, 1993), and others[1] will hold true for the future of NRMs in North America. But I would argue for a third conception of the relationship between NRMs and the rest of society, one that leads me to be more optimistic about NRMs as being compatible with the conditions of modernity.

Aspects of this third approach can be detected as far back as a series of insightful yet largely forgotten essays on the social significance of NRMs published by Stone (1978b), Westley (1978), and Colin Campbell (1978). In some ways, they accept Berger's and Hunter's analysis of the plight of modern people, and hence of their religious lives as well, but choose not to frame the response of religion, as manifested in NRMs, in the negative terms implied by Hunter's 'anti-modernist' label. They do not see the characteristics of NRMs as reactionary but rather as symptomatic of the continued and healthy evolution of the forms of religious life. There is a more neutral, if not positive, cast to their comments and conclusions.

Despite some differences, remarkable agreement exists between these three essays, such as in their similar readings of the 'new religious consciousness' that each believes has emerged in the United States since the 1960s; I can detect at least six points of agreement.

FEATURES OF A NEW RELIGIOUS CONSCIOUSNESS

First, the new religions are marked by a pronounced religious individualism. The emphasis for those joining NRMs is decidedly on what the religious involvement can do for the individual and only secondarily on its broader implications or benefits for society or the group. People's participation is motivated by the development of personal identity, and correspondingly the locus of the sacred is often seen to be within the individual and not outside (see Westley, 1978: 137). Immanence is stressed over transcendence. At least in daily practice, in meditation or chanting the names of God, for example, such is the primary experience of members.

Second, these religions are religions of experience: 'A common element that seems to characterize most of the participants of these groups is intense experiences of themselves and the sacred. The emphasis is on experience and faith rather than doctrine and belief' (Stone, 1978b: 124). As stipulated in Chapter 2, cults promise transformative experiences, and much of their activity is focused on the delivery or inducement of those experiences.

This has meant, as Stone stipulates, that the new religious consciousness found in these groups displays a more pragmatic attitude to questions of religious authority and practice. This is the third feature of NRMs commonly noted by Stone, Westley, and Campbell. 'Gurus', Stone notes (1978b: 128), 'are followed for their expertise and proficiency in encouraging charismatic experience among their followers. Their authority is based on results first, then later perhaps scripture or divine revelation.' Or as Westley puts it, religious activity in these groups 'will involve skill development and skill testing of a progressive nature. As one becomes more ritually skilled, one will gain in authority' (1978: 138). This holds true, most obviously, for groups like Scientology and other NRMs born of the human potential movement, like Silva Mind Control, the organization Westley examines in her work. But in many respects it is equally true for contemporary Neo-Paganism (Adler, 1986; Luhrmann, 1989; Hutton, 1999; Berger, 1999; Pike, 2000), a diverse range of New Age practices (Heelas, 1996; Brown, 1997; Sutcliffe, 2003),[2] the numerous groups based on various forms of Hindu and Buddhist yoga and meditation in America (Coney, 1999), and even the chanting, dancing, and the other rituals of members of Krishna Consciousness.

Fourth, the new religious consciousness is remarkably more accepting of relativism and tolerant of other religious perspectives and systems than the religions that dominated the West in the past. Many new religions clearly borrow from a diverse array of traditions, both Eastern and Western, and most of them directly acknowledge the truth of other religions. In fact, many groups find no difficulty in admitting that their path to enlightenment or salvation is but one (though perhaps a most perfect one) among many. Campbell (1978: 154) comments that the spiritual and mystic religion of today's NRMs

> carries the principle of tolerance even further than the denomination, extending it not merely to all those of one's own faith or religion but to all people. An intensely personal religion of conviction in which truth is considered polymorphous in form necessarily involves the recognition that each and every human soul can be a vehicle for divine revelation in some form or other.

Fifth, the theology, or perhaps better just the world-view, of many of these groups is holistic, or as Campbell prefers, it is monistic (Stone, 1978b: 130; Campbell, 1978: 153). Almost every kind of dualism is rejected or diminished: the traditional dualisms of God and humanity, the transcendent and the immanent, humanity and nature, the spiritual and the material, the mind and the body, the subjective and the objective, male and female, good and evil, even cause and effect (e.g. Bednarowski, 1989). As Stone says (1978: 130), for instance: 'God language refers less to He and more to thou, we, it and I. God is neither spirit nor flesh, female or male. Cosmic "energy" is the image of God most universally used. Unlimited cosmic energy is not Wholly Other but open and accessible for all to tap into.'[3]

Sixth and last, each of the above features is compatible with what Stone calls greater 'organizational openness' (1978b: 129). In different ways Stone, Westley, and Campbell suggest the religions of the future, embodied in the NRMs of the present, will be increasingly like the 'client cults' of Stark and Bainbridge (1985). In Westley's Durkheimian turn of phrase (1978: 138), since new religions will be characterized increasingly

> by the respect and awe accorded the sacred within each individual, we may expect that this will be ritually expressed by each individual's private preoccupation with the relationship of the divine within to the external, everyday personality. While people may gather in groups to celebrate the cult, the source of sacred power (and of group integration) will be acknowledged by each individual turning inward as opposed to joining together with others to worship an external symbol of group unity.

Less effort will be made to attempt to address all aspects of followers' lives, to provide a truly encompassing world-view. More attention will be given to cultivating and serving certain crucial but socially segmented psychological and spiritual needs and desires. This will be done, moreover, within flexible organizational frameworks that allow for, or even foster, different ways of 'doing the religion'. Groups as diverse as Scientology, Vajradhatu/Shambhala, Transcendental Meditation, Kripalu Yoga, Wicca, Sōka Gakkai, and a host of expressions of New Ageism, and even some forms of Christian revivalism, purposefully offer different modes of practice to their followers. Members may voluntarily select, according to their preferences, the type and intensity of their involvement from a set of options made available by the NRMs.

THE SIGNIFICANCE OF THE NEW RELIGIOUS CONSCIOUSNESS

Contrary to the popular conception of cults, then, this perspective suggests that groups like the Unification Church and Krishna Consciousness, to the extent that they still demand a total commitment from their members, are the exception and not the rule in the new religious environment. This is not to say that they will not persist or have some social and cultural significance. Rather, as stipulated in Chapter 1, up to a point it is still useful to think of NRMs as falling into two kinds or social forms. On the one hand, there are the more traditionally oriented new religions that tend to stress communal lifestyles and exclusive commitments, while, on the other hand, there are new religions that are more modern in their orientation, largely non-communal, and open to segmented and plural commitments. Too much emphasis has been placed in the past, however, by both scholars and popular observers, on the former category. The so-called totalistic cults have been in the spotlight precisely because they seem to be so out of step with the tenor of the times. They have become emblematic of the new religious life in our midst, and this misconception has helped to perpetuate the tendency to identify NRMs too exclusively with anti-modern tendencies (as Hunter does). The observations of Stone, Westley, and Campbell correct the balance somewhat. But what is more, they also make us think about the very adequacy of the pre-modern/modern dichotomy for talking about NRMs.

It is important to note, however, that Stone and Westley do not expect the communal character of religion to disappear. We are not on our way to a world of 'audience cults', to use Stark and Bainbridge's terms of reference once again. Somewhat paradoxically, the critical emphasis placed on religious experience over mere assent to doctrine is pivotal in this regard.

When intense personal experiences are facilitated through the auspices of a religious or quasi-religious organization—asanas in a yoga group, an altar call in a revival service, or a guided fantasy exercise in a human potential group—the experiences may become interpreted as religious ones. The newly awakened or reborn often attribute the source of the experience to a charismatic leader or a group's gnostic power. They are further drawn into fellowship and identification with a group that positively interprets and appreciates experiences that the everyday world discredits as deviant. While intense personal experiences contain the germ of antinomian tendencies, their first-fruits are to stimulate an identification with a community that promotes similar experiences. Thus these experiences of individual effervescence bind communities together and encourage the perpetuation of the experiences. (Stone, 1978b: 126)

In line with the observations made in Chapter 3, we also must be careful to note that none of the six primary characteristics of the new religious consciousness outlined by Stone, Westley, and Campbell is unique or truly new. They are manifestations of trends that have been developing in American religion for centuries. But most observers would agree with Stone that 'their incidence never has been documented to be as strong or as widespread' (Stone, 1978: 127; see also Bednarowski, 1989).

As well as having similar conceptions of the new religious consciousness, Stone, Westley, and Campbell seem to agree about its significance. Two points of agreement stand out: the new religious consciousness is markedly more compatible with science and the social sciences than conventional religions; likewise, it is more compatible with the new social order emerging around us, whether it is called advanced capitalism, late or high modernism, post-industrialism, or postmodernism.

Stone agrees with Wilson that most NRMs are too small and transient to be the basis for a new religious culture. But in a manner now characteristic of most students of NRMs, he argues that these groups may nevertheless 'serve as midwives for new sensibilities' (1978b: 131). Or in the words of Robbins and Bromley (1992: 4), the social and ideological innovations of NRMs 'may contribute to a subterranean cultural . . . resource pool', elements of which may move, in times of conflict and crisis, 'from [the] cultural background to [the] foreground'. Stone points to the evidence of the emergence in American society of a greater interest and trust in personal experience, intuition, holistic views, and syncretistic perspectives in fields of endeavour as diverse as medicine and business, not to mention the rapidly expanding market in humanistic and self-help psychological books on everything from being the first-born child to facing death with dignity.

He concludes that the emphasis placed by many new Eastern, human potential, and even Christian groups on one's 'inner voice', with personal experience and feelings as the best guide to truth and happiness, is part of a larger 'cultural drift' away from the austere legacy of the Protestant work ethic (Stone, 1978b: 131). North Americans are discovering that there is more to life than work, and that virtue is no longer to be measured primarily by wealth or worldly success. The ideal of rugged individualism is not as appealing as it once was. Yet Stone insists that the evidence from NRMs that points towards a rejection of the utilitarian legacy of America's Protestant past tends not to take the form, Stone insists, of 'otherworldliness or anti-rationalism'. Rather, the 'this-worldly asceticism' that sociologists since Weber (1958a) have attributed to the influence of the Protestant Reformation on the modern world is being slowly displaced by a kind of 'this-worldly mysticism' that is compatible with both the everyday demands of life in our hustle-bustle society and with those forms of science that do not reduce the world exclusively to the material (Stone 1978b: 131). With the waning of the 'charisma of reason' in our day (p. 133), this new religious consciousness is geared to the promotion of a new kind of dominant scientism. The positivist conception of science necessitated the war of science and religion. But the newer, more holistic models of science and of the universe, ranging from Bohm's theory of implicate order through chaos theory to Thomas Kuhn's conception of science, point to a more open-ended universe in which spiritual principles can find a place (Bohm, 1983; Gleick, 1987; Kuhn, 1970). A more holistic mode of scientism is emerging around us that is more receptive to the growth of many kinds of new religious activity.

Speculating further, Stone suggests that a this-worldly mysticism might even have a 'cultural survival value' because it is 'complementary to bureaucratic post-industrial society' (Stone, 1978b: 131). Giving a favourable interpretation to the diagnosis of modernity of Berger and Hunter, he comments:

> Finding satisfaction in religious experience may help accommodate late capitalism's characteristic separation of private life from vocational life, of finding meaning in consumption rather than production. . . . A mystical orientation is applied to the private sphere of life as individuals supply their own solutions to religious problems, are assured of a sense of self (or sequence of selves), and gain respite from the workaday world to return refreshed to support bureaucratic asceticism in their work-role. (Stone, 1978b: 132)

Privatized religion, in the form of this-worldly mysticism, may actually reinvigorate the role of religious beliefs and practices in the daily lives of contemporary North Americans fitting them into their busy schedules (see e.g. Dawson, 2001a).

Westley likewise observes that 'the relationship of the new religions to science' need no longer be thought of as simply 'one of rejection, substitution and escape' (1978: 140–1; see also 142). New religions are not just explaining the meaning of life in a way that the scientific world-view fails

to do. They are actively seizing on both the new cultural relativism promoted by the spread of social-scientific knowledge and some of the means
and data of the natural sciences, with regard to brain states and psychological well-being, for example, to facilitate and legitimate their existence.
Similarly, NRMs can and do benefit from the increased modern awareness
that humanity makes its own laws. Asian-based meditational practices in
particular can turn theories of the social construction of reality to their epis-
temological advantage, using them to overcome charges of solipsistic and
even narcissistic idealism. As Campbell (1978: 155) adds, the full-fledged
'rationalism, materialism and . . . self-concerned this-worldliness' of many
people in contemporary society may be 'the focus of mystical opposition
and scorn'. But 'there is no opposition to abstract, secular systems of
thought in general . . . [and this] leaves many areas in the arts, philosophy
and the sciences, where mysticism can draw on material syncretization.' He
echoes Westley in saying that, in comparison with the traditional churches
and sects of our society,

> mysticism. . . benefits most from the 'shrinking' of the world and the
> increasingly pluralistic character of modern societies. As this brings reli-
> gions into increased contact with one another it raises in an acute way the
> problem of inter-religious truth. The mystical solution is one of the sim-
> plest, avoiding the dangers of religious conflict and the difficulties of ecu-
> menicism by absorbing elements from various religions into a general
> mystical philosophy. (Campbell, 1978: 155)

These authors all draw parallels between religious and social developments. They associate the rise of the new religious consciousness they are
describing with the advance of 'social differentiation', the subdivision of
society into different institutional attachments, labour roles, and what Max
Weber calls 'spheres of action' in general. Their discussions do not offer specific connections to these developments, however. Is the new religious consciousness a mere epiphenomenon of larger social structural changes? Or is
it both a medium and a source of the cultural and social changes we are
experiencing? Because of the lack of specifics, it is very difficult to choose
between the interpretations offered by Hunter on the one hand, and by
Stone, Westley, and Campbell on the other. Are most NRMs just reactions to
modernity, or do they represent some intrinsic adaptation of religious forms
to the modern social world?

   The consensus of Stone, Westley, and Campbell does make us think
twice before too readily associating most NRMs with some countercultural
reaction to, or compensation for, the social and psychological ills of

modernity. It also shows that at least some thoughtful commentators on NRMs are not willing to accept the more pessimistic implications of the Berger and Wilson privatization thesis, which suggests that NRMs can be written off as cultural trivialities. Instead, we get intimations that the changing face of religion as found in NRMs may represent just the continued dialectical adaptation of religion to society and society to religion (see Dawson, 2004, 2005b). Religious institutions need not be the sole or even primary regulators of all aspects of social life in order for religion to continue as an important expression of cultural adaption to new social conditions. We would more readily recognize this possibility if we ceased to conceive of religion from within the overly narrow confines of a European, and probably Protestant and Enlightenment, point of view in which 'religion' is a distinct set of institutions operating within a competitive hierarchy of other institutions. 'Religion' per se cannot be equated with the organizational form of the 'church' or even a constellation of competing 'churches'. The word instead describes a dimension of ultimate meaning that is relevant to all aspects of life, even in our scientific-technological age (see Beckford's comments below).[4]

Modernism and the New Religious Movements

Little direct attention has been given to the cultural significance of NRMs since those essays of Stone, Westley, and Campbell were written more than twenty years ago. But I have encountered two fascinating analyses that can be used to support their more generous reading. In a case study of the Unification Church—which is one movement that does not show much compatibility with modernity—Arthur Parsons (1989) offers a further argument against seeing NRMs as just anti-modern.

AN ALTERNATIVE INTERPRETATION OF RELIGIOUS ACCOMMODATIONS

Parsons derives his view from an application of the insights of Eisenstadt (1956), whom he paraphrases as follows (1989: 212):

> . . . while innovative religious movements often appear to arise as responses to tensions within their secular host societies, they also tend to incorporate central cultural elements from those societies. He contends youth movements in modern societies, while they are a response to the disjunction between the expressive personalism of family life and the instrumental impersonalism of public life, also incorporate essential fea-

tures of both of these realms. They provide contexts in which diffuse affectivity can be combined with universalistic or highly rationalized moral and cosmological principles.

Whereas Wilson and Berger think many NRMs will eventually be secularized by trying to use rational arguments and bureaucracies to advance their non-rational religious aims, Parsons (1989: 213) arrives at a more optimistic conclusion by focusing on the substantive ends promoted by many groups. NRMs, he observes, 'above all strive to rationalize culture in the name of the expressive values and emotional practices that are highly legitimate in contemporary society.' In other words, he thinks these supposedly deviant religions have many similarities to the dominant culture in terms of their objectives as well as their means of achieving these. Unquestionably, we can emphasize the seemingly non-rational beliefs of the NRMs, and hence set up a dichotomy between NRMs and modernity that sees all concessions to rationality as a loss of religiousness, but in doing so we are missing something important.

> If the scholarly or public debate over specific prophetic movements becomes articulated in terms of their deviance from or rejection of conventional secular society, we fail to appreciate that their appeal and power are derived from the cultural and social fabric of their host societies. Indeed, at the core of innovative movements, in their fundamental moral principles and in their most ritualized social practices, we find components of secular society that have not been rejected but elaborated and intensified. Conformity and deviation are inextricably linked, not opposed, to each other: the more a group conforms to its host society, the more it simultaneously deviates from it. (Parsons, 1989: 223)

If its level of 'modernity' is going to affect our judgment of an NRMs significance, then, we need to understand more than simply how deviant or conformist its means and ends are.[5]

THE SURPRISING SIMILARITIES OF 'ANTI-MODERN' AND 'MODERN' NEW RELIGIOUS MOVEMENTS

Parsons's analysis tends to invalidate some of the standard ways of differentiating anti-modernist from modernist NRMs and thereby defining NRMs as culturally inconsequential because they are either anti-modern or have sold out to modernity. The doubts about the usefulness of the modern/anti-modern distinction are reinforced by a little-known yet innovative essay by

Phillip Lucas (1992), in which he describes similarities between two very different kinds of new religion: on the one hand, the Pentecostal and Charismatic movements; on the other, the various New Age movements.

The Pentecostal movement began within American Protestantism at the beginning of the twentieth century as a small fringe that stressed the return of special spiritual gifts, recorded in the New Testament, to those who believed they had experienced a special baptism of the Holy Spirit, or the holy fire. The best known of the gifts is *glossolalia*—the gift of tongues. A person speaking in tongues utters strange and continuous sounds in a kind of nonsensical language, sometimes when he or she seems to be in a trance induced by singing, praying, and occasionally even dancing. A second gift is the ability to interpret some of these utterances and make pronouncements to the congregation about their expression of God's will. Other gifts are those of prophecy and of healing by the laying on of hands. Pentecostal worship is exuberant, even somewhat disorderly at times. It represents a kind of permanent extension of the holy fervour associated with the intense revivalist camp meetings of the nineteenth century. The return of the gifts is thought to be a sign that the end of days is approaching, and the Pentecostalists are seeking to prepare themselves and others by fostering the consciousness of being born again in Christ. Today such Pentecostalist denominations as the Assemblies of God, the Church of God in Christ, the International Church of the Foursquare Gospel, and many others, constitute a major and rapidly growing segment of Christian culture in America and much of the rest of the world (Neitz, 1987; Cox, 1995). The Charismatic movement is more or less the expression of the same religious phenomena in organizations that have elected to stay associated with such traditional denominations as the Anglicans (Episcopalians) or the Catholic Church. Together, by some estimates, the Pentecostals and Charismatics constitute more than 20 per cent of American Christians. There may well be hundreds of millions of Pentecostals and Charismatics in the world.

The New Age movement is much more amorphous. In fact, it is really just a convenient name for a clustering of similar organizations of the most diverse kind, ranging from groups practising witchcraft or Neo-Paganism to various experimental forms of almost secular psychotherapies. The movement as such is united by a common stress on the sacredness of the self and on various 'spiritual' processes of self-discovery that have either been invented or recovered from numerous traditional and usually pre-modern or marginalized cultures of the world (such as Native American, Celtic, or Tibetan). In these groups the inner path of spiritual development is linked to the salvation of the world from certain contemporary and grievous errors of humanity, ranging from the pollution of the environment to the suppression of our true psychic powers. The transformation of the self through spiritual enlightenment has the potential, it is believed, to bring about the collective and radical transformation of human nature itself, thereby ushering in a New Age. In the popular consciousness, the New Age is associated with such beliefs and practices as yoga, meditation, the use of crystals for healing, macrobiotics, reincarnation, channelling, aromatherapy, the reading of auras, telepathic contact with civilizations from other worlds, astral projection, and so on (Lewis and Melton, 1993; Heelas, 1996; Hanegraaff, 1996; Brown, 1997; Sutcliffe, 2003). There is no reliable way to even guess the number of people involved in this 'movement'. But the multi-million sales of James Redfield's New Age tale *The Celestine Prophecy* (1995), which was number one on the *New York Times* bestseller list for over a hundred weeks, suggests the pervasive appeal of these ideas. Throughout North America, moreover, centres of New Age activity and training, big and small, have been established in almost every city of any size.

What is it that Lucas thinks these two seemingly very dissimilar 'religious' enthusiasms have in common? First, both the Pentecostal-Charismatic and the New Age movements stress a rediscovery of the experience of sacred power in the daily lives of ordinary people (Lucas, 1992: 194–200). The experience in question is envisioned as intense, personal, ecstatic, and susceptible to being repeated. Both movements associate these experiences with the continuous presence in human affairs of spiritual energy, whether it be *prana, mana, orgone* energy, or the Holy Spirit. They believe in contact with spiritual beings, whether spirit guides and nature spirits, or angels and demons. They both believe in establishing various functional relationships with the spirit world, relationships that can lead to the acquisition of extraordinary powers or give special assistance. Admittedly, in the kinds of experiences and the means used to acquire them, these two movements differ, but historically, socially, and culturally, each movement contributes to a new and marked democratization of spiritual experience in society.

Second, both movements represent attempts to fashion new structures of social cohesion, under the guise of 'sacred communities' (pp. 200–1). In doing so, both are distinguished by a worldwide vision, seeking to transcend 'conventional denominational, national, and ethnic boundaries'. As internationalist movements, they have adapted to 'current geopolitical realities and trends' and taken full advantage of new means of mass communication and travel, as well as mechanisms and forums for cultural exchange.

Third, at the heart of each movement is a strong emphasis on the task and means of spiritual healing, both of the mind and of the body (pp. 201–3). Underlying this preoccupation with the well-being of the individual is a common holistic belief in the interconnectedness of spirit and matter, the mind and the body, the individual and the community, and the sacred and the profane.

Fourth, both groups anticipate the arrival of a new age (pp. 203–5). New Agers usually promote a kind of 'soft' apocalypticism by which the world will be suddenly changed for the better as a result of some collective spiritual effort, while the Pentecostal-Charismatic revival adheres to biblical prophecy and is thus 'far less sanguine about the prospects of the modern world'.

Fifth, both movements display an 'anti-institutional and decentralized character' (pp. 205–7). Loose organizational structures, resembling networks far more than traditional bureaucracies, are typical of both movements, and the primary locus of authority tends to be the individual and his or her interior experience, judged in the light of its pragmatic fruits for the individual and humanity.

Like Stone, Westley, and Campbell before him, Lucas notes how these features link both the Pentecostal-Charismatic and the New Age movements to some long-standing and pervasive themes of American religious life: a messianic view of the nation, an ethos of individualism and egalitarianism, a tradition of revivalism with its emphasis on personal religious experience, and a preference for pragmatism that entails belief in the reconciliation of the religious and the scientific world-views (pp. 207–11).

Where does this leave us? Are NRMs anti-modernist or modernist? Are some anti-modernist and others modernist? It is difficult to say. The latter appears at first to be more likely; NRMs do seem to divide into some kind of conservative and liberal, or traditionalist and experimentalist, clusters. Yet as Parsons's and Lucas's analyses suggest, it is not easy to decide which movements belong in which camp and why. Both the Moonies and the Pentecostal-Charismatics, seemingly very conservative or even pre-modern movements, display features commonly associated with the modernist label. Perhaps then we are faced with a single modernist continuum of more conservative or more liberal religions? Or do the ambiguities encountered indicate that the more accurate terms of reference are modern and post-modern, respectively? Will the introduction of a post-modernist category clarify matters?

Box 8 Factors Affecting the Success of NRMs

In Box 2 we looked at the changes that Eileen Barker noticed in many of the more prominent NRMs of the post-1960s era as they achieved a degree of longevity. In a masterly complementary analysis Rodney Stark (1996a) has tried to delineate the factors that may account for this longevity in the first place. Examining the cumulative body of research now available on a variety of NRMs, he argues that NRMs will succeed to the degree that:

1. They retain cultural continuity with the conventional faiths of the societies within which they seek converts.

2. Their doctrines are non-empirical.

3. They maintain a medium level of tension with the surrounding environment—are strict, but not too strict.

4. They have legitimate leaders with adequate authority to be effective.

   (a) Adequate authority requires clear doctrinal justifications for an effective and legitimate leadership.

   (b) Authority is regarded as more legitimate and gains in effectiveness to the degree that members perceive themselves as participants in the system of authority.

5. They generate a highly motivated, volunteer, religious labour force, including many willing to proselytize.

6. They maintain a level of fertility sufficient to at least offset member mortality.

7. They compete against weak, local conventional religious organizations within relatively unregulated religious economies.

8. They sustain strong internal attachments, while remaining an open social network, able to maintain and form ties to outsiders.

9. They continue to maintain sufficient tension with their environment—remain sufficiently strict.

10. They socialize the young sufficiently well as to minimize both defection and the appeal of reduced strictness. (1996a, pp. 144–145)

If Stark is correct, and his analysis is persuasive, then some of the changes that Eileen Barker observed in the larger and more controversial NRMs may actually be detrimental to their success in the long run. A certain strictness, for example, seems to contribute to an NRMs competitive edge and enthusiasm, yet accommodation to the dominant society seems inevitable and equally necessary in other regards. Success hinges, it seems, on sustaining a delicate balance of these elements in the face of known and unknown contingencies. Investigating the play of the relevant ideological and social structural factors poses many intriguing opportunities for future research.

Drawn from Lorne L. Dawson, 'New Religious Movements.' Forthcoming in Robert Segal, ed., *Blackwell Companion to Religious Studies*. Oxford: Blackwell, 2005. Used with the permission of Blackwell Publishers.

Postmodernism and the New Religious Movements

In the essay 'Religion, Modernity, and Post-Modernity', James Beckford examines Berger's and Wilson's theories of the relationship between modernity and religion (amongst others) in the light of the data available on religion in contemporary Britain. He concludes that these approaches do not adequately capture the new realities of religious life:

> The most telling reason for questioning the received wisdoms is that none of the prevailing versions pays more than passing attention to what I believe to be the most important aspect of religious change in recent years. I am referring to the growth of parallel, yet contrasting, types of religion. On the one hand, Christian churches and Jewish groups with strict and very conservative outlooks are growing. And, on the other, a relatively new form of liberal and tolerant spirituality is spreading both inside and outside religious organizations. I shall refer to the latter as 'holistic' spirituality. The combination of these two contrasting developments wreaks havoc with prevailing ideas about religion and modernity. (Beckford, 1992: 17)

In describing some of the elements of the new spirituality, he strikes some familiar notes. Beckford (1992) specifies three 'major characteristics'. First, the new spirituality 'strains towards a holistic perspective which emphasizes the inter-connectedness between, for example, human and non-human, personal and public, physical and mental, or national and international' (p. 17). Hence its focus is not so much on the supernatural or the 'great transcendences' of the world religions as on the 'little transcendence' of the interests and limitations of the 'mundane world' (see Luckmann, 1990 as well). Second, there 'is the belief that the adoption of a holistic perspective can provide access to, or can release, new sources of power.' The extraordinary powers released are to be used, moreover, to fulfil a spiritually enlightened agenda of practical applications—improved health, food, natural environment, human rights, justice, and peace (p. 17). Third, this new spirituality is 'compatible with a wide range of specific ideologies and practices. . . . It represents a general shift in sensibility and ethos: not a specific programme of social change or a separate form of religious practice' (pp. 17–18).

It is true, Beckford admits, that the new spirituality is actively practised by only 'a tiny proportion of the population', and it 'lacks the sense of communal obligation and collective ritual attaching to public religion' (p. 18). It is not a phenomenon that can be equated with traditional conceptions of organized religion. Its influence can be detected, however, throughout contemporary life, in new ways of thinking about 'medicine, sport, leisure, education, peace, ecology, dying and grieving, self-help, gender, relations with non-human animals, social work, and even management training.' We are seeing, he says, a 'holistic shift' in society toward a kind of 'transcendent humanism'. Is this something like the new religious consciousness detected by Stone, Westley, and Campbell?

Instead of being more precise at this juncture, Beckford turns to a consideration of whether the now popular notion of post-modernity is of any help in understanding the changes he has in mind (p. 19). Given the complex and contested character of this concept, he is skeptical. If the term is merely being used to designate a period of time, say from the mid-1950s onward, then in some debatable yet trivial sense most NRMs are post-modern. But even then the application of the term denotes some shift in sensibility. Beckford summarizes the four themes most commonly associated with the new postmodernist sensibility and then considers whether they fit the new religious realities he has detected.

The concept of 'postmodernism' grew out discussions in the fields of art, literature, architecture, and philosophy about the emergence of certain rather radical new styles of thought. Philosophically the term is associated with the work of such French thinkers as Jean-François Lyotard (1984), Jean Baudrillard (1981, 1983), Michel Foucault (1972, 1982), and Jacques Derrida (1970, 1976). In their historical and philosophical analyses they have argued for a fundamental change in our intellectual agenda in the face of certain new social and cultural realities that they believed have been emerging over the last several decades. This new orientation entails the rejection, transcendence, or sometimes reversal of the guiding principles of the 'modernist' world-view, which had itself displaced the feudalistic world-view some four centuries earlier (see Rosenau, 1992). The hallmarks of the new postmodernist sensibility, Beckford suggests (1992: 19), are the following:

1. A refusal to regard positivistic, rationalistic, instrumental criteria as the sole or exclusive standard of worthwhile knowledge.

2. A willingness to combine symbols from disparate codes or frameworks of meaning, even at the cost of disjunctions and eclecticism.

3. A celebration of spontaneity, fragmentation, superficiality, irony, and playfulness.

4. A willingness to abandon the search for over-arching or triumphalist myths, narratives, or frameworks of knowledge.

These themes call to mind, Beckford acknowledges (1992: 19–20), 'a few New Age groups', particularly the Neo-Sannyassins of Bhagwan Shree Rajneesh and some other syncretistic Buddhist meditational groups in America (he names no specific groups, but I would argue that

Vajradhatu/Shambhala is a candidate—see Dawson and Eldershaw, 1998). He is quick to insist, however, that these groups are only 'the glittering baubles on the exotic fringe of religion'. They do not represent the kind of religion that is thriving in contemporary Britain. Certainly these themes have little or no relevance for understanding the ideology and practice of the growing Christian fundamentalist, Pentecostalist, and Charismatic movements. These developments 'have been resolutely transcendental rather than immanent, serious rather than playful, in good faith rather than cynical, univocal rather than fragmented, and so on' (p. 20). More problematically, though, he also asserts:

> My assessment of the new spiritualities . . . is the same. . . . Their very holism locates them much more firmly in the traditions of modernity than of post-modernity. The stress on the inter-connectedness of all living things, the heightened awareness of 'the global circumstance' . . . the strong sense of evolutionary equilibrium and change, the belief in the possibility of personal and social transformation, and the affirmation of noninstrumental rationalities are all redolent of a revised 'Enlightenment project' with the emphasis more firmly placed on the human scale and spiritual implications of science, politics and state administration. (Beckford, 1992: 21)

It is true, he observes, that the sacred canopy of the past has been fragmented and the 'juxtaposition of formerly separate religions may have created the impression . . . of a patchwork quilt' (p. 21). But the new religions and the shift in sensibility they reflect are still concerned with the pursuit of 'the truth', and they have turned more to science (of a non-reductionistic kind) than away from it. The new religious leaders of today may be *bricoleurs*—that is, they may be using what is at hand to fashion something new—but they are not exponents of the religious equivalent of an 'art for art's sake' approach to life. In most cases the few links that can be made between postmodernism and specific religions are either sophistry or redundant, since the features addressed can be accounted for equally as well within the terms of reference of modernity.[6]

NRMs: Anti-modern, Modern, or Postmodern?

So let us ask once again, with Beckford's additional comments in hand: Are we closer to identifying the cultural significance of NRMs? I think we are making progress incrementally, though the question cannot be definitively resolved. We should refrain from continuing to identify most, if not all NRMs, with some anti-modernist stance. In every NRM I can think of, the blend of traditional and modern elements, of religious and secular objectives and means, of conservative and liberal impulses is such that the anti-modernist label is bound to be misleading. Within a modernist framework, however, there would appear to be a significant division of NRMs into more traditionalist and experimentalist camps. Discerning the real points of variation between these camps requires reference to detailed studies of specific religious groups.

Likewise, with Beckford, I do not see much advantage in labelling most NRMs postmodern. As I have argued elsewhere, the terms of reference of the postmodern are still more relevant for the fine arts, architecture, and literature than for the study of social action (e.g. Dawson and Prus, 1993a, 1993b; see also Rosenau, 1992). For scholars of NRMs, an awareness of the features of the post-modern is useful but it does more to augment our descriptive vocabulary of some aspects of some new religions than to provide explanatory insights into the nature of NRMs.

In the conclusion of his analysis, Beckford makes an interesting proposal that rings true and warrants more systematic investigation. This proposal accounts for many of the seemingly postmodern features of NRMs (for example, the combination of seemingly disparate codes or frameworks of meaning) without compelling us to accept, quite contradictorily, the post-modernist meta-narrative (in which all of life, including religion, has become playful). This simpler, more accurate proposal isolates an important feature of our new religious environment that is susceptible to empirical examination. It is in keeping, moreover, with aspects of the new religious consciousness as they are described by Stone, Westley, and Campbell. Today, Beckford proposes, 'it is . . . better to conceptualize religion as a cultural resource . . . than as a social institution' (p. 23; 1989 as well). The social-structural transformations wrought by the emergence of advanced industrial societies have undermined the communal, familial, and organizational bases of religion. As a consequence, in Beckford's evocative phrase, 'religion has come adrift from its former points of social anchorage' (p. 22). Nonetheless, he argues (1992: 23):

> Religious and spiritual forms of sentiment, belief and action have survived as relatively autonomous resources. They retain the capacity to symbolize, for example, ultimate meaning, infinite power, supreme indignation and sublime compassion. And they can be deployed in the service of virtually any interest-group or ideal: not just organizations with specifically religious objectives.

There is more merit in this suggestion than the attempts to fit the data on NRMs to the postmodernist grid.[7] To explore its potential, however, carries us well beyond the scope of this introductory book.[8]

Concluding Remarks

In the epilogue to their detailed study of the Sōka Gakkai in Britain, Wilson and Dobbelaere (1994) summarize what they discovered about the nature and appeal of this successful NRM from Japan. Many aspects of the group, as they describe them, are in harmony with the observations made by Stone, Westley, Campbell, Parsons, Lucas, and Beckford on the characteristics of a new religious consciousness (see Dawson, 2001a). But Wilson and Dobbelaere continue to hold staunchly to the traditional explanatory framework, linking the appeal of Sōka Gakkai to some compensatory or oppositional response to the disjunctures of modern life. It is hard to fault them seriously for reverting to this explanatory framework when we do not yet fully understand the possible causal connections between the presumed features of modernity and the features of various specific NRMs. My point here is that we need to learn much more, by way of detailed case studies of individual NRMs,[9] about the connections between social conditions and the presence or absence, success or failure, of certain religious beliefs and practices, before we can do much more than speculate about the cultural significance of NRMs (see Dawson, 2004 and 2005b).

Contrary to the assumption of some sociologists that the study of NRMs is already passé, much of the most important work has yet to be done. With four decades of research behind us, the promise offered by the emergence of contemporary NRMs for the direct testing and development of the most basic questions of the sociology of religion has yet to be fully realized.[10] The need to know more has been, of course, a constant refrain of this text. But I hope it is now clear that we possess the means to understand cults without indulging our fears or prejudices. Common sense recommends that we be vigilant about the cults in our midst, but for this vigilance to be wise, we must be properly informed.

Notes

CHAPTER ONE

1. The *Toronto Star* and the *Globe and Mail*, respectively, for Thursday, 6 October 1994.
2. By Friday, 7 October 1994, fifty-three bodies had been found and the Quebec and Swiss authorities declared that the deaths appeared to be the result of some combination of murders and suicides. Then, much to everyone's surprise, on 21 December 1995, sixteen more followers of the movement, which had been led by the Belgian Canadian Luc Jouret and the Swiss Joseph Di Mambro, committed ritualistic suicide in a French forest near the Swiss border. On 25 March 1997, five more members committed suicide at Saint-Casimir, Quebec.

   To date there have been few studies of these events. Massimo Introvigne (1995) gives a history of the group, placing it within the long and complicated tradition of neo-Templar occult-esoteric movements in Europe. He also attempts an initial interpretation of the first tragedy in 1994. Susan Palmer (1996) and John Hall and Philip Schuyler (1997) also provide detailed and revealing analyses of the group's history, basic beliefs, and internal struggles. Palmer, in particular, offers a helpful theoretical framework for possibly understanding why the members of this group committed ritualistic murder and suicide. The most comprehensive study of this event, however, is probably to be found in the small book *Les Mythes du Temple solaire* by the Swiss historian of religions Jean-François Mayer (1996). Mayer studied the group before the tragedy and officially assisted the Swiss police in their investigation from the time the bodies were discovered. An excellent summary of his findings is provided in Mayer (1999).
3. Danny Jorgensen (1980) gives an interesting analysis of the coverage of the

Jonestown massacre in 1978 by the print media. He concludes that when the story was 'hot', in the days immediately following the tragedy, the newspapers gave an inordinate amount of selective attention to and emphasis on certain aspects of the event; they decontextualized happenings, oversimplified processes, misinformed the public, and misused the comments of so-called 'experts' to make an unusual situation fit into a largely preconceived and commonsensical understanding of deviance. The distinguished historian of religion, Jonathan Z. Smith (1982: 109), is even more scathing in his condemnation of the wholly 'pornographic' and 'polemical' character of the media coverage of the Jonestown massacre. The media treatment of the later cult-related tragedies, the Tokyo subway gas poisonings (20 March 1995), perpetrated by the Aum Shinrikyō Buddhist sect led by Shōkō Asahara, and the Heaven's Gate mass suicide at Rancho Santa Fe, California (26 March 1997), do not suggest we can expect much improvement in this coverage soon (see e.g. Richardson 1995a, 1996b; Kaplan and Marshall, 1996; Steiger and Hewes, 1997).

4. Accurate estimates are hard to come by since most new religions do not keep accurate figures, they commonly exaggerate their membership numbers, and census and other national survey data are misleading when dealing with such small percentages. Probably no more (and perhaps less) than 1 per cent or less of the American and the Canadian populations are members of a diverse array of new religions. But because the turnover in recruits to most new religions is so notoriously high (see Chapter 5), many more people may have experienced some involvement with a 'cult' than are recorded as members at any one time. One thing is clear: the real number of people joining new religions is growing at a steady pace. For example, the Canadian census figures show that there were 1,220 Scientologists in Canada in 1991, and 1,525 in 2001.The figures are small but growing, and Scientologists claim—with some justification I suspect— that many more Canadians have had some involvement with their organization. Looking at the figures for what is now a much less stigmatized religious choice, there were about 5,530 Pagans in Canada in 1991, and 21,085 in 2001 (Statistics Canada, 2003). Helen Berger (1999: 9), an American scholar of Neo-Paganism, estimates there are about 150,000 to 200,000 Neo-Pagans in the United States. Sōka Gakkai International, a Japanese Buddhist new religious movement, claims an American membership of about 300,000. Hammond and Machacek (1999) estimate that there are actually about 35,000 active members. But since the group started with about 4,000 active members in 1965, this represents significant growth.

We must remember that many people may be reluctant to publicly identify themselves with any of these unconventional groups, yet Wade Clark Roof's (1999) national surveys lead him to estimate that about 14 per cent of Americans are now what he calls 'metaphysical believers and seekers.' In other words, there are approximately 40 million people who are at least interested in new and unconventional forms of religious and spiritual practice. If only 1 per cent of Americans are actually members of such groups, that still constitutes about 2.5 to 3 million people in the United States alone.

5. There are broad similarities between the religious activities and orientations of Canadians and Americans. But as Canadians insist, and with some scholarly support (see Lipset, 1990; Handy, 1976; Mol, 1985; Reimer, 1995; Beyer, 1997), there are differences. Canadians, for instance, are simply a much less 'religious' people (see Bibby, 1987, 2002). Whereas church attendance remains relatively high in the United States, it is in sharp decline in Canada (as in Europe). However, the presence and influence of new forms of religious life in the two societies are similar enough to justify suspending consideration of such differences.

6. These are more or less the categories that Mary Farrell Bednarowski (1989) uses in her excellent study of the beliefs of various cults in *New Religions and the Theological Imagination in America*.

7. The magazine in question is *Maclean's*. The issue is 8 February 1993.

8. Let me give one fairly typical yet randomly encountered example. I recently found most of the negative stereotypes of cults repeated, without qualification, in a Canadian government report designed to help explode stereotypical ways of thinking about another social problem, namely, in the executive summary of a report by the Panel on Violence against Women, entitled *Changing the Landscape: Ending Violence—Achieving Equality* (Minister of Supply and Services Canada, 1993, cat. SW45–1/1993E). Cults, this report states, without qualification, are common sites of violence against women.

9. Even when consulted, most experts experience the frustration of seeing the careful distinctions and assessments they had laboured to convey in interviews with the press ignored or distorted in the resultant articles and media reports (for example, see the comments of Richardson in Van Driel and Richardson, 1988: 56, n. 12; Barker, 1993: 207; Beckford, 1994; Boyer, 1998; Palmer, 2004: 1–16). Barker (1995a: 301–6) presents an excellent discussion of both the necessity and the pitfalls of academics' seeking to address the cult issue publicly. Boyer (1998: 7) concludes his humorous reflections on his experiences with the media with a characteristic lament: 'For all the high-minded rhetoric about outreach, community service, and scholars' duty to educate and inform the public, the reality is often different. When academics venture into the realm of print or electronic journalism, we frequently play another role altogether: less as gurus and bearers of light than simply as fodder in the media's endless struggle to meet the one compelling, inexorable imperative of their existence: to cover all that blank paper with copy, to fill all those hours of air time with talk.'

10. Bromley and Shupe (1993: 194) explain a number of understandable reasons why scholars of religion tend to be more sympathetic to NRMs than to the anti-cult movement. But, as they stress, in the end every effort must be made to sustain a balanced perspective. We must try to avoid crossing the line separating the presentation of information from the rhetoric of interest groups vying for favour.

11. The British sociologist Bryan Wilson holds to a similar view, I have discovered (Wilson, 1982a: 133; and Wilson and Dobbelaere, 1994: 216–31), and there is a strong parallel with the general distinction made by Zald and Ash (1965) between inclusive and exclusive social movement organizations, as noted by Wallis (1984: 124–5).

12. One of the strongest critics of the reductionism of social-scientific treatments of religion is the eminent historian of religions Mircea Eliade (e.g., 1963, 1969). His views and those of others of like mind have been the subject of long and complicated debates in religious studies (see, e.g., Garrett, 1974; Segal, 1983; Dawson, 1986, 1987; and Idinopulos and Yonan, 1994).

CHAPTER TWO

1. A similar contrast of interpretive options could have been found by choosing any number of other prominent sociologists, like Bryan Wilson (1979 or 1982a) and Daniel Bell (1977). But the writings of Berger and of Stark and Bainbridge seem to have exercised a more direct influence on work in the field of NRMs.

2. Less conventionally, but still in emulation of Weber (and others), Berger also argues that the roots of the secularization of society lie in the Christian tradition itself (Berger, 1967: 110–23, 157–68). The history and theology of Christianity, he proposes, carried the 'seeds of its own destruction' in its progressive commitment to the motifs of 'transcendentalization', 'historization', and the 'rationalization of ethics', a legacy of unique world-building themes dating from at least the times of the Old Testament. Fascinating as his discussion of that theory is, however, it does not bear upon our immediate subject, the study of NRMs.

3. This same theory is presented in much greater complexity in Stark and Bainbridge (1987, reprinted in 1996), resulting in a systematic deductive theory of religion framed in terms of 344 testable propositions. In 2000, in collaboration with Roger Finke, Stark published a further simplified and revised statement of the elements of his theory of religion in *Acts of Faith: Explaining the Human Side of Religion*. At this point he repudiated his earlier use of the term 'compensators', saying the word 'implies unmeant negative connotations about the validity of religions promises'. It suffices, he asserts, to speak simply

of religions 'explanations' (2000: 289).

4.   Consult Dawson (1997) for an overview of the substantive and theoretical criticisms of church-sect-cult typologies found in the social-scientific literature of the last several decades, and a proposal for the reformulation of this mode of theorizing based on a return to the forgotten theoretical wisdom of Max Weber. Elements of this proposal will be used to justify the selective framework for the understanding of NRMs outlined in this chapter.

5.   The concept and term 'denomination', while not part of the initial formulation of church-sect typology, dates from at least Richard Niebuhr's discussion of these matters in 1929. For a discussion of the concept, see David Martin (1962).

6.   In part, as I specify elsewhere (Dawson, 1997), this is because in their other more generalized writings on church-sect theory Stark and Bainbridge have fallen prey to what Swatos (1976) calls the Troeltschian syndrome. In these writings they play upon the criterion of tension with the dominant society to differentiate churches from sects. There is an inconsistency or disjuncture, then, between the analytical frameworks they employ for distinguishing between cults and the one they employ for distinguishing between sects and churches; the net result is an incomplete typology of cults. I would argue that the measurement of tension with the dominant society used by Stark and Bainbridge and others to distinguish between churches and sects is far more complicated, problematic, and untested than the original Weberian criterion.

CHAPTER THREE

1.   As indicated in Chapter 1, the division of types of NRMs I have in mind is reminiscent of a distinction drawn by Wilson (1982a: 133). Likewise, it is similar to the contrasts drawn independently between types of new religions by Berger (1967), Stark and Bainbridge (1985), and Wallis (1984) that were discussed in Chapter 2. Here I wish to stress two things: (1) we are dealing with attributes indicative of the popular ends of a continuum, and with many mixed or intermediate forms of religious orientations and organizations found between these poles, and (2) we must avoid the inclination to reduce that continuum to the mere acceptance or rejection of modernity *per se*. What I have in mind and why is discussed in more detail in Chapter 8. The similarities between the distinctions drawn by several eminent commentators on contemporary religion suggests that we are dealing with more than a mere artifact of the analytic study of NRMs. But the distinction may become a mere artifact of analysis if it is used too cavalierly.

2.   Variants of this perspective have been presented by numerous scholars. For example: Robbins and Anthony, 1972; Anthony and Robbins, 1975; Robbins,

Anthony, and Curtis, 1975; Bird, 1979; Tipton, 1982a, 1982b; Anthony and Robbins, 1982a; Robbins and Anthony, 1982a; and to some extent Foss and Larkin, 1978; Wilson, 1982b; Levine, 1984; Wallis, 1984; Kent, 1987, 1988; Wuthnow, 1988; Palmer, 1994; Roof, 1993.

3. A related and, one might say, subsidiary aspect of arguments linking the emergence of NRMs to moral ambiguity advances the demise of American 'civil religion' in the 1970s as a causal factor. Robert Bellah has exerted a foundational influence on this interpretation as well. Those interested in this civil-religion thesis should read Bellah (1967, 1975, 1981), Robbins et al. (1976), Johnson (1981), and Anthony and Robbins (1982b, 1990).

4. See Robbins, Anthony, and Curtis (1975: 59–61) for a more elaborate discussion of this and other methodological objections to this view of the emergence of NRMs.

5. Various social structural arguments have been addressed by Robbins and Anthony, 1972; Marx and Ellison, 1975; Anthony and Robbins, 1981; Doress and Porter, 1981; Hunter, 1981; Robbins and Anthony, 1982a; Kilbourne and Richardson, 1982; Levine, 1984; Parsons, 1986, 1989; Robbins, 1988; Cartwright and Kent, 1992; Wright and D'Antonio, 1993; Palmer, 1994; and Dawson, 2004.

6. Lynn Davidman (1990) argues as well for a strong correlation between the desire for a stable family life and the conversion of young professional women to more extreme religious groups, specifically Orthodox Judaism.

7. This summary is drawn from Dawson (2005a) and used with the permission of Oxford University Press, USA. For more detailed discussions see Dawson (2004, 2005b).

8. In *Revivals, Awakenings, and Reform*, McLoughlin actually expands the scope of his analysis by arguing that the American 'awakenings' should be conceptualized in terms of Anthony F.C. Wallace's well-known anthropological theory of 'revitalization movements' (Wallace, 1956, 1966). The latter refers to periodic movements of cultural upheaval and reform commonly effected through religious means that Wallace and others think have gripped many societies around the world throughout time. The rise of Islam, for example, can be interpreted in this manner. Eister (1974), Barker (1985), Hargrove (1988), and many others (including Eldershaw and Dawson, 1995) have tried to apply elements of this broader theory to the most recent wave of NRMs in the West. Considerations of space and complexity have prompted the omission of this discussion here.

9. For example, with regard to Buddhism in the United States, two very interesting books have been published: Thomas Tweed's *The American Encounter with Buddhism, 1844–1912* (1992) and Joseph Tamney's *American Society in the Buddhist Mirror* (1992).

10. Stephen Kent (1987) also calls attention to the parallels often drawn between the

social, political, cultural, and religious unrest experienced by Americans in the sixties and seventies and that of the period in English history known as the Interregnum, the 1640s and 1650s. The Interregnum marks the time of the first phase of the English Civil War and its aftermath. As Kent meticulously documents, it too was a time in Western history when political disruption and eventual disappointment spurred the rise of sweeping and radical religious innovations—sectarian groups like the Diggers, Ranters, and Quakers whose behaviour and claims closely resemble those of many contemporary cults.

11. With this long tradition in mind, Werblowsky (1982: 35) asks playfully but fairly: 'How much of the "message" [of the NRMs] is new wine in old bottles, old wine in new bottles, old wine in old bottles, or new wine in new bottles?' The thematic and historical links between the contemporary New Age Movement and the established Western esoteric traditions is clearly delineated in Hanegraaff (1996). Many of the essays in Partridge (2003) demonstrate equally strong links between pre-modern esoteric traditions and many UFO religions.

CHAPTER FOUR

1. Insight into why specific individuals do decide to join specific NRMs is often provided in such sources as Tipton (1982a), Levine (1984), Roof (1993), Lucas (1995), Muster (1997), Layton (1998), Maaga (1998), Goldman (1999).

2. In the other classic account of relative-deprivation theory, Aberle (1962) offers a similar typology: deprivations of possessions, social deprivation, behavioural deprivation, and worth deprivation. He also expands the reference for the comparisons leading to a sense of relative deprivation to people's perceptions of their past conditions (real or imagined) and expectations for the future.

3. Wilson (1990: 195) makes the same point most succinctly: 'The idea of relative deprivation as such might be seen as an iconoclastic challenge to pure religious motivation.'

4. The importance of social networks has been discovered by many researchers. For example: Harrison, 1974; Beckford, 1975; Lofland, 1977; Bainbridge, 1978; Snow et al., 1980; Stark and Bainbridge, 1985; Rochford, 1985; Latkin et al., 1987; Palmer, 1994; Wilson and Dobbelaere, 1994; Lucas, 1995; Chancellor, 2000; and Palmer, 2004.

5. The importance of affective ties is studied by Harrison, 1974; Enroth, 1977; Lofland, 1977; Bainbridge, 1978; Galanter et al., 1979; Richardson, Stewart, and Simmonds, 1979; Levine, 1984; Barker, 1984; Rochford, 1985; Van Zandt, 1991; Palmer, 1994; Wilson and Dobbelaere, 1994; Goldman, 1999; and Chancellor, 2000.

6. Stark and Bainbridge (1987) have sought to integrate many of the points made

in this chapter into one systematic theory, framed in terms of a large series of presumably testable propositions or hypotheses (e.g., see Chapter 7 of their book). Regrettably, however, little effort has been made so far by Stark and Bainbridge or others to actually test most of these propositions. Most sociologists have been preoccupied with other aspects of their theory, dealing with secularization and the structure of religious markets (e.g., Warner, 1993; Young, 1997).

7.   Brock Kilbourne, 'Equity or Exploitation? The Case of the Unification Church', *Review of Religious Research* 28 (1986): 143–50, also documents the role of youthful idealism in predisposing people to joining the Moonies.

8.   The same impression is conveyed by Chancellor's (2000: 34-57) independent account of why people joined the Children of God/The Family.

9.   Chancellor (2000: 58, n. 1 and 35-36) rightly notes that insufficient attention has been given to the nature and significance of the theologies or doctrinal teaching of NRMs, in part because the study of NRMs 'has been entrusted primarily to social scientists'. Jamie Hubbard (1998) provides an excellent account of why this has happened and a forceful argument for its reversal (see also Bednarowski, 1989).

CHAPTER FIVE

1.   Deprogrammers are those who have attempted, as Ted Patrick says (1976), to 'fight fire with fire' by physically removing young people, against their will, from NRMs and subjecting them, on behalf of their parents and others, to an often gruelling critique of the new religion they have joined until their confidence in their new beliefs is broken. Deprogramming is illegal now. It has been replaced by various forms of voluntary 'exit counselling'. Consult Shupe and Bromley (1980) for a history, description, and discussion of the first years of the anti-cult movement and deprogramming, and Shupe, Bromley and Darnell (2004) for an updating of the situation.

2.   See, for example: Robbins and Anthony, 1979b; Robbins and Anthony, 1982b; Bromley and Richardson, 1983; Coleman, 1984; Barker, 1984; Levine, 1984; Robbins, 1984; Richardson, 1985, 1995c; Wright, 1987; Society for the Scientific Study of Religion, 1988; Rochford et al., 1989; Anthony, 1990; Dawson, 1990, 1996; Shinn, 1993; Anthony and Robbins, 2004.

3.   At my own large and decidedly scientifically oriented university, for example, an affiliated Catholic college sponsored a public lecture entitled 'Cults: "Works of the Devil"' (7 November 1995). The speaker, previously employed by the Archdiocese of Toronto to 'educate' high school students about cults, presented the standard brainwashing scenario espoused by the anti-cult movement without qualification, other than the addition of the

inflammatory supposition that NRMs are literally the work of the Devil and his minions. Although many of the students in the audience were sceptical or even offended, many of the older members of the audience, drawn from the larger non-academic community, seemed to accept much of what was said, though little or no reliable evidence had been supplied. The scenario was largely repeated, with only a little more sophistication, when a neighbouring university sponsored a lecture by Ron Loomis, a past president of the Cult Awareness Network and long time anti-cult activist (27 February 1997).

4. See Anthony and Robbins (1994) for an excellent overview of the emergence of the brainwashing literature and the connection with Chinese POW camps.

5. In a limited sense Singer is using the term descriptively if, as she implies at points, she is simply describing new religions that have proved to be harmful (such as Jim Jones and the Peoples Temple and the Solar Temple) and then assigning the name 'cult' exclusively to them. But this approach is disingenuous since the term 'cult' clearly has a much broader connotation in public usage. Moreover, her more sweeping rhetoric at other points belies her claim to any restricted meaning.

6. Of course, if there is no brainwashing, then there also would be little or no need for such largely self-proclaimed specialists as Hassan and Singer, 'exit counsellors' ready to treat the 'victims' and advise the public.

7. The term conversion is often used rather loosely and this is not the place to rectify this state of affairs. But a conversion is thought to entail an extensive 'reorganization of identity, meaning, [and] life' rooted in a transformation of the 'informing aspect' of one's biography (Travisano, 1981: 594, 600–1). In agreement with Bankston et al. (1981), Heirich (1977), Lofland and Skonovd (1981: 375), and Snow and Machalek (1984: 1970), I think a conversion is to be differentiated on this basis (by degree) from such related phenomena as 'adhesion' (the renewal of an existing faith), alternation (the transitory adoption of an alternative orientation), or mere affiliation (simply identifying with some group).

8. At the request of several leading anti-cult psychologists in 1983, the American Psychological Association (APA) created a task force to investigate Deceptive and Indirect Methods of Persuasion and Control. A report was submitted three years later to the APA's Board of Social and Ethical Responsibility. On the advice provided by its own independent reviewers the board rejected the report concluding that it lacked appropriate scientific rigour. This and a series of other briefs submitted to American courts by several other academic professional societies (e.g. the American Sociological Association), indicating doubts as to the scientific credibility of claims about brainwashing in cults, led to a protracted and interesting legal battle that ultimately went against the

interests of the anti-cult movement (see Anthony, 1990; Richardson, 1997; Anthony, 1999).

9. Bromley (2001) goes on to offer a sophisticated, though speculative, analysis of the well-springs of the brainwashing debate in the social tensions stemming from the ever greater disembedding of individuals as agents from the traditional social contexts in which they operate. He traces various developments in the social order over the last several decades that 'have the effect of preserving autonomy, expanding requirements for voluntarism, and promoting self-directedness' in society. This structural transformation has fostered movements advocating ever stauncher demands for individual autonomy and also countermovements concerned about the consequences of the modern processes of disembedding. The brainwashing debate is a sub-element of this larger social conflict. At one point, Bromley succinctly summarizes the complex contrast he has in mind (2001: 339–340):

> Although the dominant institutions in Western societies have moved rapidly towards . . . individual disembeddedness, conflict remains over how individual essence and individual-group relationships will be authorized. Pursuant to the present argument, I distinguish two loosely organized coalitions, the religion and mental health coalitions. Constituent partners in the former coalition tend to include the religion movements, some denominational bodies, religious liberty organizations, and religion scholars working from a structural perspective. Institutional authorization derives from the assertion of a transcendental power that is the ultimate source of individual essence and social relationships. The constitutional privileging of religion presents a formidable obstacle to challenging this source of authorization. Constituent partners in the latter coalition tend to include the religion countermovements, a segment of health professionals, some regulatory institutions, and religion scholars working from a social-psychological perspective. Institutional authorization derives from the assertion of the individual as the fundamental reality upon which all social relationships are constructed. The recent expansion of provisions in state and national legislation defining and protecting individual rights against institutional claims has created strong momentum towards extension of such provisions across all institutional sectors. Although there are numerous individuals and groups that do not conform to this profile, the two coalitions do offer competing definitions of and authorization for individual-group relationships.

10. My (2001b) critique of Kent's revival of the brainwashing scenario similarly demonstrates that the information he uses to support a negative interpreation lends itself equally plausibly to a more neutral explanation of the events, policies, and behaviour in question.

Chapter Six

1. The analysis in this section of the chapter was first presented in Dawson (2000). It is reproduced with the permission of Taylor and Francis.
2. See, for example: Swatsky, 1978; Bromley and Shupe, 1979; Miller, 1983; Kent, 1987; Lewis, 1988; Jenkins, 2000.
3. Lynn Davidman (1990) comes to remarkably similar conclusions about the young women converting to a strict form of Orthodox Judaism.
4. Goldman (1999) offers a similar and more detailed analysis.

Chapter Seven

1. In *Cults in Our Midst*, for example, Margaret Singer (1995: 3) quite typically begins her polemic against NRMs by highlighting the potential for cults to be violent:

   > Twice in less than fifteen years we have been shown the deadly ends to which cult followers can be led. In 1978, aerial photos of 912 brightly clad followers of Jim Jones, dead by cyanide laced drinks and gunshots in a steamy Guyanese jungle, were shown in magazines and on television. . . . And in early 1993, television programs showed the Koresh cult's shoot-out, then several weeks later its flaming end on the Texas plains. How many more Jonestowns and Wacos will have to occur before we realize how vulnerable all humans are to influence? In the time between these two episodes, nearly a hundred cult children and mothers died from lack of care in Indiana and there were reports of numerous other children and adults abused in cults. . . . Cult members who once were ordinary citizens have been persuaded by each of these and other groups to carry out group whims—including murder, suicide, and other violent acts—at the behest of the cult leader.

2. Excellent review essays summarizing what we know about the individual incidents of mass violence in NRMs are provided in Hall et al., 2000 and Bromley and Melton, 2002.
3. There are conflicting reports of the precise number of people who died at Jonestown; Singer, above, says 912, while Chidester (1988) says 914, and other sources cite both these and other slightly different numbers.
4. Fifty-three members died on 7 October 1994. Another sixteen took their own lives fourteen months later, and five more on 22 March 1997 (see Mayer, 1999).
5. Of course, as specified in Chapter 1, there are exceptions to every generalization about NRMs. For instance, the Church of Scientology instituted the infamous 'Fair Game Law' for one year. This 'law' stipulated that enemies of

Scientology 'may be deprived of property or injured by any means by any Scientologist. . . . [They] may be tricked, sued or lied to or destroyed' (L.R. Hubbard, 'Penalties for Lower Conditions', *Hubbard Communications Office Policy Letter*, 21 October 1968, as quoted in Kent, 1996: 26). Though this policy was formally cancelled, many commentators continue to suspect that some retaliatory activities continue, in effect, to be condoned by at least some elements of the church. I can only say that my own dealings with the Church of Scientology have been most cordial and I have never been informed of any acts of violence perpetrated by members of this group.

6. Robbins (1986) contains a fascinating description of another apocalyptic group that committed suicide, the Russian Old Believers.

7. CS (O-chlorobenzalmalononitrile) gas is extremely irritating and even lethal to children; the military use of this gas was banned by the Chemical Weapons Convention signed by the United States (and ninety-nine other countries) in 1993 (Wright, 1995b: 168, 329).

8. For some detailed and very persuasive presentations of this reading of events, see Barkun (1994), Tabor (1995), Ammerman (1995), Sullivan (1996) and Docherty (2001). As Sullivan's and Docherty's independent analyses of documents and the transcripts of negotiations demonstrates, neither the BATF nor the FBI made much effort to take the Branch Davidians' religious convictions seriously, let alone to understand their point of view. When they belatedly realized the error of their ways, officials systematically distorted the truth about their failure to consult religious experts (see Sullivan, 1996: 222–4).

9. The authoritative research of Roof and McKinney (1988) identifies 15.8 per cent of Americans as Conservative Protestants, and apocalyptic beliefs are pivotal to their self-understanding. To this number, of course, could be added many others from other religious orientations.

10. For an excellent account of the extraordinary charismatic powers of a decidedly plain and unobtrusive man, see Lucas's discussions of Earl Blighton, the founder and leader of a small but successful NRM (Lucas, 1995).

11. Both Palmer (1988) and Latkin (1992) offer insights into this process as it occurred in one particularly notorious instance: the ill-fated Rajneesh commune in Oregon (1981–5). Mayer (1999) and Hall and Schuyler (2000) provide similar information for the Solar Temple.

12. See Richardson, Stewart, and Simmonds (1979) for a good description of a battle between factions representing charismatic and rational-legal forms of authority in an NRM.

13. See, for example, the near hagiography of L. Ron Hubbard in *What is Scientology?* (1993: 25–55).

14. Once again, there are exceptions to every generalization about NRMs. Wallis (1982) presents Moses David of the Children of God/The Family as a classic

illustration of the charismatic leader who tries to avoid the consequences of the routinization of charisma. But Davis and Richardson (1976; Richardson and Davis, 1983) argue that Moses David had purposefully introduced more organizational uniformity to the group homes around the world, from an early point in the movement's development, in order to make his followers less dependent on him and reduce his burden as leader. Richardson believes that the importance and influence of single charismatic leaders in NRMs is usually exaggerated, in part because we do not know enough about the organizational structure and daily operation of most NRMs. Nevertheless, in each of the prominent cases of cult violence discussed here, the influence of a strong charismatic leader does seem to have been crucial.

15. Ironically, of course, as Stark and Bainbridge point out (1996: 245): 'The realities of recruitment to high-tension sects and cults will favor social isolation.' As indicated in Chapter 4, the majority of converts to NRMs are not very attached to conventional society in the first place. They are also people who have chosen to accept a set of specific and general religious compensators in lieu of pursuing various scarce rewards in the larger society, precisely because the absence of these material, social, and psychological rewards made them feel deprived. The intrinsic tendency for these kinds of groups to become increasingly isolated and cut off from avenues of recruitment accounts, Stark and Bainbridge (1996: 243–54) think, for the short life of most NRMs.

16. One member had, however, left Heaven's Gate just a few days before. His account of events has yet to be published.

17. It seems that Jim Jones was also quite ill towards the end, though probably from his misuse of various prescription drugs (Maaga, 1998).

18. This interpretation receives support from the narrow-minded reactions of law-enforcement agents to the suggestion that they receive some formal instruction in dealing with religious issues, as recorded and reported by Sullivan (1996: 229–31; see Docherty, 2001 as well).

19. Jayne Seminare Docherty (2001) presents a fascinating analysis of how the prolonged negotiations between the Branch Davidians and the FBI at Waco went so grievously wrong, after a promising start, because of the many points of conflict between their worldviews.

> Waco was a confrontation between the Branch Davidians for whom God acts in History, and FBI agents, for whom religion is an individual, private concern. For the Branch Davidians, the Waco standoff was a confrontation between God and the evil powers of a secular state that refused to be governed by God's law. For the FBI negotiators, the Waco standoff was a confrontation between the legitimate powers of the state and a group deluded by religious fervor or duped by a con man using religion as a cover for immoral and criminal activities. (Docherty, 2001: 69)

Operating with divergent 'naming, framing and blaming stories' the two parties were unable to find sufficient common ground and soon became fatally polarized.

20. The account provided by Chidester is enriched by Mary McCormich Maaga's (1998) further study of documents, tapes, transcripts, and interviews with ex-members of The Peoples Temple. Maaga's careful analysis casts even more light on daily life in Jonestown, calling attention in particular to the unrecognized and important role played by a group of white middle-class women in the leadership of the religion towards the end (see Layton 1998 as well). A comprehensive archive of data on The Peoples Temple and Jonestown is provided by the web site 'Alternative Considerations of Jonestown and Peoples Temple' (http://jonestown.sdsu.edu) sponsored by the Department of Religious Studies at San Diego State University in California.

CHAPTER EIGHT

1. This rather pessimistic pattern of interpretation even slips into Robbins and Bromley's essay on social experimentation and the significance of the NRMs (1992). In this paper Robbins and Bromley argue that the experimentation of NRMs arises in response to various structural conditions in modern society. They then use Hunter's analysis along with Bromley and Busching's discussion of contractual and covenantal forms of social relations to delineate briefly the kinds of conditions they have in mind. Bromley and Busching depict NRMs as a reaction to the shift from pre-modern covenantal relations to modern contractual relations, and much like Berger, they propose that the religious response 'might take the form of either creating [new] pre-modern/covenantal social forms or adapting to the requisites of modern/contractual social forms' (Robbins and Bromley, 1992: 5). Once again we are faced with an either/or scenario that does not bode well for attributing any long-term positive significance to the NRMs of today.

2. As Hanegraaff stresses throughout his detailed analysis of the literature of the New Age movement, 'the absolute primacy accorded to personal experience can be considered the central aspect of New Age beliefs about God' (1996: 185). 'The ultimate reality of the gods', he goes on to say, 'does not really matter as long as they can be addressed and their presence experienced....' In the end, New Agers 'address the gods *because it works*. Whether the reality they contact is metaphysical or intrapsychic is felt to be of secondary importance' (emphasis in the original; 1996: 197).

3. See Beckford's article, 'Holistic Imagery and Ethics in New Religious and Healing Movements' (1984), and Hanegraaff on New Age conceptions of holism and its identification with healing and personal growth (1996: 42–61,

119–58).

4. I can think of few better illustrations of the view I am seeking to briefly describe than the movie *Contact* (1997), which stars Jody Foster and is based on a novel by the famous astronomer, an opponent of organized religion, Carl Sagan.

5. I have found this line of analysis to be most useful for an understanding of the nature and improbable success of Vajradhatu (now also known as Shambhala), a Western NRM based on Tibetan Buddhism (Eldershaw and Dawson, 1995; Dawson and Eldershaw, 19987). See my analysis of Sōka Gakkai as well (Dawson, 2001).

6. In a later essay Beckford (1996) extends this same critical line of analysis, examining Bauman's (1992), Giddens's (1991), and Beck's (1992) tentative discussions of post-modern religion.

7. Robbins and Bromley (1992: 22) are taken with Beckford's suggestion as well.

8. There is a strong resonance between Beckford's theoretical suggestion and the empirical findings of Bibby (1987 and 2003) in Canada and Davie (1994 and 2000) in Britain and the rest of Europe (see Lambert 2004 as well). Both provide ample evidence that while organized religion in its traditional forms is in serious trouble there continues to be a sustained interest in so-called 'religious questions' and 'spiritual matters'. Roof's (1999) comprehensive empirical analysis of the religiosity of American baby boomers likewise reveals a shift in religious preferences and the emergence of a significant new constituency of 'metaphysical and spiritual seekers'.

9. As advocated by Pitchford, Bader, and Stark (2001), and admirably displayed by Mary Farrell Bednarowski (1989) and Susan J. Palmer (1994).

10. There are a number of important issues of this type that were addressed only briefly or not at all in this introductory text. Some of these are (1) the fundraising activities of NRMs and the conflicts these create both within and outside of religious groups (e.g. Richardson, 1988); (2) the nature of the religious experiences, including altered states of consciousness, cultivated in many NRMs (e.g. Barker, 1984; Brown 1997; Cox, 1977; Levine, 1984; Palmer, 1994; Preston, 1981; Puttick, 1997; Whitehead, 1987; Wilson and Dobbelaere, 1994; Wilson, 1984, 1990); (3) the organizational structure and innovations of NRMs (e.g. Davis and Richardson, 1976; Richardson, Stewart, and Simmonds, 1979; Lofland and Richardson, 1984; Hammond and Machacek, 1999); (4) the complex history of legal struggles involving 'cults' (e.g. Anthony 1990; Anthony and Robbins, 1992, 1995; Richardson, 1991, 1995b, 1997, 2004a) and state efforts to regulate NRMs (e.g. Richardson, 2004b); (5) the factors affecting the success or the failure of NRMs (e.g. Stark, 1987, 1996a; Wilson, 1987; Stark and Iannaccone, 1997).

Bibliography

Aberle, David
  1962 'Millennial Dreams in Action'. Pp. 209–14 in S.L. Thrupp, ed., *Comparative Studies in Society and History,* Supplement II. The Hague, The Netherlands: Mouton.

Adams, R.L., and R.J. Fox
  1972 'Mainlining Jesus: The New Trip'. *Society* 9(4): 50–6.

Adler, Margot
  1986 *Drawing Down the Moon: Witches, Druids, Goddess-Worshippers, and Other Pagans in America Today.* Boston: Beacon Press.

Adorno, T.W., E. Frenkel-Brunswick, D.J. Levinson, and R.N. Sanford
  1950 *The Authoritarian Personality.* New York: Harper and Brothers.

Aidala, Angela
  1985 'Social Change, Gender Roles, and New Religious Movements'. *Sociological Analysis* 46(3): 287–314.

Alfred, H.R.
  1976 'The Church of Satan'. Pp. 180–202 in C. Glock and R. Bellah, eds, *The New Religious Consciousness.* Berkeley, CA: University of California Press.

Ammerman, Nancy T.
  1987 *Bible Believers: Fundamentalists in the Modern World.* New Brunswick, NJ: Rutgers University Press.

  1995 'Waco, Federal Law Enforcement, and Scholars of Religion'. Pp. 282–96 in S.A. Wright, ed., *Armageddon in Waco: Critical Perspectives on the Branch Davidian Conflict.* Chicago: University of Chicago Press.

Anthony, Dick
  1990 'Religious Movements and Brainwashing Litigation: Evaluating Key

Testimony'. Pp. 295–344 in T. Robbins and D. Anthony, eds, *In Gods We Trust: New Patterns of Religious Pluralism in America*. 2nd edn. New Brunswick, NJ: Transaction.

1999   'Pseudoscience and Minority Religions: An Evaluation of the Brainwashing Theories of Jean-Maire Abgrall'. *Social Justice Research* 12(4): 421–56.

2001   'Tactical Ambiguity and Brainwashing Formulations: Science or Pseudo-Science?' Pp. 215–317 in B. Zablocki and T. Robbins, eds, *Misunderstanding Cults*. Toronto: University of Toronto Press.

———, and Bruce Ecker
1987   'The Anthony Typology: A Framework for Assessing Spiritual and Consciousness Groups'. Pp. 35–106 in D. Anthony, B. Ecker, and K. Wilber, eds, *Spiritual Choices: The Problem of Recognizing Authentic Paths to Inner Transformation*. New York: Paragon.

———, and Thomas Robbins
1975   'The Meher Baba Movement: Its Effects on Post-Adolescent Social Alienation'. Pp. 479–511 in I. Zaretsky and M. Leone, eds, *Religious Movements in Contemporary America*. Princeton, NJ: Princeton University Press.

1981   'New Religions, Families, and Brainwashing'. Pp. 263–74 in T. Robbins and D. Anthony, eds, *In Gods We Trust: New Patterns of Religious Pluralism in America*. 1st edn. New Brunswick, NJ: Transaction.

1982a   'Contemporary Religious Ferment and Moral Ambiguity'. Pp. 243–63 in E. Barker, ed., *New Religious Movements: A Perspective for Understanding Society*. New York: Edwin Mellen Press.

1982b   'Spiritual Innovation and the Decline of American Civil Religion'. Pp. 229–48 in M. Douglas and S. Tipton, eds, *Religion and America: Spirituality in a Secular Age*. Boston: Beacon Press.

1990   'Civil Religion and Recent American Religious Ferment'. Pp. 475–502 in T. Robbins and D. Anthony, eds, *In Gods We Trust: New Patterns of Religious Pluralism in America*. 2nd edn. New Brunswick, NJ: Transaction.

1992   'Law, Social Science and the "Brainwashing" Exception to the First Amendment'. *Behavioral Sciences and the Law* 10(1): 5–27.

1994   'Brainwashing and Totalitarian Influence'. Pp. 457–71 in *Encyclopedia of Human Behavior*, Vol. 1. San Diego, CA: Academic Press.

1995   'Negligence, Coercion and the Protection of Religious Belief'. *Journal of Church and State* 37(3): 509–36.

1997   'Religious Totalism, Exemplary Dualism and the Waco Tragedy'. Pp. 261–84 in T. Robbins and S. Palmer, eds, *Millennium, Messiahs and Mayhem*. New York: Routledge.

2004   'Conversion and "Brainwashing" in New Religious Movements'. Pp. 243–97 in J.R. Lewis, ed., *The Oxford Handbook of New Religious Movements*. New York: Oxford University Press.

Aronoff, Jodi, Steven J. Lynn, and Peter Malinowski
2000   'Are Cultic Environments Psychologically Harmful?' *Clinical Psychology Review* 20(1): 91–111.

Atwood, James D., and Ronald B. Flowers
1983   'Early Christianity as a Cult Movement'. *Encounter* 44(3): 245–61.

Austin, Roy L.
1977   'Empirical Adequacy of Lofland's Conversion Model'. *Review of Religious Research* 18: 282–7.

Babbie, Earl, and Donald Stone
1977   'An Evaluation of the est Experience by a National Sample of Graduates'. *Bioscience Communications* 3: 123–40.

Bader, Chris, and Alfred Demaris
1996   'A Test of the Stark and Bainbridge Theory of Affiliation with Religious Cults and Sects'. *Journal for the Scientific Study of Religion* 35(3): 285–303.

Bainbridge, William Sims
1978   *Satan's Power: Ethnography of a Deviant Psychotherapy Cult*. Berkeley, CA: University of California Press.

1997   *The Sociology of Religious Movements*. New York: Routledge.

2002   *The Endtime Family: Children of God*. Albany, NY: State University of New York Press.

————, **and Rodney Stark**
1979   'Cult Formation: Three Compatible Models.' *Sociological Analysis* 40, 1979: 283–95

1980   'Scientology: To Be Perfectly Clear'. *Sociological Analysis* 41(2): 128–36.

Balch, Robert W.
1980   'Looking behind the Scenes in a Religious Cult: Implications for the Study of Conversion'. *Sociological Analysis* 41(2): 137–43.

1995a   'Waiting for the Ships: Disillusionment and the Revitalization of Faith in Bo and Peep's UFO Cult'. Pp. 137–66 in J.R. Lewis, ed., *The Gods Have Landed: New Religions from Other Worlds*. Albany, NY: State University of New York Press.

1995b   'Charisma and Corruption in the Love Family: Toward a Theory of Corruption in Charismatic Cults'. Pp. 155–79 in D.G. Bromley, ed., *Religion and the Social Order*, Vol. 5. Greenwich, CT: JAI Press.

————, **G. Farnsworth, and S. Wilkins**
1983   'When the Bombs Drop'. *Sociological Perspectives* 26(2): 137–58.

————, John Domitrovitch, Barbara Lynn Markdale, and Vanessa Morrison
1997   'Fifteen Years of Failed Prophecy: Coping with Cognitive Dissonance in a Baha'i Sect'. Pp. 73—90 in T. Robbins and S.J. Palmer, eds, *Millennium, Messiahs, and Mayhem*. New York: Routledge.

———— and David Taylor
2002   'Making Sense of Heaven's Gate Suicides'. Pp. 209–28 in D.G. Bromley and J.G. Melton, eds, *Cults, Religion and Violence*. Cambridge: Cambridge University Press.

Bankston, William B., Craig J. Forsyth, and H. Hugh Floyd, Jr
1981   'Toward a General Model of the Process of Radical Conversion: An Interactionist Perspective on the Transformation of Self-Identity'. *Qualitative Sociology* 4(4): 279–97.

Barker, Eileen
1984   *The Making of a Moonie. Choice or Brainwashing?* Oxford: Basil Blackwell.

1985   'New Religious Movements: Theoretical Issues'. Pp. 36–57 in P.E. Hammond, ed., *The Sacred in a Secular Age*. Berkeley, CA: University of California Press.

1989   *New Religious Movements: A Practical Introduction*. London: Her Majesty's Stationery Office.

1993   'Will the Real Cult Please Stand Up? A Comparative Analysis of Social Constructions of New Religious Movements'. Pp. 193–211 in D.G. Bromley and J.K. Hadden, eds, *Religion and the Social Order*, Vol. 3, *The Handbook on Cults and Sects in America, Part B*. Greenwich, CT: JAI Press.

1995a   'The Scientific Study of Religion? You Must Be Joking!' *Journal for the Scientific Study of Religion* 34(3): 287–310.

1995b   'Plus ça change . . .' *Social Compass* 42(2): 165–80.

Barkun, Michael
1994   'Reflections after Waco: Millennialists and the State'. Pp. 41–9 in J.R. Lewis, ed., *From the Ashes: Making Sense of Waco*. Lanham, MD: Rowman and Littlefield.

Bateson, C. Daniel, and W. Larry Ventis
1982   *The Religious Experience: A Social-Psychological Perspective*. New York: Oxford University Press.

Baudrillard, Jean
1981   *For a Critique of the Political Economy of the Sign*. St Louis, MO: Telos Press.

1983   *Simulations*. New York: Semiotext(e).

Bauman, Zygmunt
1992   *Intimations of Postmodernity*. London: Routledge.

Baumeister, Roy F.
1986   *Identity: Cultural Change and the Struggle for Self*. New York: Oxford University Press.

Beck, Ulrich
1992   *Risk Society: Towards a New Modernity.* London: Sage.

Beckford, James
1975   *The Trumpet of Prophecy: A Sociological Study of Jehovah's Witnesses.* New York: Oxford and Halsted Press.

1978   'Accounting for Conversion'. *British Journal of Sociology* 29(2): 249–62.

1984   'Holistic Imagery and Ethics in New Religious and Healing Movements'. *Social Compass* 31(2–3): 259–72.

1985   *Cult Controversies: The Societal Response to the New Religious Movements.* London: Tavistock.

1989   *Religion in Advanced Industrial Society.* London: Unwin Hyman.

1992   'Religion, Modernity and Post-modernity'. Pp. 11–23 in B. Wilson, ed., *Religion: Contemporary Issues.* London: Bellew.

1994   'The Media and New Religious Movements'. Pp. 143–8 in J.R. Lewis, ed., *From the Ashes: Making Sense of Waco.* Lanham, MD: Rowan and Littlefield.

1996   'Postmodernity, High Modernity and New Modernity: Three Concepts in Search of Religion'. Pp. 30–47 in K. Flanagan and P.C. Jupp, eds, *Postmodernity, Sociology and Religion.* New York: St Martin's Press.

1999   'The Mass Media and New Religious Movements'. Pp. 103-19 in B. Wilson and J. Cresswell, eds, *New Religious Movements: Challenge and Response.* London: Routledge.

Bednarowski, Mary Farrell
1989   *New Religions and the Theological Imagination in America.* Bloomington, IN.: Indiana University Press.

1992   'The New Age and Feminist Spirituality'. Pp. 167–78 in J.R. Lewis and J. Gordon Melton, eds, *Perspectives on the New Age.* Albany, NY: State University of New York Press.

Bell, Daniel
1977   'The Return of the Sacred: The Argument on the Future of Religion'. *British Journal of Sociology* 28: 419–49.

Bellah, Robert
1967   'Civil Religion in America'. *Daedalus* 96(1): 1–21.

1975   *The Broken Covenant.* New York: Seabury.

1976   'New Religious Consciousness and the Crisis of Modernity'. Pp. 333–52 in C. Glock and R. Bellah, eds, *The New Religious Consciousness.* Berkeley, CA: University of California Press.

1981   'Religion and the Legitimation of the American Republic'. Pp. 39–50 in T. Robbins and D. Anthony, eds, *In Gods We Trust: New Patterns of Religious*

Pluralism in America. 1st edn. New Brunswick, NJ: Transaction.

Berger, Helen A.

1999   *A Community of Witches: Contemporary Neo-Paganism and Witchcraft in the United States.* Columbia, SC: University of South Carolina Press.

————, **Evan A. Leach, and Leigh S. Shaffer**

2003   *Voices from the Pagan Census: A National Survey of Witches and Neo-pagans in the United States.* Columbia, SC: University of South Carolina Press.

Berger, Peter L.

1967   *The Sacred Canopy.* New York: Doubleday.

1969   *A Rumor of Angels.* New York: Doubleday.

1999   *The Desecularization of the World.* Grand Rapids, MI: Eerdmans.

————, **and Thomas Luckmann**

1966   *The Social Construction of Reality: A Treatise in the Sociology of Knowledge.* New York: Doubleday.

————., **and Richard Neuhaus**

1970   *Movement and Revolution.* New York: Doubleday.

————, **Brigitte Berger, and Hansfried Kellner**

1974   *The Homeless Mind: Modernization and Consciousness.* New York: Vintage.

Beyer, Peter

1994   *Religion and Globalization.* Thousand Oaks, CA: Sage.

1997   'Religious Vitality in Canada: The Complementarity of Religious Market and Secularization Perspectives'. *Journal for the Scientific Study of Religion* 36 (2): 272–88.

————, **ed.**

2001   *Religion in the Process of Globalization.* Würzburg, Germany: Ergon.

Bibby, Reginald

1987   *Fragmented Gods: The Poverty and Potential of Religion in Canada.* Toronto: Irwin.

2002   *Restless Gods: The Renaissance of Religion in Canada.* Toronto: Stoddard.

Bird, Frederick

1979   'The Pursuit of Innocence: New Religious Movements and Moral Accountability'. *Sociological Analysis* 40(4): 335–46.

1993   'Charisma and Leadership in New Religious Movements'. Pp. 75–92 in D.G. Bromley and J.K. Hadden, eds, *Religion and the Social Order*, Vol. 3, *The Handbook on Cults and Sects in America,* Part A. Greenwich, CT: JAI Press.

————, **and Bill Reimer**

1982   'Participation Rates in New Religious Movements'. *Journal for the Scientific Study of Religion* 21(1): 1–14.

Blumer, Herbert

1951   'Collective Behavior'. Pp. 208–10 in A.M. Lee, ed., *Principles of Sociology*. New York: Barnes and Noble.

1969   *Symbolic Interactionism: Perspective and Method*. Berkeley, CA: University of California Press.

Bohm, David

1983   *Wholeness and the Implicate Order*. London: Ark Paperbacks.

Boyer, Paul

1992   *When Time Shall Be No More: Prophecy Belief in Modern American Culture*. Cambridge, MA: Belknap Press of Harvard University Press.

1998   'Dealing with the Media Circus: Confessions of a "Cult" Expert'. *Bulletin of the Council of Societies for the Study of Religion* 27(1): 5–7, reprinted from the 18 April issue of *The Chronicle of Higher Education*.

Bradney, Anthony

1999   'Children of a Newer God: The English Courts, Custody Disputes, and NRMs'. Pp. 210–23 in S.J. Palmer and C.E. Hardman, eds., *Children in New Religions*. New York: Routledge.

Bretton-Granatoor, Gary

1997   *A Jewish Response to Cults*. New York: URJ Press.

Brodin, Jenny-Ann

2003   'A Matter of Choice: A Micro-level Study of How Swedish New Agers Choose Their Religious Beliefs and Practices'. *Rationality and Society* 15(3): 381–405.

Bromley, David G.

1988   'Deprogramming as a Mode of Exit from New Religious Movements: The Case of the Unificationist Movement'. Pp. 185–204 in D.G. Bromley, ed., *Falling from the Faith: Causes and Consequences of Religious Apostasy*. Newbury Park, CA: Sage.

1998   'Listing (In Black and White) Some Observations on (Sociological) Thought Reform'. *Nova Religio* 1(2): 250–65.

2001   'A Tale of Two Theories: Brainwashing and Conversion as Competing Political Narratives'. Pp. 318–48 in B. Zablocki and T. Robbins, eds, *Misunderstanding Cults*. Toronto: University of Toronto Press.

2002   'Dramatic Denouements'. Pp. 11–41 in D.G. Bromley and J.G. Melton, eds, *Cults, Religion and Violence*. Cambridge: Cambridge University Press.

2004   'Leaving the Fold: Disaffiliating from New Religious Movements'. Pp. 298–314 in J.R. Lewis, ed., *The Oxford Handbook of New Religious Movements*. New York: Oxford University Press.

——, and E. Breschel

1992   'General Population and Institutional Elite Support for Social Control of New

Religious Movements: Evidence from National Survey Data'. *Behavioral Sciences and the Law* 10: 39–52.

———, and Bruce C. Busching

1988   'Understanding the Structure of Contractual and Covenantal Social Relations: Implications for the Sociology of Religion'. *Sociological Analysis* 49 (supp.): 15–32.

———, and Jeffrey K. Hadden, eds

1993   *Religion and the Social Order,* Vol. 3, *The Handbook on Cults and Sects in America, Parts A and B.* Greenwich, CT: JAI Press.

———, and Phillip E. Hammond, eds

1987   *The Future of New Religious Movements.* Macon, GA: Mercer University Press.

———, and J. Gordon Melton, eds

2002   *Cults, Religion and Violence.* Cambridge: Cambridge University Press.

———, and James T. Richardson, eds

1983   *The Brainwashing/Deprogramming Controversy: Sociological, Psychological, Legal and Historical Perspectives.* Lewiston, NY: Edwin Mellen Press.

———, and Thomas Robbins

1993   'The Role of Government in Regulating New and Nonconventional Religions'. Pp. 205–41 in J. Wood and D. Davis, eds, *The Role of Government in Monitoring and Regulating Religion in Public Life.* Waco, TX: Baylor University, Dawson Institute for Church-State Studies.

———, and Anson D. Shupe, Jr

1979a   'The Tnevnoc Cult'. *Sociological Analysis* 40(4): 361–6.

1979b   'Just a Few Years Seem like a Lifetime: A Role Theory Approach to Participation in Religious Movements'. Pp. 159–86 in L. Kriesberg, ed., *Research in Social Movements, Conflict and Change,* Vol. 2. Greenwich, CT: JAI Press.

1980   *The Moonies in America.* Beverly Hills, CA: Sage.

1986   'Affiliation and Disaffiliation: A Role Theory Interpretation of Joining and Leaving New Religious Movements'. *Thought* 61: 197–211.

1993   'Organized Opposition to New Religious Movements'. Pp. 177–98 in D.G. Bromley and J.K. Hadden, eds, *Religion and the Social Order,* Vol. 3, *The Handbook on Cults and Sects in America, Part A.* Greenwich, CT: JAI Press.

1994   'The Modern North American Anti-Cult Movement 1971–1991: A Twenty-Year Retrospective'. Pp. 3–31 in A. Shupe and D.G. Bromley, eds, *Anti-Cult Movements in Cross-Cultural Perspective.* New York: Garland.

2004   'Leaving the Fold: Disaffiliation from New Religious Movements'. Pp. 298–314 in J.R. Lewis, ed., *The Oxford Handbook of New Religious Movements.* New York: Oxford University Press.

————, Anson D. Shupe, Jr, and Donna L. Oliver

1982   'Perfect Families: Visions of the Future in a New Religious Movement'. *Marriage and Family Review* 4 (314): 119–29.

————, Anson D. Shupe, Jr, and J.C. Ventimiglia

1983   'The Role of Anecdotal Atrocities in the Social Construction of Evil'. Pp. 139–60 in D.G. Bromley and J.T. Richardson, eds, *The Brainwashing/Deprogramming Controversy: Sociological, Psychological, Legal and Historical Perspectives.* Lewiston, NY: Edwin Mellen Press.

————, and Edward D. Silver

1995   'The Davidian Tradition: From Patronal Clan to Prophetic Movement'. Pp. 43–72 in S.A. Wright, ed., *Armageddon in Waco.* Chicago: University of Chicago Press.

Brown, Michael F.

1997   *The Channeling Zone: American Spirituality in an Anxious Age.* Cambridge, MA: Harvard University Press.

Bruce, Steve

2002   *God is Dead: Secularization in the West.* Oxford: Blackwell.

Calley, Malcolm

1965   *God's People: West Indian Pentecostal Sects in England.* London: Oxford University Press.

Campbell, Bruce F.

1978   'A Typology of Cults'. Sociological Analysis 39(3): 228–40.

1980   *Ancient Wisdom Revived: A History of the Theosophical Movement.* Berkeley, CA: University of California Press.

Campbell, Colin

1978   'The Secret Religion of the Educated Classes'. *Sociological Analysis* 39(2): 146–56.

Canada Panel on Violence Against Women

1993   *Changing the Landscape: Ending Violence Against Women.* Ottawa: Supply and Services Canada, cat. SW45–11, 1993E.

Carter, Lewis F.

1990   *Charisma and Control in Rajneeshpuram.* Cambridge: Cambridge University Press.

Cartwright, Robert H., and Stephen A. Kent

1992   'Social Control in Alternative Religions: A Familial Perspective'. *Sociological Analysis* 53(4): 345–61.

Chancellor, James D.

2000   *Life in the Family: An Oral History of the Children of God.* Syracuse, NY: Syracuse University Press.

Chidester, David
1988   *Salvation and Suicide: An Interpretation of Jim Jones, the Peoples Temple, and Jonestown.* Bloomington, IN: Indiana University Press.

Church of Scientology
1993   *What Is Scientology?* Los Angeles, CA: Bridge Publications.

Clark, John, M.D. Langone, R.E. Schacter, and R.C.D. Daly
1981   *Destructive Cult Conversion: Theory, Research, and Treatment.* Weston, MA: American Family Foundation.

Coates, Priscilla D.
1994   'The Cult Awareness Network'. Pp. 93–101 in A. Shupe and D.G. Bromley, eds, *The Anti-Cult Movements in Cross-Cultural Perspective.* New York: Garland.

Cohn, Norman
1961   *The Pursuit of the Millennium: Revolutionary Millenarians and Mystical Anarchists of the Middle Ages.* Oxford: Oxford University Press.

Coleman, John
1984   'New Religions and the Myth of Mind Control'. *American Journal of Orthopsychiatry* 54(2): 322–5.

Coney, Judith
1999   *Sohaja Yoga: Socializing Processes in a South Asian New Religious Movement.* Richmond, Surrey: Curzon.

Conway, Flo, and Jim Siegelman
1978   *Snapping: America's Epidemic of Sudden Personality Change.* Philadelphia, PA: J.B. Lippincott.

Couch, Carl J.
1989   'From Hell to Utopia and Back to Hell: Charismatic Relationships'. *Symbolic Interaction* 12(2): 265–79.

Cowan, Douglas E.
2003   *Bearing False Witness? An Introduction to the Christian Countercult Movement.* Westport, CT: Praeger.

——, and Jeffrey K. Hadden
2004   'God, Guns, and Grist for the Media's Mill: Constructing the Narratives of New Religious Movements and Violence'. *Nova Religio* 8(2): 64–82.

Cox, Harvey
1977   *Turning East: The Promise and Peril of the New Orientalism.* New York: Simon and Schuster.

1995   *Fire from Heaven: The Rise of Pentecostal Spirituality and the Reshaping of Religion in the Twenty-First Century.* Reading, MA: Addison-Wesley.

Davidman, Lynn

1990   'Women's Search for Family and Roots: A Jewish Religious Solution to a Modern Dilemma'. Pp. 385–407 in T. Robbins and D. Anthony, eds, *In Gods We Trust: New Patterns of Religious Pluralism in America*. 2nd edn. New Brunswick, NJ: Transaction.

————, and Janet Jacobs

1993   'Feminist Perspectives on New Religious Movements'. Pp. 173–90 in D.G. Bromley and J.K. Hadden, eds, *Religion and the Social Order*, Vol. 3, *The Handbook on Cults and Sects in America, Part B*. Greenwich, CT: JAI Press.

Davie, Grace

1994   *Religion in Britain since 1945: Believing without Belonging*. Oxford: Blackwell.

2000   *Religion in Modern Europe: A Memory Mutates*. Oxford: Oxford University Press.

Davis, Rex, and James Richardson

1976   'The Organization and Functioning of the Children of God'. *Sociological Analysis* 37(4): 321–39.

Dawson, Lorne L.

1986   'Neither "Nerve" nor "Ecstasy": Comment on the Wiebe-Davis Exchange'. *Studies in Religion* 15: 145–51.

1987   'On References to the Transcendent in the Scientific Study of Religion: A Qualified Idealist Proposal'. *Religion* 17(4): 227–50.

1988   *Reason, Freedom and Religion: On Closing the Gap between the Humanistic and Scientific Study of Religion*. New York: Peter Lang.

1990   'Self-Affirmation, Freedom, and Rationality: Theoretically Elaborating "Active" Conversions'. *Journal for the Scientific Study of Religion* 29: 141–63.

1993   'Libido and Cognition: The Integrated Use of Freud and Piaget in the Study of Religious Experience'. *Journal of Psychology and Religion* 2–3: 71–100.

1994a   'Human Reflexivity and the Nonreductive Explanation of Religious Action'. Pp. 143–61 in T.A. Idinopulos and E.A. Yonan, eds, *Religion and Reductionism—Essays on Eliade, Segal, and the Challenge of the Social Sciences for the Study of Religion*. Leiden, The Netherlands: E.J. Brill.

1994b   'Accounting for Accounts: How Should Sociologists Treat Conversion Stories?' *International Journal of Comparative Religion and Philosophy* 1(1 & 2): 46–66.

1996   'Who Joins New Religious Movements and Why: Twenty Years of Research and What Have We Learned?' *Studies in Religion* 25(2): 193–213.

1997   'Creating "Cult" Typologies: Some Strategic Considerations'. *Journal of Contemporary Religion* 12(3): 363–81.

1998a   'Anti-Modernism, Modernism, and Postmodernism: Struggling with the

Cultural Significance of New Religious Movements'. *Sociology of Religion* 59(2): 131–51.

1998b   'The Cultural Significance of New Religious Movements and Globalization: A Theoretical Prolegomenon'. *Journal for the Scientific Study of Religion* 37(3): forthcoming.

1999   'When Prophecy Fails and Faith Persists: A Theoretical Overview'. *Nova Religio* 3 (1): 60–82.

2000   'Religious Cults and Sex'. Pp. 323–26 in C.D. Bryant, ed., *The Encyclopedia of Criminology and Deviant Behaviour.* New York: Taylor and Francis.

2001a   'The Cultural Significance of New Religious Movements: The Case of Sōka Gakkai'. *Sociology of Religion* 62(3): 337–64.

2001b   'Raising Lazarus: A Methodological Critique of Stephen Kent's Revival of the Brainwashing Model'. Pp. 379–400 in B. Zablocki and T. Robbins, eds, *Misunderstanding Cults*. Toronto: University of Toronto Press.

2002   'Crises of Charismatic Legitimacy and Violent Behaviour in New Religious Movements'. Pp. 80–101 in D.G. Bromley and J.G. Melton, eds, *Cults, Religion and Violence*. Cambridge: Cambridge University Press.

2004   'The Socio-Cultural Significance of Modern New Religious Movements'. Pp. 68–99 in J.R. Lewis, ed., *Oxford Handbook of New Religious Movements*. New York: Oxford University Press.

2005a   'The Meaning and Significance of New Religious Movements'. Forthcoming in D.G. Bromley, ed., *Teaching New Religious Movements*. New York: Oxford University Press.

2005b   'Privatization, Globalization and Religious Innovation: Giddens' Theory of Modernity and the Refutation of Secularization', Forthcoming in J.A. Beckford and J. Walliss, eds, *Religion and Social Theory: Classical and Contemporary Debates*. London: Ashgate.

2005c   'New Religious Movements'. Forthcoming in Robert Segal, ed., *Blackwell Companion to Religious Studies*. Oxford: Blackwell, 2005.

2004   *Cults and New Religious Movements: A Reader.* Oxford: Blackwell.

————, and Lynn Eldershaw
1998   'Shambhala Warriorship: Investigating the Adaptations of Imported New Religious Movements'. Pp. 199–228 in B. Ouellet and R. Bergeron, eds, *Les Sociétés devant le nouveau pluralisme religieux*. Montreal: Fides.

————, and Robert C. Prus
1993a   'Interactionist Ethnography and Postmodernist Discourse: Affinities and Disjunctures in Approaching Human Lived Experience'. Pp. 147–77 in N. Denzin, ed., *Studies in Symbolic Interaction*, vol. 15, Greenwich, CT: JAI Press.

1993b   'Human Enterprise, Intersubjectivity, and the Ethnographic Other: A Reply to Denzin and Fontana'. Pp. 193–200 in N. Denzin, ed., *Studies in Symbolic Interaction*, vol. 15, Greenwich, CT: JAI Press.

Deikman, Arthur J.
1990   *The Wrong Way Home: Uncovering the Patterns of Cult Behavior in American Society.* Boston: Beacon.

Dein, Simon
1997   'Lubavitch: A Contemporary Messianic Movement'. *Journal of Contemporary Religion* 12(2): 191–204.

Delgado, Richard
1980   'Limits to Proselytizing'. *Society* 17: 25–32.

1985   'Cults and Conversion: The Case for Informed Consent'. Pp. 111–28 in T. Robbins, W.C. Shepherd, and J. McBride, eds, *Cults, Culture, and the Law.* Chico, CA: Scholars Press.

DeRosa, Elaine
1989   'Challenging Cults, Cultivating Family'. *The Greater Phoenix Jewish News.* Retrieved from www.rickross.com on 17 Nov. 2004.

Derrida, Jacques
1970   'Structure, Sign and Play in the Discourse of the Human Sciences'. Pp. 247–72 in R. Macksey and E. Donato, eds, *The Languages of Criticism and the Sciences of Man.* Baltimore: Johns Hopkins University Press.

1976   *Of Grammatology.* Baltimore: John Hopkins University Press.

Docherty, Jane Seminare
2001   *Learning Lessons from Waco: When the Parties Bring Their Gods to the Negotiation Table.* Syracyuse, NY: Syracuse University Press.

Doress, Irvin, and Jack Nusan Porter
1981   'Kids in Cults'. Pp. 297–302 in T. Robbins and D. Anthony, eds, *In Gods We Trust: New Patterns of Religious Pluralism in America.* 1st edn. New Brunswick, NJ: Transaction.

Downton, James V.
1979   *Sacred Journeys: The Conversion of Young Americans to Divine Light Mission.* New York: Columbia University Press.

Durkin, John, Jr, and Andrew Greeley
1991   'A Model of Religious Choice under Uncertainty: On Responding Rationally to the Nonrational'. *Rationality and Society* 3(3): 178–96.

Ebaugh, Helen Rose Fuchs
1988   *Becoming an EX: The Process of Role Exit.* Chicago: University of Chicago Press.

Eisenstadt, S.N.
1956   *From Generation to Generation: Age Groups and Social Structure.* Glencoe, IL: Free Press.

Eister, Allan W.

1974   'Culture Crises and New Religious Movements: A Paradigmatic Statement of a Theory of Cults'. Pp. 612–27 in I. Zaretsky and M. Leone, eds, *Religious Movements in Contemporary America*. Princeton, NJ: Princeton University Press.

Eldershaw, Lynn, and Lorne L. Dawson

1995   'Refugees in the Dharma: The Buddhist Church of Halifax as a Revitalization Movement'. Pp.1–45 in *North American Religion*, Vol. 4. Waterloo, ON: Wilfrid Laurier University Press.

Eliade, Mircea

1963   *Patterns of Comparative Religion*. New York: Meridian.

1969   *The Quest: History and Meaning in Religion*. Chicago: University of Chicago Press.

Ellison, Christopher G., and John P. Bartkowski

1995   '"Babies are Being Beaten": Exploring Child Abuse Allegations at Ranch Apocalypse'. Pp 111–49 in S.A. Wright, ed., *Armageddon in Waco*. Chicago: University of Chicago Press.

Ellwood, Robert S., and Harry B. Partin

1988   *Religious and Spiritual Groups in Modern America*. 2nd edn. Englewood Cliffs, NJ: Prentice-Hall.

Emberley, Peter C.

2002   *Divine Hunger: Canadians on Spiritual Walkabout*. Toronto: HarperCollins.

Enroth, Ronald

1977   *Youth, Brainwashing, and the Extremist Cults*. Grand Rapids, MI: Zondervan.

Erikson, Erik H.

1968   *Identity, Youth and Crisis*. New York: W.W. Norton.

Festinger, Leon, Henry W. Riecken, and Stanley Schachter

1956   *When Prophecy Fails*. New York: Harper and Row.

Feuerstein, Georg

1990   *Holy Madness: The Shock Tactics and Radical Teachings of Crazy-wise Adepts, Holy Fools, and Rascal Gurus*. New York: Penguin Books.

Fichter, Joseph H.

1983   'Family and Religion Among the Moonies'. Pp. 289–304 in W.V. D'Antonio and J. Aldous, eds, *Families and Religion: Conflict and Change in Modern Society*. Beverly Hills, CA: Sage.

Fields, Rick

1981   *How the Swans Came to the Lake: A Narrative History of Buddhism in America*. Berkeley, CA: Shambhala Publications.

Finke, Roger, and Rodney Stark
1992   *The Churching of America, 1776–1990.* New Brunswick, NJ: Rutgers University Press.

Foss, Daniel A., and Ralph W. Larkin
1978   'Worshipping the Absurd: The Negation of Social Causality among the Followers of Guru Maharaj Ji'. *Sociological Analysis* 39(2): 157–64.

Foucault, Michel
1972   *The Archaeology of Knowledge.* London: Tavistock.

1982   *This Is Not a Pipe.* Berkeley, CA: University of California Press.

Frankl, Razelle
1987   *Televangelism: The Marketing of Popular Religion.* Carbondale, IL: Southern Illinois University Press.

Freed, Josh
1980   *Moonwebs: Journey into the Mind of a Cult.* Toronto: Dorset.

Freud, Sigmund
1921   *Group Psychology and the Analysis of the Ego.* London: Hogarth.

Galanter, Marc
1980   'Psychological Introduction into the Large Group: Findings from a Modern Religious Sect'. *American Journal of Psychiatry* 137(12): 1574–9.

1989   *Cults: Faith, Healing and Coercion.* New York: Oxford University Press.

————, **and Peter Buckley**
1983   'Psychological Consequences of Charismatic Religious Experience and Meditation'. Pp. 194–204 in D.G. Bromley and J.T. Richardson, eds, *The Brainwashing/Deprogramming Controversy: Sociological, Psychological, Legal and Historical Perspectives.* Lewiston, NY: Edwin Mellen Press.

————, **Richard Rabkin, Judith Rabkin, and Alexander Deutsch**
'The "Moonies": A Psychological Study of Conversion and Membership in a Contemporary Religious Sect'. *American Journal of Psychiatry* 136: 165–70.

Gardner, William L., and Bruce J. Avolio
1998   'The Charismatic Relationship: A Dramaturgical Perspective'. *The Academy of Management Review* 23: 32–58.

Garrett, William
1974   'Troublesome Transcendence: The Supernatural in the Scientific Study of Religion'. *Sociological Analysis* 35(3): 167–80.

Gartrell, C. David, and Zane K. Shannon
1985   'Contacts, Cognitions, Conversion: A Rational Choice Approach'. *Review of Religious Research* 27(1): 32–48.

Giddens, Anthony
1990   *The Consequences of Modernity.* Cambridge: Polity Press.

1991   *Modernity and Self-Identity: Self and Society in the Late Modern Age.* Cambridge: Polity Press.

Ginsburg, G.P., and J.T. Richardson
1998   '"Brainwashing" Evidence in the Light of Daubert'. Pp. 265–88 in H. Reece, ed., *Law ard and Science.* Oxford: Oxford University Press.

Gitlin, Todd
1987   *The Sixties: Years of Hope, Days of Rage.* New York: Bantam.

Gleick, James
1987   *Chaos: Making a New Science.* New York: Penguin.

Glock, Charles Y.
1964   'The Role of Deprivation in the Origin and Evolution of Religious Groups'. Pp. 24–36 in R. Lee and M. Marty, eds, *Religion and Social Conflict.* New York: Oxford University Press.

————, and Robert N. Bellah, eds
1976   *The New Religious Consciousness.* Berkeley, CA: University of California Press.

Goldman, Marion S.
1995   'From Promiscuity to Celibacy: Women and Sexual Regulation at Rajneeshpuram'. Pp. 203–19 in M. Neitz and M.S. Goldman. eds, *Sex, Lies and Sanctity: Religion and Deviance in Contemporary North America.* Greenwich, CT: JAI Press.

1999   *Passionate Journeys: Why Successful Women Joined a Cult.* Ann Arbor, MI: University of Michigan Press.

Greenfield, Robert
1975   *The Spiritual Supermarket.* New York: E.P. Dutton.

Greil, Arthur L.
1993   'Explorations Along the Sacred Frontier: Notes on Para-religions, Quasi-religions, and Other Boundary Phenomena'. Pp. 153–72 in D.G. Bromley and J.K. Hadden, eds, *Religion and the Social Order,* Vol. 3, *The Handbook on Cults and Sects in America, Part A.* Greenwich, CT: JAI Press.

————, and David R. Rudy
1984   'What Have We Learned from Process Models of Conversion? An Examination of Ten Case Studies'. *Sociological Focus* 17(4): 305–23.

Gurney, Joan Neff, and Kathleen J. Tierney
1982   'Relative Deprivation and Social Movements: A Critical Look at Twenty Years of Theory and Research'. *The Sociological Quarterly* 23(4): 33–47.

Gurr, Ted
1970   *Why Men Rebel.* Princeton, NJ: Princeton University Press.

Gussner, R.E., and S.D. Berkowitz
1988   'Scholars, Sects, and Sanghas I: Recruitment to Asian-Based Meditation

Groups in North America'. *Sociological Analysis* 49(2): 136–70.

Hall, John R.
1987   *Gone from the Promised Land.* New Brunswick, NJ: Transaction.

1990   'The Apocalypse at Jonestown'. Pp. 269–93 in T. Robbins and D. Anthony, eds, *In Gods We Trust: New Patterns of Religious Pluralism in America.* 2nd edn. New Brunswick, NJ: Transaction.

2000   'Finding Heaven's Gate'. Pp. 149–82 in J.R. Hall et al., *Apocalypse Observed.* New York: Routledge.

2002   'Mass Suicide and the Branch Davidians'. Pp. 149–69 in D.G. Bromley and J.G. Melton, eds, *Cults, Religion and Violence.* Cambridge: Cambridge University Press.

———, **and Philip Schuyler**
2000   'The Mystical Apocalypse of the Solar Temple'. Pp. 111–48 in J.R. Hall et al. *Apocalypse Observed.* New York: Routledge.

———, **with Philip D. Schuyler and Sylvaine Trinh**
2000   *Apocalypse Observed: Religious Movements, the Social Order, and Violence in North America, Europe, and Japan.* New York: Routledge.

———, **and Sylvaine Trinh**
2000   'The Violent Path of Aum Shinrikyō'. Pp. 76–110 in J.R. Hall et al. *Apocalypse Observed.* New York: Routledge.

Hammond, Phillip
1987   'Cultural Consequences of Cults'. Pp. 261–73 in D. Bromley and P. Hammond, eds, *The Future of New Religious Movements.* Macon, GA: Mercer University Press.

———, **and David Machacek**
1999   *Sōka Gakkai in America: Accommodation and Conversion.* New York: Oxford University Press.

Hamnett, Ian
1973   'Sociology of Religion and Sociology of Error'. *Religion* 3(1): 1–12.

Handy, Robert T.
1976   *A History of the Churches in the United States and Canada.* New York: Oxford University Press.

Hanegraaff, Wouter J.
1996   *New Age Religion and Western Culture.* Leiden, The Netherlands: E.J. Brill.

Hannigan, James A.
1991   'Social Movement Theory and the Sociology of Religion: Toward a New Synthesis'. *Sociological Analysis* 52(3): 311–32.

Hardyck, A., and M. Braden
1962   'Prophecy Fails Again: A Report on a Failure to Replicate'. *Journal of Abnormal*

and Social Psychology 65(2): 136–41.

Hargrove, Barbara
1988 'Religion, Development, and Changing Paradigms'. *Sociological Analysis* 48 (Supplementary issue): 33–48.

Harrison, Michael
1974 'Sources of Recruitment to Catholic Pentecostalism'. *Journal for the Scientific Study of Religion* 13(1): 49–64.

Hassan, Steven
1988 *Combatting Cult Mind-Control.* Rochester, VT: Park Street Press.

1994 'Strategic Intervention Therapy: A New Form of Exit-Counselling for Cult Members'. Pp. 103–25 in A. Shupe and D.G. Bromley, eds, *The Anti-Cult Movements in Cross-Cultural Perspective.* New York: Garland.

Heelas, Paul
1996 *The New Age Movement: The Celebration of the Self and the Sacralization of Modernity.* Oxford: Blackwell.

Heirich, Max
1977 'Change of Heart: A Test of Some Widely Held Theories about Religious Conversion'. *American Journal of Sociology* 83(3): 653–80.

Herberg, Will
1955 *Protestant, Catholic, Jew.* New York: Doubleday.

Heymann, Phillip B. (Deputy Attorney General)
1993 *Lessons of Waco: Proposed Changes in Federal Law Enforcement.* Washington, D.C.: U.S. Department of Justice.

Hine, Virginia H.
1974 'The Deprivation and Disorganization Theories of Social Movements'. Pp. 646–61 in I. Zaretsky and M. Leone, eds, *Religious Movements in Contemporary America.* Princeton, NJ: Princeton University Press.

Hinkle, L.E., and Wolff, H.E.
1956 'Communist Interrogation and the Indoctrination of "Enemies of the States"'. *American Medical Association Archives of Neurological Psychology* 76: 117–27.

Holt, John B.
1940 'Holiness Religion: Culture Shock and Social Reorganization'. *American Sociological Review* 5 (Oct.): 740–7.

Homer, Michael W.
1999 'The Precarious Balance Between Freedom of Religion and The Best Interests of the Child'. Pp. 187–209 in S.J. Palmer and C.E. Hardman, eds, *Children in New Religions.* New York: Routledge.

Hoover, Stewart M.
1994 *Religion in Public Discourse: The Role of the Media.* Report for the Center for

Mass Media Research, School of Journalism and Mass Communication, University of Colorado, Boulder.

Hubbard, Jamie
1998   'Embarassing Superstition, Doctrine, and the Study of New Religious Movements'. *Journal of the American Academy of Religion* 66 (1): 59–92.

Hubbard, L. Ron
1975   *Dianetics: The New Science of Mental Health.* Los Angeles: Bridge. Originally published 1950.

Hunter, Edward
1951   *Brainwashing in Red China.* New York: Vanguard Press.

Hunter, James D.
1981   'The New Religions: Demodernization and the Protest against Modernity'. Pp. 1–19 in B. Wilson, ed., *The Social Impact of New Religious Movements.* New York: Rose of Sharon Press.

1983   *American Evangelicalism.* New Brunswick, NJ: Rutgers University Press.

Hutton, Ronald
1999   *The Triumph of the Moon: A History of Modern Pagan Witchcraft.* Oxford: Oxford University Press.

Huxley, Aldous
1970   *The Perennial Philosophy.* New York: Harper and Row. Originally published 1944.

Idinopulos, Thomas A., and Edward A. Yonan, eds
1994   *Religion and Reductionism: Essays on Eliade, Segal, and the Challenge of the Social Sciences for the Study of Religion.* Leiden, The Netherlands: E.J. Brill.

Introvigne, Massimo
1995   'Ordeal by Fire: The Tragedy of the Solar Temple'. *Religion* 25(2): 267–83.

———, and Jean-François Mayer
2002   'Occult Masters and the Temple of Doom: The Fiery End of the Solar Temple,' in David G. Bromley and J. Gordon Melton, eds, *Cults, Religion and Violence.* Cambridge: Cambridge University Press, 2002: 170–88.

———, and J. Gordon Melton
1997   'The Attack Upon Religious Groups in Present-Day Europe: A Special Report'. Paper presented to the American Academy of Religion, San Francisco.

Jacobs, Janet Liebman
1984   'The Economy of Love in Religious Commitment: The Deconversion of Women from Nontraditional Religious Movements'. *Journal for the Scientific Study of Religion* 23: 155–71.

1989   *Divine Disenchantment: Deconverting from New Religions.* Bloomington, IN:

Indiana University Press.

Janis, Irving

1972   *Victims of Groupthink: A Psychological Study of Foreign Policy Decisions and Fiascoes.* Boston: Houghton Mifflin.

Jenkins, Phillip

2000   *Mystics and Messiahs: Cults and New Religions in American History.* New York: Oxford University Press.

Johnson, Benton

1961   'Do Holiness Sects Socialize in Dominant Values?' *Social Forces* 39 (May): 309–16.

1977   'Sociological Theory and Religious Truth'. *Sociological Analysis* 38(4): 368–88.

1981   'A Sociological Perspective on New Religions'. Pp. 51–66 in T. Robbins and D. Anthony, eds, *In Gods We Trust: New Patterns of Religious Pluralism in America.* 1st edn. New Brunswick, NJ: Transaction.

Johnson, Doyle Paul

1979   'Dilemmas of Charismatic Leadership: The Case of the People's Temple'. *Sociological Analysis* 40(4): 315–23.

Jones, Constance A.

1994   'Church Universal and Triumphant: A Demographic Profile'. Pp. 39–53 in J.R. Lewis and J.G. Melton, eds, *Church Universal and Triumphant in Scholarly Perspective.* Stanford, CA: Center for Academic Publication.

Jorgensen, Danny L.

1980   'The Social Construction and Interpretation of Deviance—Jonestown and the Mass Media'. *Deviant Behavior* 1(3–4): 309–32.

Judah, J. Stillson

1974   *Hare Krishna and the Counter-Culture.* New York: John Wiley.

Kanter, Rosabeth M.

1972   *Commitment and Community: Communes and Utopias in Sociological Perspective.* Cambridge, MA: Harvard University Press.

Kaplan, David E., and Andrew Marshall

1996   *The Cult at the End of the World.* New York: Crown.

Karr, Alphonse

1849   *Les Guêpes* VI, January.

Kelly, Aidan A.

1990   *Cults and the Jewish Community: Representative Works of Anti-Cult Literature.* Detroit: Garland.

Kent, Stephen A.

1987   'Puritan Radicalism and the New Religious Organizations: Seventeenth-

Century England and Contemporary America'. Pp. 3–46 in R.F. Tomasson, ed., *Comparative Social Research,* Vol. 10. Greenwich, CT: JAI Press.

1988   'Slogan Chanters to Mantra Chanters: A Mertonian Deviance Analysis of Conversion to Religiously Ideological Organizations in the Early 1970s'. *Sociological Analysis* 49(2): 104–18.

1996   'Scientology's Relationship with Eastern Religious Traditions'. *Journal of Contemporary Religion* 11(1): 21–36.

2001a   *From Slogans to Mantras: Social Protest and Religious Conversions in the Late Vietnam War Era.* Syracuse, NY: Syracuse University Press.

2001b   'Brainwashing Programs in The Family/Children of God and Scientology'. Pp. 349–78 in B. Zablocki and T. Robbins, eds, *Misunderstanding Cults.* Toronto: University of Toronto Press.

Kephart, William M. and William W. Zellner
1991   *Extraordinary Groups.* 4th ed. New York: St. Martin's Press.

Kilbourne, Brock
1986   'Equity or Exploitation? The Case of the Unification Church'. *Review of Religious Research* 28(2): 143–50.

,———, and James T. Richardson
1982   'Cults versus Families: A Case of Misattribution of Cause?' Pp. 81–100 in F. Kaslow and M.B. Sussman, eds, *Cults and the Family.* New York: Haworth Press.

1989   'Paradigm Conflict, Types of Conversion, and Conversion Theories'. *Sociological Analysis* 50(1): 1–21.

Kleiver, Lonnie D.
1999   'Meeting God in Garland: A Model of Religious Tolerance'. *Nova Religio* 3(1): 45–53.

Knox, Willem, Wim Meeus, and Harm't Hart
1991   'Religious Conversion of Adolescents: Testing the Lofland and Stark Model of Religious Conversion'. *Sociological Analysis* 52(3): 227–40.

Kuhn, Thomas
1970   *Structure of Scientific Revolutions.* 2nd edn. Chicago: University of Chicago Press.

Lambert, Yves
2004   'A Turning Point in Religious Evolution in Europe'. *Journal of Contemporary Religion* 19(1): 29–45.

Langone, Michael D., ed.
1993   *Recovery from Cults: Help for Victims of Psychological and Spiritual Abuse.* New York: W.W. Norton.

Latkin, Carl

1987   'Rajneeshpuram, Oregon—An Exploration of Gender and Work Roles, Self-concept, and Psychological Well-being in an Experimental Community'. Doctoral diss., University of Oregon, Eugene, OR.

1992   'Seeing Red: A Social-Psychological Analysis of the Rajneeshpuram Conflict'. *Sociological Analysis* 53(3): 257–71.

————, **R. Hagan, R. Littman, and N. Sundberg**

1987   'Who Lives in Utopia? A Brief Report on the Rajneeshpuram Research Project'. *Sociological Analysis* 48(1): 73–81.

Layton, Deborah

1998   *Seductive Poison: A Jonestown Survivor's Story of Life and Death in the Peoples Temple.* New York: Anchor Books.

Levine, Saul V.

1984   *Radical Departures: Desperate Detours to Growing Up.* New York: Harcourt Brace Jovanovich.

Levitt, Cyril

1984   *Children of Privilege: Student Revolt in the Sixties.* Toronto: University of Toronto Press.

Lewis, James R.

1986   'Reconstructing the Cult Experience: Post-Involvement Attitudes as a Function of Mode of Exit and Post-Involvement Socialization'. *Sociological Analysis* 47(2): 151–9.

1988   'Apostates and the Legitimation of Repression: Some Historical and Empirical Perspectives on the Cult Controversy'. *Sociological Analysis* 48(4): 386–96.

————, **and David G. Bromley**

1987   'The Cult Withdrawal Syndrome: A Case of Misattribution of Cause?' *Journal for the Scientific Study of Religion* 26(4): 508–22.

————, **and J. Gordon Melton, eds**

1993   *Perspectives on the New Age.* Albany, NY: State University of New York Press.

1994   *Sex, Slander, and Salvation. Investigating the Family/Children of God.* Stanford, CA: Center for Academic Publication.

Lewy, Guenter

1974   *Religion and Revolution.* New York: Oxford University Press.

Lifton, Robert Jay

1961   *Thought Reform and the Psychology of Totalism.* New York: Norton.

1997   'Reflections on Aum Shinrikyō'. Pp. 112–20 in C. Strozier and M. Flynn, eds, *The Year 2000: Essays on the End.* New York: New York University Press.

1999   *Destroying the World to Save It: Aum Shinrikyō, Apocalyptic Violence, and the New Global Terrorism.* New York: Henry Holt.

Lippert, Randy
1990   'The Construction of Satanism as a Social Problem in Canada'. *Canadian Journal of Sociology* 15(4): 417–39.

Lipset, Seymour Martin
1990   *Continental Divide: The Values and Institutions of the United States and Canada.* New York: Routledge.

Lofland, John F.
1977   *Doomsday Cult: A Study of Conversion, Proselytization and Maintenance of Faith.* Enlarged edn. New York: Irvington.

———, and James T. Richardson
1984   'Religious Movement Organizations: Elemental Forms and Dynamics'. Pp. 29–51 in L. Kriesberg, ed., *Research in Social Movements, Conflict and Change,* Vol. 7. Greenwich, CT: JAI Press.

———, and Norman Skonovd
1981   'Conversion Motifs'. *Journal for the Scientific Study of Religion* 20(4): 373–85.

———, and Rodney Stark
1965   'Becoming a World-Saver: A Theory of Conversion to a Deviant Perspective'. *American Sociological Review* 30(6): 863–74.

Loomis, Ronald N.
1997   'Cults on Campus: The Appeal, The Danger'. Public lecture delivered at Wilfrid Laurier University, Waterloo, ON, 27 February.

Lucas, Phillip C.
1992   'The New Age Movement and the Pentecostal/Charismatic Revival: Distinct Yet Parallel Phases of a Fourth Great Awakening?' Pp. 189–211 in James R. Lewis and J. Gordon Melton, eds, *Perspectives on the New Age.* Albany, NY: State University of New York Press.

1995   *The Odyssey of a New Religion. The Holy Order of MANS from New Age to Orthodoxy.* Bloomington, IN: Indiana University Press.

———, and Thomas Robbins
2004   *New Religious Movements in the 21st Century.* New York: Routledge.

Luckmann, Thomas
1990   'Shrinking Transcendence, Expanding Religion'. *Sociological Analysis* 50(2): 127–38.

Luhrmann, Tanya
1989   *Persuasions of the Witch's Craft.* Cambridge, MA: Harvard University Press.

Lyotard, Jean-François
1984   *The Postmodern Condition: A Report on Knowledge.* Minneapolis: University of Minnesota Press.

Maaga, Mary McCormich

1998   *Hearing the Voices of Jonestown.* Syracuse, NY: Syracuse University Press.

Machacek, David and Bryan Wilson, eds.

2000   *Global Citizens: The Sōka Gakkai Buddhist Movement in the World.* New York: Oxford University Press.

Machalek, Richard, and David A. Snow

1993   'Conversion to New Religious Movements'. Pp. 53–74 in D.G. Bromley and J.K. Hadden, eds, *Religion and the Social Order,* Vol. 3, *The Handbook on Cults and Sects in America, Part B.* Greenwich, CT: JAI Press.

Martin, David

1962   'The Denomination'. *British Journal of Sociology* 13(2): 1–14.

Martin, Walter

1977   *The Kingdom of Cults.* Minneapolis: Bethany Fellowship.

Marx, John H., and David L. Ellison

1975   'Sensitivity Training and Communes: Contemporary Quests for Community'. *Pacific Sociological Review* 18(4): 442–62.

Marx, Karl

1972   'Contribution to the Critique of Hegel's Philosophy of Right: Introduction'. Pp. 37–52 in K. Marx and F. Engels, *On Religion.* Moscow: Progress.

Mauss, Armand

1993   'Research in Social Movements and in New Religious Movements: The Prospects for Convergence'. Pp. 127–51 in D.G. Bromley and J.K. Hadden, eds, *Religion and the Social Order,* Vol. 3, *The Handbook on Cults and Sects in America, Part A.* Greenwich, CT: JAI Press.

Mayer, Jean-François

1996   *Les Mythes du Temple Solaire.* Geneva, Switzerland: Georg.

1999   '"Our Terrestrial Journey is Coming to an End": The Last Voyage of the Solar Temple'. *Nova Religio* 2: 172–96.

2001   'Field Notes: The Movement for the Restoration of the Ten Commandments of God'. *Nova Religio* 5 (1): 203–10.

McCarthy, John, and Mayer N. Zald

1977   'Resource Mobilization and Social Movements: A Partial Theory'. *American Journal of Sociology* 82(6): 1212–41.

McLellan, Janet

1999   *Many Petals of the Lotus: Five Asian Buddhist Communities in Toronto.* Toronto: University of Toronto Press.

McLoughlin, William G.

1978   *Revivals, Awakenings, and Reform: An Essay on Religion and Social Change in America, 1607–1977.* Chicago: University of Chicago Press.

Meerlo, Joost

1956   *The Rape of the Mind.* New York: Grosset and Dunlap.

Melton, J. Gordon

1985   'Spiritualization and Reaffirmation: What Really Happens when Prophecy Fails?' *American Studies* 26(2): 17–29.

1987   'How New Is New? The Flowering of the "New" Religious Consciousness Since 1965'. Pp. 46–56 in D. Bromley and P. Hammond, eds, *The Future of New Religious Movements.* Macon, GA: Mercer University Press.

1992a   *The Encyclopedic Handbook of Cults in America.* 2nd rev. edn. New York: Garland.

1992b   'Violence and the Cults'. Pp. 361–93 in J.G. Melton, *The Encyclopedic Handbook of Cults in America.* 2nd edn. New York: Garland.

1994   'Sexuality and the Maturation of the Family'. Pp. 71–95 in J.R. Lewis and J.G. Melton, eds, *Sex, Slander, and Salvation: Investigating the Family/Children of God.* Stanford, CA: Center for Academic Publication.

1995   'The Changing Scene of New Religious Movements: Observations from a Generation of Research'. *Social Compass* 42(2): 265–76.

2000   *The Church of Scientology.* Salt Lake City: Signature Books.

2004   'An Introduction to New Religions'. Pp. 16–35 in J.R. Lewis, ed., *The Oxford Handbook of New Religious Movements.* New York: Oxford University Press.

————, **and David G. Bromley**

2002   'Challenging Misconceptions about the New Religions-Violence Connection'. Pp. 42–56 in D.G. Bromley and J.G. Melton, eds, *Cults, Religion and Violence.* Cambridge: Cambridge University Press.

Miller, Donald

1983   'Deprogramming in Historical Perspective'. Pp. 15–28 in D.G. Bromley and J.T. Richardson, eds, *The Brainwashing/Deprogramming Controversy: Sociological, Psychological, Legal and Historical Perspectives.* Lewiston, NY: Edwin Mellen Press.

1997   *Reinventing American Protestantism.* Berkeley, CA: University of California Press.

Miller, Timothy, ed.

1991   *When Prophets Die: The Postcharismatic Fate of New Religious Movements.* Albany, NY: State University of New York Press.

1995   *America's Alternative Religions.* Albany, NY: State University of New York Press.

Mills, Edgar W., Jr

1982   'Cult Extremism: The Reduction of Normative Dissonance'. Pp. 75–87 in K. Levi, ed., *Violence and Religious Commitment.* University Park, PA:

Pennsylvania State University Press.

Milne, Hugh

1986   *Bhagwan: The God That Failed.* London: Caliban.

Mol, Hans J.

1976   *Identity and the Sacred: A Sketch for a New Social Scientific Theory of Religion.* New York: Free Press.

1985   *Faith and Fragility: Religion and Identity in Canada.* Burlington, ON: Trinity Press.

Monk, Maria

1876   *Awful Disclosures of Maria Monk, as Exhibited in a Narrative of her Sufferings*
[1836]   *During her Residence of Five Years as a Novice and Two Years as a Black Nun in Hotel Dien Nunnery, at Montreal.* Rev. ed. New York: The Truth Seeker.

Moore, H. Lawrence

1985   *Religious Outsiders and the Making of Americans.* New York: Oxford University Press.

Muster, Nori J.

1997   *Betrayal of the Spirit: My Life Behind the Headlines of the Hare Krishna Movement.* Urbana, IL: University of Illinois Press.

Needleman, Jacob

1970   *The New Religions.* New York: E.P. Dutton.

Neitz, Mary Jo

1987   *Charisma and Community: A Study of Religious Commitment within the Charismatic Renewal.* New Brunswick, NJ: Transaction.

Nelson, Geoffrey K.

1984   'Cults and New Religions: Toward a Sociology of Religious Creativity'. *Sociology and Social Research* 68(3): 301–25.

Niebuhr, H. Richard

1929   *The Social Sources of Denominationalism.* New York: Henry Holt.

1951   *Christ and Culture.* New York: Harper and Row.

Oakes, Len

1997   *Prophetic Charisma: The Psychology of Revolutionary Religious Personalities.* Syracuse, NY: Syracuse University Press.

O'Gorman, Edith

1871   *Trials and Persecution of Miss Edith O'Gorman, Otherwise Sister Teresa de Chantal, of St. Joseph's Convent, Hudson City, N.J.* Hartford, CT: Conneticut Publishing Company.

Palmer, Susan Jean

1988   'Charisma and Abdication: A Study of the Leadership of Bhagwan Shree Rajneesh'. *Sociological Analysis* 49(2): 119–35.

1994   *Moon Sisters, Krishna Mothers, Rajneesh Lovers: Women's Roles in New Religions.* Syracuse, NY: Syracuse University Press.

1996   'Purity and Danger in the Solar Temple'. *Journal of Contemporary Religion* 11(3): 303–18.

1999   'Frontier Families: The Children of Island Pond'. Pp. 153–71 in S.J. Palmer and C.E. Hardman, eds, *Children in New Religions.* New York: Routledge.

2004   *Aliens Adored: Raël's UFO Religion.* New Brunswick, NJ: Rutgers University Press.

————, and Natalie Finn
1992   'Coping with Apocalypse in Canada: Experiences of Endtime in la Mission de l'Esprit Saint and the Institute of Applied Metaphysics'. *Sociological Analysis* 53(4): 397–415.

Parsons, Arthur S.
1986   'Messianic Personalism: A Role Analysis of the Unification Church'. *Journal for the Scientific Study of Religion* 25(2): 141–61.

1989   'The Secular Contribution to Religious Innovation: A Case Study of the Unification Church'. *Sociological Analysis* 50(3): 209–27.

Parsons, Talcott
1951   *The Social System.* Glencoe, IL: Free Press.

1971   *The System of Modern Societies.* Englewood Cliffs, NJ: Prentice-Hall.

Patrick, Ted, and Tom Dulack
1976   *Let Our Children Go!* New York: E.P. Dutton.

Partridge, Christopher
2003   *UFO Religions.* London: Routledge.

Penton, M. James
1985   *Apocalypse Delayed: The Story of the Jehovah's Witnesses.* Toronto: University of Toronto Press.

Pfeifer, Jeffrey E.
1992   'The Psychological Framing of Cults: Schematic Representations and Cult Evaluations'. *Journal of Applied Social Psychology* 22(7): 531–44.

1999   'Perceptual Biases and Mock Juror Decision Making: Minority Religions in Court'. *Social Justice Research* 12 (4): 409–19.

Pike, Sarah
2000   *Earthly Bodies, Magical Selves.* Berkeley, CA: University of California Press.

Pitchford, Susan, Christopher Bader, and Rodney Stark
2001   'Doing Field Studies of Religious Movements: An Agenda'. *Journal for the Scientific Study of Religion* 40(3): 379–92.

Poling, T., and J. Kenny

1986   *The Hare Krishna Character Type: A Study in Sensate Personality.* Lewiston, NY: Edwin Mellen Press.

Prebish, Charles, and Kenneth Ken'ichi Tanaka

1998   *The Faces of Buddhism in America.* Berkeley, CA: University of California Press.

Preston, David L.

1981   'Becoming a Zen Practitioner'. *Sociological Analysis* 42(1): 47–55.

Pritchard, Linda K.

1976   'Religious Change in Nineteenth-Century America'. Pp. 297–330 in Charles Glock and Robert Bellah, eds, *The New Religious Consciousness.* Berkeley, CA: University of California Press.

Puttick, Elizabeth

1997   *Women in New Religions: In Search of Community, Sexuality and Spiritual Power.* New York: St Martin's Press.

1999   'Women in New Religious Movements'. Pp. 143–62 in B. Wilson and J. Cresswell, eds, *New Religious Movements: Challenge and Response.* London: Routledge.

Rambo, Lewis R.

1993   *Understanding Religious Conversion.* New Haven, CT: Yale University Press.

Raschke, Carl

1980   *The Interruption of Eternity: Modern Gnosticism and the Origins of the New Religious Consciousness.* Chicago: Nelson-Hall.

Reader, Ian

1996   *A Poisonous Cocktail? Aum Shinrikyō's Path to Violence.* Copenhagen: Nordic Institute of Asian Studies Books.

2000   *Religious Violence in Contemporary Japan: The Case of Aum Shinrikyo.* Honolulu: University of Hawaii Press.

2002   'Dramatic Confrontations: Aum Shinrikyō Against the World'. Pp. 189–208 in D.G. Bromley and J.G. Melton, eds, *Cults, Religion and Violence.* Cambridge: Cambridge University Press.

Reimer, Samuel H.

1995   'A Look at Cultural Effects on Religiosity: A Comparison Between the United States and Canada'. *Journal for the Scientific Study of Religion* 34(4): 445–57.

Rescher, Nicholas

1988   *Rationality.* Oxford: Clarendon Press.

Richardson, James T.

1980   'Conversion Careers'. *Society* (March/April): 47–50.

1985   'The   Active   vs.   Passive   Convert: Paradigm   Conflict   in

Conversion/Recruitment Research'. *Journal for the Scientific Study of Religion* 24(2): 163–79.

1991   'Cult/Brainwashing Cases and Freedom of Religion'. *Journal of Church and State* 33(1): 55–74.

1992a   'Public Opinion and the Tax Evasion of Reverend Moon'. *Behavioral Sciences and the Law* 10(1): 53–63.

1992b   'Mental Health of Cult Consumers: Legal and Scientific Controversy'. Pp. 233–44 in J. Schumaker, ed., *Religion and Mental Health*. Oxford: Oxford University Press.

1993a   'Definitions of Cult: From Sociological-Technical to Popular-Negative'. *Review of Religious Research* 34(4): 348–56.

1993b   'A Social Psychological Critique of "Brainwashing" Claims about Recruitment to New Religions'. Pp. 75–97 in D.G. Bromley and J.K. Hadden, eds, *Religion and the Social Order,* Vol. 3, *The Handbook on Cults and Sects in America,* Part B. Greenwich, CT: JAI Press

1993c   'Religiosity as Deviance: The Negative Religious Bias in the Use and Misuse of the DMS-III'. *Deviant Behavior* 14(1): 1–21.

1994   'Update on "The Family": Organizational Change and Development in a Controversial New Religious Group'. Pp. 27–39 in J.R. Lewis and J.G. Melton, eds, *Sex, Slander, and Salvation: Investigating the Family/Children of God.* Stanford, CA: Center for Academic Publication.

1995a   'Manufacturing Consent about Koresh: A Structural Analysis of the Role of Media in the Waco Tragedy'. Pp. 153–76 in S.A. Wright, ed., *Armageddon in Waco.* Chicago: University of Chicago Press.

1995b   'Legal Status of Minority Religions in the United States'. *Social Compass* 42(2): 249–64.

1995c   'Clinical and Personality Assessment of Participants in New Religions'. *The International Journal for the Psychology of Religion* 5(3): 145–70.

1996a   'Journalistic Bias toward New Religious Movements in Australia'. *Journal of Contemporary Religion* 11(3): 289–302.

1996b   '"Brainwashing" Claims and Minority Religions Outside the United States: Cultural Diffusion of a Questionable Concept in the Legal Arena'. *Brigham Young University Law Review* (4): 873–904.

1997   'Sociology and the New Religions: "Brainwashing", the Courts, and Religious Freedom'. Pp. 115–37 in P. Jenkins and S. Kroll-Smith, eds, *Witnessing for Sociology: Reflexive Essays on Sociologists in Court.* New York: Praeger.

1999   'Social Control of New Religions: From "Brainwashing" Claims to Child Sex Abuse Accusations'. Pp. 172-86 in S.J. Palmer and C.E. Hardman, eds.

Children in New Religions. New York: Routledge.

2004a 'Legal Dimensions of New Religions'. Pp. 163–83 in J.R. Lewis, ed., *The Oxford Handbook of New Religious Movements*. New York: Oxford University Press.

——, ed.
1988 *Money and Power in New Religions*. Lewiston, NY: Edwin Mellen Press.

2004b *Regulating Religion: Case Studies from Around the Globe*. New York: Kluwer.

——, Robert Balch, and J. Gordon Melton
1993 'Problems of Research and Data in the Study of New Religions'. Pp. 213–29 in D.G. Bromley and J.K. Hadden, eds, *Religion and the Social Order*, Vol. 3, *The Handbook on Cults and Sects in America, Part B*. Greenwich, CT: JAI Press.

——, and David G. Bromley
1983 'Classical and Contemporary Brainwashing Models: A Comparison and Critique'. Pp. 29–45 in D.G. Bromley and J.T. Richardson, eds, *The Brainwashing/Deprogramming Controversy: Sociological, Psychological, Legal and Historical Perspectives*. Lewiston, NY: Edwin Mellen Press.

——, and Rex Davis
1983 'Experiential Fundamentalism: Revisions of Orthodoxy in the Jesus Movement'. *Journal of the American Academy of Religion* 51(3): 397–425.

——, and Massimo Introvigne
2001 '"Brainwashing" Theories in European Parliamentry and Administrative Reports on "Cults and Sects"'. *Journal for the Scientific Study of Religion* 40: 143–68.

——, Jan van der Lans, and Frans Derks
1986 'Leaving and Labeling: Voluntary and Coerced Disaffiliation from Religious Social Movements'. Pp. 97–126 in L. Kriesberg, ed., *Research in Social Movements, Conflicts and Change*. Greenwich, CT: JAI Press.

——, and Mary Stewart
1977 'Conversion Process Models and the Jesus Movement'. *American Behavioral Scientist* 20(6): 819–38.

——, Mary White Stewart, and Robert B. Simmonds
1979 *Organized Miracles: A Study of a Contemporary, Youth, Communal, Fundamentalist Organization*. New Brunswick, NJ: Transaction.

Robbins, Thomas
1984 'Constructing Cultist "Mind Control"'. *Sociological Analysis* 43(3): 241–56.

1986 'Religious Mass Suicide before Jonestown: The Russian Old Believers'. *Sociological Analyis* 47(1): 1–20.

1988 *Cults, Converts, and Charisma*. Newbury Park, CA: Sage.

2002   'Sources of Volatility in Religious Movements'. Pp. 57–79 in D.G. Bromley and J.G. Melton, eds, *Cults, Religion and Violence*. Cambridge: Cambridge University Press.

———, **and Dick Anthony**

1972   'Getting Straight with Meher Baba: A Study of Mysticism, Drug Rehabilitation and Postadolescent Role Conflict'. *Journal for the Scientific Study of Religion* 11(2): 122–40.

1979a   'The Sociology of Contemporary Religious Movements'. Pp. 75–89 in A. Inkeles, ed., *Annual Review of Sociology*. Palo Alto, CA: Annual Reviews Inc.

1979b   'Cults, Brainwashing, and Counter-Subversion'. *Annals of the American Academy of Political and Social Science* 446 (Nov.): 78–90.

1982a   'Cults, Culture, and Community'. Pp. 57–79 in F. Kaslow and M.B. Sussman, eds, *Cults and the Family*. New York: Haworth Press.

1982b   'Deprogramming, Brainwashing and the Medicalization of Deviant Religious Groups'. *Social Problems* 29(3): 283–97.

1984   'Constructing Cultist "Mind Control"'. *Sociological Analysis* 45: 241–56

1987   'New Religions and Cults in the United States'. Pp. 394–405 in Mircea Eliade, ed., *The Encyclopedia of Religion*. New York: Macmillan.

1995   'Sects and Violence: Factors Enhancing the Volatility of Marginal Religious Movements'. Pp. 236–59 in S.A. Wright, ed., *Armageddon in Waco*. Chicago: University of Chicago Press.

———, **and Dick Anthony, eds**

1981   *In Gods We Trust: New Patterns of Religious Pluralism in America*. 1st edn. New Brunswick, NJ: Transaction.

1990   *In Gods We Trust: New Patterns of Religious Pluralism in America*. 2nd edn. New Brunswick, NJ: Transaction.

———, **Dick Anthony, and Thomas Curtis**

1975   'Youth Culture Religious Movements: Evaluating the Integrative Hypothesis'. *The Sociological Quarterly* 16(4): 48–64.

———, **Dick Anthony, Thomas Curtis, and Madaline Doucas**

1976   'The Last Civil Religion: The Unification Church of Reverend Sun Myung Moon'. *Sociological Analysis* 37(2): 111–25.

———, **and David Bromley**

1992   'Social Experimentation and the Significance of American New Religions: A Focused Review Essay'. Pp. 1–28 in M. Lynn and D. Moberg, eds, *Research in the Social Scientific Study of Religion*, Vol. 4. Greenwich, CT: JAI Press.

———, **and Susan J. Palmer, eds**

1997   *Millennium, Messiahs and Mayhem*. London: Routledge.

Robertson, R., and J. Chirico
1985   'Humanity, Globalization and Worldwide Religious Resurgence: A Theoretical Exploration'. *Sociological Analysis* 46(3): 219–42.

Rochford, E. Burke, Jr
1985   *Hare Krishna in America*. New Brunswick, NJ: Rutgers University Press.

1988   'Movement and Public Conflict: Values, Finances and the Decline of Hare Krishna'. Pp. 271–303 in J.T. Richardson, ed., *Money and Power in New Religions*. Lewiston, NY: Edwin Mellen Press.

——, and Jennifer Heinlein
1998   'Child Abuse in the Hare Krishna Movement: 1971-1986'. *ISKCON Communications Journal* 6 (1): 43–69.

——, Sherly Purvis, and NeMar Eastman
1989   'New Religions, Mental Health, and Social Control'. Pp. 57–82 in M. Lynn and D. Moberg, eds, *Research in the Social Scientific Study of Religion*, Vol. 1. Greenwich, CT: JAI Press.

Roof, Wade Clark
1993   *A Generation of Seekers: The Spiritual Journeys of the Baby Boom Generation*. San Francisco: Harper-Collins.

1999   *Spiritual Marketplace: Baby Boomers and the Remaking of American Religion*. Princeton, NJ: Princeton University Press.

——, and William McKinney
1988   *American Mainline Religion: Its Changing Shape and Future*. New Brunswick, NJ: Rutgers University Press.

Rose, Susan
1987   'Woman Warriors: The Negotiation of Gender in a Charismatic Community'. *Sociological Analysis* 48(3): 245–58.

Rosenau, Pauline Marie
1992   *Post-Modernism and the Social Sciences*. Princeton, NJ: Princeton University Press.

Rosenfeld, Jean E.
2000   'The Justus Freemen Crisis: The Importance of the Analysis of Religion in Avoiding Violent Outcomes'. Pp. 323–44 in C. Wessinger, ed., *Millenialism, Persecution and Violence: Historical Cases*. Syracuse, NY: Syracuse University Press.

Ross, Colin A.
1995   *Satanic Ritual Abuse: Principles of Treatment*. Toronto: University of Toronto Press.

Saliba, John A.
1993   'The New Religions and Mental Health'. Pp. 99–113 in D.G. Bromley and

J.K. Hadden, eds, *Religion and the Social Order*, Vol. 3, *The Handbook on Cults and Sects in America, Part B*. Greenwich, CT: JAI Press.

2004   'Psychology and the New Religious Movements'. Pp. 317–32 in J.R. Lewis, ed., *The Oxford Handbook of New Religious Movements*. New York: Oxford University Press.

Sargent, William
1957   *Battle for the Mind*. London: Heinemann.

Schein, Edgar, I. Schneier, and C. Becker
1961   *Coercive Persuasion*. New York: Norton.

Schultze, Quentin J.
1991   *Televangelism and American Culture*. Grand Rapids, MI: Baker Book House.

Segal, Robert
1983   'In Defence of Reductionism'. *Journal of the American Academy of Religion* 51(2): 97–124.

Seggar, John, and Phillip Kunz
1972   'Conversion: Evaluation of a Step-Like Process of Problem-Solving'. *Review of Religious Research* 13(3): 178–84.

Selengut, Charles
1988   'American Jewish Converts to New Religious Movements'. *The Jewish Journal of Sociology* 30(2): 95–109.

Sherkat, Darren E.
1997   'Embedding Religious Choices: Integrating Preferences and Social Constraints into Rational Choice Theories of Religious Behavior'. Pp. 65–85 in L. Young, ed., *Rational Choice Theory and Religion: Summary and Assessment*. New York: Routledge.

Shaffir, William
1993   'Jewish Messianism Lubavitch-Style: An Interim Report'. *The Jewish Journal of Sociology* 35: 115–28.

1994   'Interpreting Adversity: Dynamics of Commitment in a Messianic Redemption Campaign'. *The Jewish Journal of Sociology* 36: 43–53.

1995   'When Prophecy is not Validated: Explaining the Unexpected in a Messianic Campaign'. *The Jewish Journal of Sociology* 37: 119–36.

Shinn, Larry D.
1993   'Who Gets to Define Religion? The Conversion/Brainwashing Controversy'. *Religious Studies Review* 19(3): 195–207.

Shupe, Anson D., Jr, and David G. Bromley
1980   *The New Vigilantes: Deprogrammers, Anti-Cultists and the New Religions*. Beverly Hills, CA: Sage.

1994   'The Modern Anti-Cult Movement, 1971–1991: A Twenty-Year Retrospective'. Pp. 3–31 in A. Shupe and D.G. Bromly, eds, *The Anti-Cult Movements in Cross-Cultural Perspective*. New York: Garland.

———, and Susan E. Darnell
2004   'The North American Anti-Cult Movement: Vicissitudes of Success and Failure'. Pp. 184–201 in J.R. Lewis, ed., *The Oxford Handbook of New Religious Movements*. New York: Oxford University Press.

Singelenberg, Richard
1988   '"It Separated the Wheat from the Chaff": The "1975" Prophecy and Its Impact among Dutch Jehovah's Witnesses'. *Sociological Analysis* 50: 23–40.

Singer, Margaret T.
1979   'Coming out of the Cults'. *Psychology Today* (Jan.): 72–82.

1995   *Cults in Our Midst: The Hidden Menace in Our Everyday Lives*. San Francisco, CA: Jossey-Bass.

Singer, Merrill
1988   'The Social Context of Conversion to a Black Religious Sect'. *Review of Religious Research* 29(4): 177–92.

Skolnik, Jerome H.
1969   *The Politics of Protest*. New York: Simon and Schuster.

Smith, Jonathan Z.
1982   'The Devil in Mr. Jones'. Pp. 102–34 in J.Z. Smith, *Imagining Religion: From Babylon to Jonestown*. Chicago, IL: University of Chicago Press.

Snow, David, and Richard Machalek
1982   'On the Presumed Fragility of Unconventional Beliefs'. *Journal for the Scientific Study of Religion* 21: 15–26.

1984   'The Sociology of Conversion'. Pp. 167–90 in Ralph H. Turner and James F. Short, eds, *Annual Review of Sociology*. Palo Alto, CA: Annual Reviews Inc.

———, and Cynthia L. Phillips
1980   'The Lofland-Stark Conversion Model: A Critical Reassessment'. *Social Problems* 27(4): 430–47.

———, Louis A. Zurcher, Jr, and Sheldon Ekland-Olson
1980   'Social Networks and Social Movements: A Microstructural Approach to Differential Recruitment'. *American Sociological Review* 45(5): 787–801.

Society for the Scientific Study of Religion et al.
1988   *Brief Amicus Curiae*. Submitted in The Court of Appeal for the State of California, Fourth Appellate District, Division One, 29 Feb.

Solomon, Trudy
1981   'Integrating the "Moonie" Experience: A Survey of Ex-members of the

Unification Church'. Pp. 275–95 in T. Robbins and D. Anthony, eds, *In Gods We Trust: New Patterns of Religious Pluralism in America*. 1st edn. New Brunswick, NJ: Transaction Press.

Spencer, Metta
1985   *Foundations of Modern Sociology*. 4th edn. Scarborough, ON: Prentice-Hall.

Spickhard, James V.
1994   'When None Dare Call it Evil: A Sociological Framework for Evaluating Abuse in Religions'. Pp. 251–60 in M. Neitz and M.S. Goldmann, eds, *Sex, Lies and Sanctity: Religion and Deviance in Contemporary North America*. Greenwich, CT: JAI Press.

Stacey, J.
1990   *Brave New Families: Stories of Domestic Upheaval in Late Twentieth Century America*. New York: Basic Books.

Staples, Clifford L., and Armand Mauss
1987   'Conversion or Commitment? A Reassessment of the Snow and Machalek Approach to the Study of Conversion'. *Journal for the Scientific Study of Religion* 26(2): 133–47.

Stark, Rodney
1987   'How New Religions Succeed: A Theoretical Model'. Pp. 11–29 in D.G. Bromley and P.E. Hammond, eds, *The Future of New Religious Movements*. Macon, GA: Mercer University Press.

1996a   'Why Religious Movements Succeed or Fail: A Revised General Model'. *Journal of Contemporary Religion* 11: 133–46.

1996b   *The Rise of Christianity: A Sociologist Reconsiders History*. Princeton, NJ: Princeton University Press.

———, **and William Sims Bainbridge**
1979   'Of Churches, Sects, and Cults: Preliminary Concepts for a Theory of Religious Movements'. *Journal for the Scientific Study of Religion* 18(2): 117–33.

1985   *The Future of Religion: Secularization, Revival and Cult Formation*. Berkeley, CA: University of California Press.

1987   *A Theory of Religion*. New York: Peter Lang, 1987. Repr. New Brunswick, NJ: Rutgers University Press, 1996.

———, **and Roger Finke**
1993   'A Rational Approach to the History of American Cults and Sects'. Pp. 109–25 in D.G. Bromley and J.K. Hadden, eds, *Religion and the Social Order*, Vol. 3, *The Handbook on Cults and Sects in America, Part A*. Greenwich, CT: JAI Press.

2000   *Acts of Faith: Explaining the Human Side of Religion*. Berkeley, CA: University of California Press.

————, and Laurence R. Iannaccone

1993   'Rational Choice Propositions About Religious Movements'. Pp. 241–61 in D.G. Bromley and J.K. Hadden, eds, *Religion and the Social Order*, Vol. 3, *The Handbook on Cults and Sects in America, Part A*. Greenwich, CT: JAI Press.

1997   'Why the Jehovah's Witnesses Grow so Rapidly: A Theoretical Application'. *Journal of Contemporary Religion* 12(2): 133–57.

Statistics Canada

Religion in Canada, 2001 Census (retrieved from www.statscan.ca)

Steiger, Brad, and Hayden Hewes

1997   *Inside Heaven's Gate*. New York: Signet Books.

Stillson, Judah J.

1967   *The History and Philosophy of Metaphysical Movements in America*. Philadelphia, PA: Westminster Press.

Stone, Donald

1978a   'On Knowing How We Know about New Religions'. Pp. 141–52 in J. Needleman and G. Baker, eds, *Understanding New Religions*. New York: Seabury Press.

1978b   'New Religious Consciousness and Personal Religious Experience'. *Sociological Analysis* 39(2): 123–34.

Stone, Jon R.

2000   *Expecting Armageddon: Essential Readings in Failed Prophecy*. New York: Routledge.

Straus, Roger

1976   'Changing Oneself: Seekers and the Creative Transformation of Life Experience'. Pp. 252–73 in J. Lofland, ed., *Doing Social Life*. New York: Wiley and Sons.

1979   'Religious Conversion as a Personal and Collective Accomplishment'. *Sociological Analysis* 40(2): 158–65.

Streiker, Lowell D.

1984   *Mind-bending: Brainwashing, Cults and Deprogramming in the 1980s*. Garden City, NY: Doubleday.

Strozier, Charles B.

1994   *Apocalypse: On the Psychology of Fundamentalism in America*. Boston: Beacon Press.

Sullivan, Lawrence E.

1996   '"No Longer the Messiah": US Federal Law Enforcement Views of Religion in Connection with the 1993 Siege of Mount Carmel Near Waco, Texas'. *Numen* 43(2): 213–34.

Suttcliffe, Steven J.
  2003   *Children of the New Age: A History of Spiritual Practices.* London: Routledge.

Swantko, Jean A.
  1999   'The Twelve Tribes' Communities, The Anti-Cult Movement, and Government's Response'. *Social Justice Research* 12(4): 341–64.

Swatos, William H., Jr
  1976   'Weber or Troeltsch?: Methodology, Syndrome, and the Development of Church-Sect Theory'. *Journal for the Scientific Study of Religion* 15(2): 129–44.

Swatsky, Rodney
  1978   'Moonies, Mormons, and Mennonites: Christian Heresy and Religious Toleration'. Pp. 20–40 in M.D. Bryant and H.W. Richardson, eds, *A Time for Consideration: A Scholarly Appraisal of the Unification Church.* New York: Edwin Mellen Press.

Szubin, Adam, C.J. Jensen III, and R. Gress
  2000   'Interacting with Cults: A Policing Model'. *FBI Law Enforcement Bulletin* 69: 16–25.

Tabor, James D.
  1995   'Religious Discourse and Failed Negotiations: The Dynamics of Biblical Apocalypticism at Waco'. Pp. 263–81 in S.A. Wright, ed., *Armageddon in Waco.* Chicago: University of Chicago Press.

———, **and Eugene Gallagher**
  1995   *Why Waco?* Berkeley, CA: University of California Press.

Takbaaki, Sanada
  1979   'After Prophecy Fails: A Reappraisal of a Japanese Case'. *Japanese Journal of Religious Studies* 6: 217–37.

Tamney, Joseph B.
  1992   *American Society in the Buddhist Mirror.* New York: Garland.

Tipton, Steven M.
  1982a   *Getting Saved from the Sixties.* Berkeley, CA: University of California Press.

  1982b   'The Moral Logic of Alternative Religions'. Pp. 79–107 in M. Douglas and S. Tipton, eds, *Religion and America.* Boston: Beacon Press.

Tiryakian, Edward
  1967   'A Model of Social Change and Its Lead Indicators'. Pp. 59–67 in S. Klausner, ed., *The Study of Total Societies.* Garden City, NY: Doubleday.

  1972   'Towards a Sociology of Esoteric Culture'. *American Sociological Review* 78 (Nov.): 491–512.

Toch, Hans
  1965   *The Social Psychology of Social Movements.* Indianapolis, IN: Bobbs-Merrill.

Traungot, Michael

1998   "The Farm'. Pp. 41–62 in W.W. Zellner and M. Petrowsky, eds. *Sects, Cults and Spiritual Communities*. Westport, CT: Praeger.

Travisano, Richard

1981   'Alternation and Conversion as Qualitatively Different Transformations'. Pp. 237–48 in G. Stone and H. Farberman, eds, *Social Psychology through Symbolic Interaction*. New York: John Wiley and Sons.

Troeltsch, Ernst

1931   *The Social Teachings of the Christian Churches,* Vol. I. London: George Allen and Unwin.

Tumminia, Diana

1998   'How Prophecy Never Fails: Interpretive Reason in a Flying Saucer Group'. *Journal of Contemporary Religion* 59: 157–70.

Turner, Bryan

1978   'Recollection and Membership: Converts' Talk and the Ratiocination of Commonality'. *Sociology* 12: 316–24.

Turner, Victor

1968   *The Ritual Process*. Chicago: Aldine.

Tweed, Thomas A.

1992   *The American Encounter with Buddhism, 1844–1912: Victorian Culture and the Limits of Dissent*. Bloomington, IN: Indiana University Press.

Underwood, Barbara, and B. Underwood

1979   *Hostage to Heaven*. New York: Clarkson N. Potter.

Van Driel, Barend, and James T. Richardson

1988   'Print Media Coverage of New Religious Movements: A Longitudinal Study'. *Journal of Communication* 38(3): 37–61.

Van Fossen, Anthony B.

1988   'How Do Movements Survive Failures of Prophecy?' Pp. 193–212 in L. Kriesberg, B. Mitsztal and J. Mucha, eds, *Research in Social Movements, Conflicts and Change*. 10. Greenwich, CT: JAI Press.

Van Zandt, David E.

1991   *Living in the Children of God*. Princeton, NJ: Princeton University Press.

Wallace, Anthony F.C.

1956   'Revitalization Movements'. *American Anthropologist* 58: 264–81.

1966   *Religion: An Anthropological View*. New York: Random House.

Wallis, Roy

1977   *The Road to Total Freedom: A Sociological Analysis of Scientology*. New York: Columbia University Press.

1979   'Sex, Marraige and the Children of God'. Pp. 74-90 in R. Wallis, *Salvation and Protest: Studies in Social and Religious Movements*. London: Frances Pinter.

1982   'The Social Construction of Charisma'. *Social Compass* 29(1): 25–39.

1984   *The Elementary Forms of New Religious Life*. London: Routledge and Kegan Paul.

————, and Steve Bruce

1983   'Accounting for Action: Defending the Common Sense Heresy'. *Sociology* 17(1): 97–111.

1986   'Sex, Violence and Religion: Antinomianism and Charisma'. Pp. 115–27 in R. Wallis and S. Bruce, *Sociological Theory, Religion and Collective Action*. Belfast: Queen's University Press.

Walliss, John

2004   *Apocalyptic Trajectories: Millennnarianism and Violence in the Contemporary World*. Oxford: Peter Lang.

Warner, Stephen R.

1988   *New Wine in Old Skins: Evangelicals and Liberals in a Small Town Church*. Berkeley, CA: University of California Press.

1993   'Work in Progress toward a New Paradigm for the Sociological Study of Religion in the United States'. *American Journal of Sociology* 98(5): 1044–93.

Weber, Max

1949   *The Methodology of the Social Sciences*. Trans. and ed. E.A. Shils and H.A. Finch. New York: Free Press.

1958a   *The Protestant Ethic and the Spirit of Capitalism*. Trans. T. Parsons. New York: Charles Scribner's Sons.

1958b   *From Max Weber. Essays in Sociology*. Trans. and ed. H.H. Gerth and C.W. Mills. New York: Oxford University Press.

1963   *The Sociology of Religion*. Trans. Ephraim Fischoff. Boston: Beacon Press.

1964   *The Theory of Social and Economic Organization*. Trans. A.M. Henderson. Ed. Talcott Parsons. New York: Free Press.

Werblowsky, R.J. Zwi

1982   'Religions New and Not So New: Fragments of an Agenda'. Pp. 32–46 in E. Barker, ed., *New Religious Movements: A Perspective for Understanding Society*. New York: Edwin Mellen Press.

Wessinger, Catherine

1999   'Religious Studies Scholars, FBI Agents, and the Montana Freemen Standoff'. *Nova Religio* 3: 36–44.

2000   *How the Millennium Comes Violently*. New York: Seven Bridges Press.

Westley, Frances

1978   '"The Cult of Man": Durkheim's Predictions and New Religious Movements'. *Sociological Analysis* 39(2): 135–45.

1983   *The Complex Forms of the Religious Life: A Durkheimian View of New Religious Movements.* Chico, CA: Scholars Press.

Whitehead, Harriet

1987   *Renunciation and Reformulation: A Study of Conversion in an American Sect.* Ithaca, NY: Cornell University Press.

Whitsel, Bradley C.

2003   *The Church Universal and Triumphant.* Syracuse, NY: Syracuse University Press.

Wilson, Bryan R.

1961   *Sects and Society.* Berkeley, CA: University of California Press.

1970   *Religious Sects: A Sociological Study.* London: Weidenfeld and Nicolson.

1975   *The Noble Savages: The Primitive Origins of Charisma and Its Contemporary Survival.* Berkeley, CA.: University of California Press.

1976   *The Contemporary Transformation of Religion.* Oxford: Clarendon Press.

1978   'When Prophecy Failed'. *New Society* 26: 183–84.

1979   'The Return of the Sacred'. *Journal for the Scientific Study of Religion* 18(3): 268–80.

1982a   *Religion in Sociological Perspective.* Oxford: Oxford University Press.

1982b   'The New Religions: Preliminary Considerations'. Pp. 16–31 in E. Barker, ed., *New Religious Movements: A Perspective for Understanding Society.* New York: Edwin Mellen Press.

1987   'Factors in the Failure of the New Religious Movements'. Pp. 30–45 in D.G. Bromley and P.E. Hammond, eds, *The Future of New Religious Movements.* Macon, Ga: Mercer University Press.

1988   '"Secularization": Religion in the Modern World'. Pp. 953–66 in Stewart Sutherland et al., eds, *The World's Religions.* London: Routledge.

1990   *The Social Dimension of Sectarianism.* Oxford: Clarendon Press.

1993   'Historical Lessons in the Study of Sects and Cults'. Pp. 53–73 in D.G. Bromley and J.K. Hadden, eds, *Religion and the Social Order,* Vol. 3, *The Handbook on Cults and Sects in America, Part A.* Greenwich, CT: JAI Press.

————, **and Karel Dobbelaere**

1994   *A Time to Chant: The Sōka Gakkai Buddhists in Britain.* Oxford: Clarendon Press.

Wilson, Stephen R.

1984   'Becoming a Yogi: Resocialization and Deconditioning as Conversion Processes'. *Sociological Analysis* 45(4): 301–14.

1990   'Personal Growth in a Yoga Ashram: A Symbolic Interactionist Interpretation'. Pp. 137–66 in D. Moberg and M.L. Lynn, eds, *Research in the Social Scientific Study of Religion*, Vol. 7. Greenwich, CT: JAI Press.

Wolf, David

2004   'Child Abuse and the Hare Krishnas: History and Response'. Pp. 321–44 in E.E. Bryant and M.L. Ekstrand, eds, *The Hare Krishna Movement: The Postcharismatic Fate of a Religious Transplant*. New York: Columbia University Press.

Wood, Allen Tate, with Jack Vitch

1979   *Moonstruck: A Memoir of My Life in a Cult*. New York: William Morrow.

Wright, Stuart A.

1984   'Post-Involvement Attitudes of Voluntary Defectors from Controversial New Religious Movements'. *Journal for the Scientific Study of Religion* 23(2): 172–82.

1986   'Dyadic Intimacy and Social Control in Three Cult Movements'. *Sociological Analysis* 47 (2): 137–50.

1987   *Leaving Cults: The Dynamics of Defection*. Washington, DC: Society for the Scientific Study of Religion Monograph Series, no. 7.

1998   'Chen Tao: A Case Study in the Failure of Prophecy'. Paper presented at the Society for the Scientific Study of Religion, Montreal.

————, ed.

1995a   'Another View of the Mt Carmel Standoff'. Pp. xiii–xxvi in S. Wright, ed., *Armageddon in Waco*. Chicago: University of Chicago Press.

1995b   *Armageddon in Waco: Critical Perspectives on the Branch Davidian Conflict*. Chicago: University of Chicago Press.

————, and William V. D'Antonio

1993   'Families and New Religions'. Pp. 219–38 in D.G. Bromley and J.K. Hadden, eds, *Religion and the Social Order*, Vol. 3, *The Handbook on Cults and Sects in America, Part A*. Greenwich, CT: JAI Press.

————, and Helen Rose Ebaugh

1993   'Leaving New Religions'. Pp. 117–38 in D. Bromley and J. Hadden, eds, *Religion and the Social Order*, Vol. 3, *The Handbook on Cults and Sects in America, Parts A and B*. Greenwich, CT: JAI Press.

Wuthnow, Robert

1982   'World Order and Religious Movements'. Pp. 47–65 in E. Barker, ed., *New Religious Movements: A Perspective for Understanding Society*. New York: Edwin Mellen Press.

1985   'The Cultural Context of Contemporary Religious Movements'. Pp. 43–56 in T. Robbins, W.C. Sheperd, and J. McBride, eds, *Cults, Culture, and the Law*. Chico, CA: Scholars Press.

1988   *The Restructuring of American Religion*. Princeton, NJ: Princeton University Press.

Yinger, J. Milton
1970   *The Scientific Study of Religion*. New York: Macmillan.

Young, Lawrence, ed.
1997   *Rational Choice Theory and Religion: Summary and Assessment*. New York: Routledge.

Young, John L., and Ezra E.H. Griffiths
1992   'A Critical Evaluation of Coercive Persuasion as Used in the Assessment of Cults'. *Behavioural Sciences and the Law* 10: 89–101.

Zablocki, Benjamin
1996   'Reliability and Validity of Apostate Accounts in the Study of Religious Communities'. Paper presented to the Association for the Sociology of Religion, New York City.

2001   'Towards a Demystification and Disinterested Scientific Theory of Brainwashing'. Pp. 159–214 in B. Zablocki and T. Robbins, eds, *Misunderstanding Cults*. Toronto: University of Toronto Press.

Zald, Mayer, and Roberta Ash
1965   'Social Movement Organizations: Growth, Decay and Change'. *Social Forces* 44: 327–41.

Zarestsky, I., and M.P. Leone, eds
1974   *Religious Movements in Contemporary America*. Princeton, NJ: Princeton University Press.

Zaroulis, Nancy, and Gerald Sullivan
1984   *Who Spoke Up? American Protest against the War in Vietnam, 1963–1975*. Garden City, NY: Doubleday.

Zygmunt, J.F.
1970   'Prophetic Failure and Chiliastic Identity: The Case of Jehovah's Witnesses'. *American Journal of Sociology* 75(6): 926–48.

1972   'When Prophecies Fail: A Theoretical Perspective on Comparative Evidence'. *American Behavioral Scientist* 16(2): 245–67.

Index

abuse: child, 132–5, 140; sexual, 132, 140

'adjustive socialization', 46

adolescents: social ties and, 78–9; see also age

Aethurius Society, 3

affective ties: conversion and, 78

age: conversion and, 78–9, 83–4

Aidala, Angela, 127

alienation, 17, 55–6

aliens: groups associated with, 3, 9–10; see also specific groups

ambiguity, moral, 43–6, 181

American Family Foundation, 8

amplification, deviance, 154, 161, 176

Anabaptists, 126–7, 146

anomie, 16–17, 44, 56

anti–cult movement, 1, 7–8, 27–8; brainwashing and, 96–116; child abuse accusations and, 132–5

antinomianism, 126–7

apocalyptic beliefs, 145, 146–52; basis of, 147–50; behavioural consequences of, 150–2; failures of, 168–75

asceticism, 128–9

Ashara, 158

Asian traditions; see Eastern traditions

Aum Shinrikyō, 143, 158, 177

authority: delegation of, 155; results–based, 183; types of, 152–3

awakenings, religious, 62–6; schisms and, 64

baby boomers, 41–6, 48

Bader, Chris, and Alfred Demaris, 24, 79, 85

Baha'is Under the Provision of the Covenant, 169, 170, 172, 173

Bainbridge, William Sims, and Rodney Stark, 60–2

Balch, Robert, 78, 164–5

Baptists, 147

Barker, Eileen, 34–6, 193, 194; on converts, 77–8, 79, 83, 86, 87, 90, 92, on brainwashing, 105, 107, 110, 111–12, 115

Barton, Winnifred, 171

BATF (Bureau of Alcohol, Tobacco and Firearms), 149, 175–6

Beckford, James, 11, 195–8

Bellah, Robert, 40–3

Berg, David, (Moses David), 127, 131–2, 134, 135, 156, 160

Berger, Peter, 14–20, 24–5, 52, 181, 187, 195

bias: anti–cult, 7–8; pro–cult, 10–11

Bible: apocalyptic beliefs and, 147–9

Bird, Frederick, and Bill Reimer, 111

Black Hebrew Nation, 76

Bo and Peep UFO cult, 78, 164–5

Book of Revelation, 147–9
boundaries: violence and, 162, 163–4
Boyer, Paul, 146
Brahma Kumaris, 129
brainwashing, 6, 95–124; case against, 103–16; case for, 97–103; criminal and civil cases and, 95, 96; member retention and, 119–24; theories of, 105–6; three phases of, 99–100
Branch Davidians, 2, 7, 8, 99, 133, 142, 143, 145, 149, 175–6; isolation and, 162, 163
Bromley, David, 121–2, 176–7
Bromley, David, and Anson D. Shupe, Jr, 66–7, 117
Buddhism, 8–9, 23, 45

cadres, 37–8
Campbell, Bruce, 30
Campbell, Colin, 182–9
Catholic Charismatic Renewal, 51, 80, 93, 191–3
Catholicism, 3, 32, 125; conversion and, 86
Chancellor, James, 87, 131
charisma: leaders and, 27, 28–9, 145–6, 152–61; nature of, 153; resisting routinization of, 156–60; see also leadership, charismatic
Chen Tao, 169
Chidester, David, 178
children: 'of privilege,' 72; sexuality of, 128; taken by authorities, 132–5; see also abuse, child
Children of God/The Family, 87, 156, 160, 177; conversion and, 83, 87, 100; family nature of, 51;'flirty fishing' and, 104, 128; sexual deviance and, 126, 127–8, 131–5
Christianity, 3; apocalyptic beliefs and, 146–5, 147–50; conservative, 23, 45, 48; as cult, 23; fundamentalist, 7; growth in, 41–2; history of, 69–70; mystical organizations of, 150; new religions of, 69; see also Catholicism;

churches; Protestantism; religion; specific groups
Christian Science, 85
'churched', 24
churches: conventional, 24; definition of, 26–7; sects and, 26–9; sects and cults and, 23–4; weakness of, 24; see also religion; specific groups
Church of Satan, 3, 84
Church of the True Word, 169, 172, 173
Church Universal and Triumphant, 3, 4, 34, 84, 177
CIA (Central Intelligence Agency), 106
Citizens Freedom Foundation, 8
Clark, John, 97
class: conversion and, 85
'coercive persuasion', 96
cognitive dissonance, 174–5
'combination', 46
commitment: degree of, 83
communes: gender roles in, 137
community: family–like NRMs and, 51–2; shift from, 59
'compensation', 47
compensators, 21, 62; specific, 81; supernatural, 22–3
consciousness, new religious, 183–5; significance of, 185–9
conversion, 71–94; active/passive, 117–19; brainwashing and, 95–119; rationality of, 93; total, 75; verbal, 75; see also converts; recruitment
converts: social attributes of, 82–90
costs: rewards and, 21
Council on Mind Abuse, 8
counterculture: in 1960s, 40–4, 72; Fourth Awakening and, 65
courts: brainwashing and, 115–16; religious freedoms and, 7
cult(s): audience, 33, 36–7; churches and, 23–4; client, 33–4, 36–7; definition of, 28–9; 'experts' on, 1; sects and, 23–4, 27–9, 31; as term, 10, 27–8; theories of religion and, 24–5; traits of, 28–9; typologies of, 29–34,

36–8; see also New Religious
  Movements; specific groups
Cult Awareness Network, 8, 116
cult movement, 33–4, 36
'cult scare', 27
cultural significance: NRMs and, 179–99
culture: as human creation, 15
custody: child abuse accusations and,
  133

David, Moses; see Berg, David
Davidians; see Branch Davidians
Davidman, Lynn, 140–1
deception, 103–4, 116
Dein, Simon, 170, 174
deinstitutionalization, 49, 52–6
denial: failure of apocalyptic prophecies
  and, 174–5
'deployable agents', 120
deprivation: economic, 72–3; relative,
  71–5; types of, 73
deprogramming, 7, 95, 108–9, 113, 116
deviance, sexual, 125–41; social movements and, 72
'deviance amplification', 154, 161, 176
Diagnostic and Statistical Manual of Mental
  Disorders, The, 114
Dianetics: The Modern Science of Mental
  Health, 33
Di Mambro, Joseph, 165–6
disembedding: social life and, 56–8
dislocation: NRMs and, 39–40
dissonance: cognitive, 174–5; management of, 174–5; normative, 166
Divine Light Mission/Elan Vital, 3, 45,
  46–7
Do and Ti, 150, 158, 159, 165; see also
  Heaven's Gate

Eastern traditions: groups associated
  with, 3, 45–6, 66, 68, 80, 84–5, 92;
  see also specific groups
Ebaugh, Helen Rose Fuchs, 113
education: conversion and, 84–5
Ellwood, Robert S., and Harry B. Partin,

68
Enroth, Ronald, 97–8, 102–3, 106
'Entrepreneur Model of Cult Innovation',
  61
est (Erhard Seminar Training), 3, 33, 45,
  84
evangelism, 23; awakenings and, 63–4
exclusivity: conversion and, 81, 83
'exit counselling', 109, 113, 116; see also
  deprogramming
experience: ecstatic or transfiguring, 29;
  personal, 185–6; positive, 94; religious,
  93–4; religions of, 183
expert systems: modernity and, 56–7
expressive relationships, 50, 52
externalization, 15

families: spiritual, 51; surrogate, 49–52
Family, The; see Children of God/The
  Family
Farm, The, 127
FBI (Federal Bureau of Investigation),
  149, 175
Festinger, Leon, Henry W. Riecken, and
  Stanley Schachter, 168, 175
Finke, Roger, and Rodney Stark, 32
First Great Awakening, 62, 63, 64
Fourth Great Awakening, 63, 64–6
'free love', 126–8
fundamentalists, 'returning', 80

Galanter, Marc, 109–10, 115, 163–4
Gampo Abbey, 9
gender, 126, 136–42; ambiguity and,
  140; conversion and, 85–6; roles and,
  136–42
Giddens, Anthony, 56–8
globalization, 4, 56–7
Glock, Charles, 72–4
glossolalia, 181
Goldman, Marion S., 83, 85, 87
Great Awakenings, 62–6
Greil, Arthur L., and David R. Rudy, 76
'groupthink', 166, 167
Gurney, Joan Neff, and Kathleen J.

Tierney, 74
guru–disciple relationship, 129–30; see also leadership, charismatic
Gussner, R.E., and S.D. Berkowitz, 80, 85, 92

Hammond, Phillip, and David Machacek, 83, 84, 85
Hamnett, Ian, 12
Hardyck, A., and M. Braden, 173
Hassan, Steven, 97–8, 99, 102–3, 106
Heaven's Gate, 3, 142, 150, 158, 159, 165; conversion and, 78, 84; isolation and, 163, 164
Hermetic Orthodoxy, 3
Hine, Virginia, 75
Hinkle, Lawrence, 106
'holistic shift', 195–6
holistic world–view, 184
Holy Order of MANS, 44
Hoover, Stewart, 7
Hubbard, Jamie, 70
Hubbard, L. Ron, 33, 155, 157
human error: failure of apocalyptic prophecies and, 172–3
human potential movement: groups associated with, 3, 45
Hunter, Edward, 99, 105–6
Hunter, James Davison, 52–4, 56, 187, 188
hypnosis, 102

Ichigen no Miya, 169, 170, 171–2
identity: construction of, 57–8; meaningful, 53–4; subjective, 57–8
ideological alignments, weak, 80
individualism, utilitarian, 41–5
innovation: cults and, 23
Institute of Applied Metaphysics, 169, 174
institutionalization, 52–3
instrumental relationships, 50
integration, cultural, 4
intensive interaction: conversion and, 78
internalization, 15

International Society for Krishna Consciousness; see Krishna Consciousness
intervention: violence and, 176–8
irrationality, 12–13
isolation: violence and, 162

Jacobs, Janet Liebman, 110
Janis, Irving, 167
Jehovah's Witnesses, 147, 169, 171, 172, 174
Jesus: esoteric teachings and, 69
Jesus Movement groups, 45
Jews: conversion and, 86, 88–90
John of Patmos, 147
Johnson, Benton, 12, 52, 54–6
Jones, Jim, 84, 158, 159, 160, 162–3; see also Peoples Temple
Jonestown massacre, 2, 142, 145; see also Peoples Temple
Jouret, Luc, 150, 165
Judaism, 3

Keech, Marion, 168
Kennedy, John F.: 'groupthink' and, 167
Kent, Stephen, 43, 119, 121
knowledge, esoteric, 29
Knox, Willem, Wim Meeus, and Harm't Hart, 76
Korean War: brainwashing and, 97, 106
Koresh, David, 2, 7, 149, 159, 162; see also Branch Davidians
Krishna Consciousness, 3, 4, 27, 29, 34, 45, 47; conversion and, 83, 86, 87, 88; deception and, 104; gender roles and, 138–9; sex and, 129

Latkin, Carl, R. Hagan, R. Littman, and N. Sundberg, 83, 85, 86, 88
'Law of Love', 127, 135
leadership, charismatic, 145–6, 152–61; crises of, 160–1; precariousness of, 154–5; see also charisma
Levine, Saul, 91–2, 113
lifestyle experimentation: in 1960s, 40–3

Lifton, Robert, 99, 105–6, 120
Lofland, John F., and Rodney Stark, 75–6
Lofland–Stark Model of Conversion,
    75–6, 78
loneliness: conversion and, 79
'love–bombing', 101–2, 106–7
Love Our Children Inc., 8
Lubavitch Hasidim, 169, 170, 172, 174
Lucas, Phillip, 44, 191–3
Luckmann, Thomas, 15

Machalek, Richard, and David A. Snow,
    85
McLoughlin, William, 62–6
Marx, Karl, 39
meaningfulness, 16–17
media: cults and, 5–8
mediating structures, 50, 52
Meerloo, Joost, 99, 105–6
'me generation', 44
Melton, J. Gordon, 27, 66, 67, 144, 170,
    171, 173
membership: level of commitment and,
    37–8; mode of, 32–3, 36–8
men: NRM membership and, 126, 136,
    137, 138–9
Methodists, 147
Millerite movement, 146, 169, 173
Mills, Edgar, Jr, 166
'mind control', 96
Mission de l'Esprit Saint, 169, 170
modernity: late, 49; NRMs' compatibility
    with, 182, 186, 189–93; NRMs'
    response to, 58; NRMs' orientation to,
    11, 185; structural changes in, 56–8;
    structural dilemma of, 54–6
modernization, 182
Moon, Reverend Sun Myung, 1, 4
Moonies; see Unification Church
moral ambiguity, 43–6, 47–8
Mormons, 32, 146–7
motivations: NRM membership and,
    71–94; relative–deprivation theory and,
    71–5; sectarian membership and,
    72–3; stereotypical, 71

Movement for the Restoration of the Ten
    Commandments, 143, 163
MSIA ('Messiah'), 1
Münster, Thomas, 146
mysticism, 'this–wordly', 187, 188

Naropa Institute, 9
Neitz, Mary Jo, 93
Nelson, Geoffrey, 12
Neo–Pagan groups: conversion and, 84,
    88
new age: anticipation of, 193
New Age groups, 2, 4, 44, 69, 191–3
New Christian Right, 48, 63
New Religious Movements (NRMs), 2; as
    adaptations of religion, 60; anti–mod-
    ern, 190–3, 197–9; changes in, 34–6;
    continuity of, 48–9, 67–8; cultural
    change and, 39–62; emergence of,
    39–70; established, 29, 36; as experi-
    mentation, 180; as expression of cul-
    tural continuity, 62–70, 182–9; fami-
    ly–like, 51; formation of, 24, 60–2;
    hostility towards, 5–8; models of for-
    mation, 60–2; modern, 190–3, 197–9;
    moral ambiguity and, 43–6; nature of,
    25; 'newness' of, 66–7; postmodern,
    195–9; rates of activity of, 24; as resis-
    tance, 180; social and cultural signifi-
    cance of, 25; social world and, 31; suc-
    cess of, 34–6, 193–4; as successor
    movements', 40–3; survival of, 182;
    theories of religion and, 24–5; violence
    and, 5–6, 142–78; see also cults; specif-
    ic groups
Nichirin Soshu; see Sōka Gakkai
Niebuhr, H. Richard, 31–2, 69
nomos, 16–17, 19
normalcy/deviance, sexual, 129–30
'normative dissonance', 166
normlessness, 16
Noyes, John Humphrey, 127

objectivation, 15
occult revival: groups associated with, 3

Oneida Community, 127
Order of the Solar Temple; see Solar Temple
Ordre du Temple solaire, L'; see Solar Temple
organization: changes in, 29; forms of, 32–3, 36–8; openness of, 184
Osho Foundation; see Rajneeshpuram

Palmer, Susan Jean, 83, 84, 85, 92, 136–7, 138–42
Palmer, Susan Jean, and Natalie, Finn, 171, 174
paranoia, leaders', 154–5
Parsons, Arthur, 189–90
particularism: conversion and, 81
Paul: conversion of, 117–18
Peasants' War, 146
Pentecostal movement, 76, 191–3
Peoples Temple, 2, 133, 142, 143, 145, 160, 178; isolation and, 162–4
personal relationships, 57–8
Pfeifer, Jeffrey, 6–7
pluralism, 18
post–industrialism: compatibility with, 186
postmodernism, 195–9; NRMs' compatibility with, 186
private life: deinstitutionalization of, 53–6; public life and, 50, 53–6
prophets: NRM leaders as, 69, 153
proselytization: failure of apocalyptic prophecies and, 170
protest, political, 40–4
Protestantism, 3; apocalyptic beliefs and, 146; awakenings and, 63; liberal, 23; conversion and, 86
psychiatry: cults and, 5
'Psychopathology Model of Cult Innovation', 61
public life: institutionalization of, 53–6; private life and, 50, 53–6
Puttick, Elizabeth, 125, 131
Pyschosynthesis, 3

Raëlians, 3, 4, 34; conversion and, 84, 85, 86
Rajneesh, Bhagwan Shree, 83–4, 155–6
Rajneesh Foundation; see Rajneeshpuram
Rajneeshpuram, 3; conversion and, 83–4, 86, 87, 88; gender roles and, 138–9; trance and, 107–8; sexual deviance and, 127, 128
Ramtha, 3
rationality, 12–13
rationalization, 182; failure of apocalyptic prophecies and, 170–3
reaffirmation: failure of apocalyptic prophecies and, 173–4
reality: social construction of, 15
recruitment: brainwashing and, 100–3; public places and, 77; see also conversion; converts
'redirection', 47
reductionism: avoidance of, 11–13, 70, 75
reintegration, social, 45, 48–9
relative deprivation theory, 71–5; criticisms of, 74–5
relativism: acceptance of, 183–4
religion: as anti–modern, 180; background in, 86–90; as business, 18–20, 25, 37; changing, 59–60; commercialization of, 37; as cultural resources, 198–9; decline of, 42, 59–60; economies of, 22; esoteric, 68–70; future of, 21–2; history of, 68–70; monopoly and, 25; persistence of, 20; as pre–modern, 180; privatized, 18, 187; sociology of, 12, 14–25; theories of, 15–17, 20–2; US history of, 62–8; see also churches; specific groups
Rescher, Nicholas, 13
revival, religious: sects and, 23
'Revolutionary Sex', 127
rewards, 21, 62; conversion and, 80–1
Richardson, James T., 6, 7, 114, 132, 135
Richardson, James T., Robert Balch, and J. Gordon Melton, 110–12

Richardson, James T., and Mary Stewart, 80

risk: trust and, 57–8

Robbins, Thomas, 39–40, 107, 121, 122–3

Robbins, Thomas, and Dick Anthony, 30–1, 52, 40, 145, 152

Robbins, Thomas, Dick Anthony, and Thomas Curtis, 46–7

Robbins, Thomas, and David Bromley, 138, 186

Rochford, E. Burke, Jr, 83, 87

roles, 16; 53; gender, 136–42

Roof, Wade Clark, 48

Ross, Rick, 88

routinization: authority and, 155, 156–60

Rouxists, 169, 174

sacred: profane and, 30

Sacred Canopy, The, 14

sacred communities, 192

sacred power: rediscovery of, 192

Sadler, William Samuel, 9

Saliba, John A., 113, 114–5

salvation, 29–30

Sargent, William, 99, 105–6

Schein, Edgar, I. Schneier, and C. Becker, 99, 105–6, 120

science: compatibility with, 186–8; modernity and, 56–7; social, 4–5, 10, 12

scientism, 187

Scientology, 3, 4, 20, 29, 33, 45, 47; conversion and, 83, 84, 86, 88, 100; leadership and, 155, 157; organization of, 37–8

Sea Org, 38, 155

Second Great Awakening, 62, 63, 64

sectarianism, 24

sects, 23–4; churches and, 26–9, 31; cults and churches and, 23–4; definition of, 26–7; formation of, 24; types of, 29–30

secularism: conversion and, 88

secularization, 25, 59–60; definition of, 17–18; NRMs and, 179–89; theories of, 17–20, 22–4

Seekers, 168, 169

seekership: conversion and, 80, 81–2, 87, 89

Selengut, Charles, 88–90

self–actualization, 57–8

services: cults' provision of, 33–4

Seventh Day Adventists, 146, 173

sex: moral relativity and, 129–31; religious significance of, 131–2; see also gender; sexual deviance

sex–complementarity groups, 138

sex–polarity groups, 138–9

sexual deviance, 125–41; guru–disciple relationship and, 129–30

sex–unity groups, 138

Shaffir, William, 170, 172, 174

Shambhala International, 3, 8–9, 45, 157

'shift–to–risk', 166, 167–8

Silva Mind–Control, 3

Singer, Margaret, 77; on brainwashing, 97–8, 99–100, 102–3, 106, 107–8, 116

Singer, Merrill, 76

Smith, Joseph, 146

Snow, David, and Richard Machalek, 174–5

Snow, David, and Cynthia L. Phillips, 76

social encapsulation, 146, 162–8

social functions: religious institutions and, 59

socialization, 'adjustive', 46

social movements: Fourth Awakening and, 65; 'irrationalist' theories of, 71–2

social networks: conversion and, 77–8

social psychology: social encapsulation and, 166–7

social structure: changing, 49–58

social ties, weak extra–cult, 78–9, 81

sociology, 4–5, 8, 10–12

Sōka Gakkai, 3, 199; conversion to, 76, 77, 83, 84, 85, 87

Solar Temple, 1–2, 142, 143, 150,

151–2, 160, 165–6, 177; conversion
and, 84; isolation and, 162,163
Spickard, James, 129
spiritual healing, 192–3
spirituality, 2
spiritualization: failure of apocalyptic
prophecies and, 171
'spiritual needs', 12
Stark, Rodney, 193
Stark, Rodney, and William Sims
Bainbridge, 14; on converts, 79, 80,
80–1, 85, 86–7, 88, 93; theory of religion and, 20–5, 40; typology and,
31–2, 33, 34, 36
Stark, Rodney, and Roger Finke, 14,
67–8
Stark, Rodney, and Laurence Iannaccone,
144
stigma: seekership and, 81–2
Stone, Donald, 13, 182–9
'strategic intervention therapy', 116
Straus, Roger, 117
'Subculture–Evolution Model of Cult
Innovation', 61–2
supernatural: role of, 20–1, 22–3
synthesis: NRMs as, 4

televangelists, 64
tension management, 47–8
test of faith: failure of apocalyptic
prophecies and, 172
Theosophy, 3, 4, 34, 36, 66
Third Great Awakening, 62–4
'this–worldly mysticism', 187, 188
'thought reform', 96
Tipton, Steven M., 43, 44–5, 48
'Tnevnoc Cult', 66–7
tolerance: other religions and, 183–4
tradition: orientation to, 11, 185
training: recruitment and, 100–1
trances, 107–8
Transcendental Meditation, 3
transformation, 4
Troeltsch, Ernst, 26
Trungpa Rinpoche, Chogyam, 8–9, 157,

160
trust: risk and, 57–8
Turner, Ralph, 16
typologies: church–sect, 26–9;
church–sect–cult, 31–3

UFOs: groups associated with, 3, 4
Unarians, 169, 174
'unchurched', 24; conversion and, 80
Unification Church, 1, 4, 29, 34, 45, 47,
103–4; conversion to, 75–6, 77–8, 79,
80, 83, 86, 87, 88–90, 92, 100; brainwashing and, 111–12, 114; deception
and, 103–4; family nature of, 51; sex
and, 128–9; voluntary defectors from,
109–10
United States: religious history of, 62–8
universalization: expressive roles and, 52;
'of reflexivity', 56–7
Universal Link, 169
Urantia, 9–10
utilitarian individualism, 41–5

Vajradhatu/Shambhala, see Shambhala
values, changing: emergence of NRMs
and, 40–9
Van Driel, Barend, 6
Vedanta Society, 66
violence, 142–78; anticipation of, 151;
charismatic leadership and, 111; recent
examples of, 142–6; social encapsulation and, 162–8

Waco, see Branch Davidians
Wallis, Roy, 31, 37, 83, 84, 86, 156
Weber, Max, 18, 26, 31, 153, 154
Westley, Frances, 182–9
Wiccan groups, 3, 84
Wilson, Bryan R., 170, 195; on converts,
74–5, 82, 51–2, 59–60; on leadership,
153, 154; typology of, 27, 29
Wilson, Bryan R., and Karel Dobbelaere,
76, 77,, 83, 84, 85, 87, 199
Wolff, Harold, 106
women: NRM membership and, 126,

129–30, 136–42
world–building, 15+
'world of love', 54–6
'world of work', 54–6
Wright, Stuart, 109, 110, 113, 132
Wuthnow, Robert, 3, 47

Yinger, J. Milton, 27, 28
young adults: social ties and, 78–9; *see
   also* age

Zablocki, Benjamin, 119–21, 123